T0407922

NATURAL DISASTER RESEARCH, PREDICTION AND MITIGATION

# HURRICANE SANDY REBUILDING STRATEGY AND PROGRESS UPDATE

# NATURAL DISASTER RESEARCH, PREDICTION AND MITIGATION

Additional books in this series can be found on Nova's website under the Series tab.

Additional e-books in this series can be found on Nova's website under the e-book tab.

NATURAL DISASTER RESEARCH, PREDICTION AND MITIGATION

# HURRICANE SANDY REBUILDING STRATEGY AND PROGRESS UPDATE

## LORAYNE TUCKER
### EDITOR

nova
publishers

*New York*

**Library of Congress Cataloging-in-Publication Data**

ISBN: 978-1-63321-826-0

*Published by Nova Science Publishers, Inc. † New York*

# CONTENTS

# PREFACE

Hurricane Sandy struck the East Coast with incredible power and fury, wreaking havoc in communities across the region. Entire neighborhoods were flooded. Families lost their homes. Businesses were destroyed. Infrastructure was torn apart. After all the damage was done, it was clear that the region faced a long, hard road back. That is why President Obama pledged to work with local partners every step of the way to help affected communities rebuild and recover. On August 19, 2013, the Hurricane Sandy Rebuilding Task Force released its Rebuilding Strategy for the Sandy impacted region. The Rebuilding Strategy included a long-term plan for rebuilding that guides Sandy supplemental spending to drive regional coordination and make communities more resilient to future disasters. The Rebuilding Strategy also aligns federal, state and local policies to achieve goals that are important to the long-term rebuilding of the region in the most economically efficient, ecologically robust and innovative ways possible. This book discusses the Hurricane Sandy Rebuilding Strategy in detail.

Chapter 1 - On October 29, 2012 multiple weather systems – including Hurricane Sandy – collided over the most densely populated region in the nation, with devastating and tragic results. At least 159 people in the United States were killed as either a direct or indirect result of Sandy.

More than 650,000 homes were damaged or destroyed and hundreds of thousands of businesses were damaged or forced to close at least temporarily. The power of nature was set loose on our nation's largest city and some of our smallest coastal towns, with results that would have previously seemed unimaginable. Lives were lost, millions of homes were upended, families were made homeless in a single night, and entire communities were in shock at the scale of the loss.

The government's response began before the storm hit and by the day it made landfall more than 1,500 personnel from the Federal Emergency Management Agency (FEMA) were on the ground along the East Coast. Federal, State, and local emergency responders rescued and provided basic services to individuals, assessed damage, and began guiding families and businesses to the assistance available to help them get back on their feet. As of July 2013, FEMA and the Small Business Administration (SBA) had helped more than 270,000 individuals or households and 3,900 businesses to get back on their feet through $3.8 billion in SBA recovery loans and FEMA individual assistance.

Chapter 2 - On August 19, 2013, the Hurricane Sandy Rebuilding Task Force released its Rebuilding Strategy for the Sandy impacted region. The Rebuilding Strategy included a long-term plan for rebuilding that guides Sandy Supplemental spending to drive regional coordination and make communities more resilient to future disasters. The Rebuilding Strategy also aligns federal, state and local policies to achieve seven goals that are important to the long-term rebuilding of the region in the most economically efficient, ecologically robust and innovative ways possible. These goals are:

- Promoting Resilient Rebuilding through Innovative Ideas and a Thorough Understanding of Current and Future Risk
- Ensuring a Regionally Coordinated, Resilient Approach to Infrastructure Investment
- Restoring and Strengthening Homes and Providing Families with Safe, Affordable Housing Options
- Supporting Small Businesses and Revitalizing Local Economies
- Addressing Insurance Challenges, Understanding, and Affordability
- Building State and Local Capacity to Plan for and Implement Long-Term Recovery and Rebuilding
- Improving Data Sharing Between Federal, State, and Local Officials

The Rebuilding Strategy identified 69 specific recommendations across these broad goals as well as specific member agencies[1] to lead the implementation of each of them. Since the publication of the Rebuilding Strategy, these agencies have continued to work closely together to move the recommendations forward and deliver on their commitments to the region and the President.

This report includes an update on the implementation of the Rebuilding Strategy goals and an additional section on the internal efforts to improve data sharing and accountability through the Sandy Program Management Office (PMO). This report is organized by each of the seven Rebuilding Strategy goals and the PMO; recommendations are grouped according to these goals. Each section of this report includes background information from the original Rebuilding Strategy, identifies the relevant leading agencies[1], and includes brief updates on highlighted areas of progress made since the publication of the Rebuilding Strategy through the spring of 2014. A full list of the Rebuilding Strategy recommendations is included as an appendix to this document.

In: Hurricane Sandy Rebuilding Strategy and Progress Update       ISBN: 978-1-63321-826-0
Editor: Lorayne Tucker                                      © 2014 Nova Science Publishers, Inc.

*Chapter 1*

# HURRICANE SANDY REBUILDING STRATEGY: STRONGER COMMUNITIES, A RESILIENT REGION[*]

## *Hurricane Sandy Rebuilding Task Force*

## EXECUTIVE SUMMARY

On October 29, 2012 multiple weather systems – including Hurricane Sandy[1] – collided over the most densely populated region in the nation, with devastating and tragic results. At least 159 people in the United States were killed as either a direct or indirect result of Sandy.[2]

More than 650,000 homes were damaged or destroyed and hundreds of thousands of businesses were damaged or forced to close at least temporarily.[3] The power of nature was set loose on our nation's largest city and some of our smallest coastal towns, with results that would have previously seemed unimaginable. Lives were lost, millions of homes were upended, families were made homeless in a single night, and entire communities were in shock at the scale of the loss.

The government's response began before the storm hit and by the day it made landfall more than 1,500 personnel from the Federal Emergency Management Agency (FEMA) were on the ground along the East Coast.[4] Federal, State, and local emergency responders rescued and provided basic services to individuals, assessed damage, and began guiding families and businesses to the assistance available to help them get back on their feet. As of July 2013, FEMA and the Small Business Administration (SBA) had helped more than 270,000 individuals or households and 3,900 businesses to get back on their feet through $3.8 billion in SBA recovery loans and FEMA individual assistance.

---

[*] This is an edited, reformatted and augmented version of document issued August 2013.

## Rebuilding Challenges and the Creation of the Hurricane Sandy Rebuilding Task Force

In recognition of the size and magnitude of the storm and the rebuilding challenges facing the region, President Obama signed an Executive Order on December 7, 2012 creating the Hurricane Sandy Rebuilding Task Force and designating the Secretary of Housing and Urban Development, Shaun Donovan, as Chair. The Federal Government's experience from previous disasters taught that it was vital to have a team focused exclusively on long-term rebuilding immediately after the storm hit; working in tandem with the elements of the National Disaster Recovery Framework (NDRF), the Task Force was established to ensure the recovery benefitted from cabinet-level focus and coordination. The President charged the Task Force with identifying and working to remove obstacles to resilient rebuilding while taking into account existing and future risks and promoting the long-term sustainability of communities and ecosystems in the Sandy-affected region.

In January 2013, Congress passed and the President signed the Disaster Relief Appropriations Act, 2013 (Sandy Supplemental), which provided about $50 billion in funding to support rebuilding in the region.

This Rebuilding Strategy establishes guidelines for the investment of the Federal funds made available for recovery and sets the region on the path to being built back smarter and stronger with several outcomes in mind:

- Aligning this funding with local rebuilding visions.
- Cutting red tape and getting assistance to families, businesses, and communities efficiently and effectively, with maximum accountability.
- Coordinating the efforts of the Federal, State, and local governments and ensuring a region- wide approach to rebuilding.
- Ensuring the region is rebuilt in a way that makes it more resilient – that is, better able to with-stand future storms and other risks posed by a changing climate.

Resilience involves enabling the region to respond effectively to a major storm, recover quickly from it, and adapt to changing conditions, while also taking measures to reduce the risk of significant damage in a future storm. Sustainability involves ensuring the long-term viability of the people and economy of the region and its natural ecosystems, which requires consideration of the risks posed by a changing climate, the practicality of maintaining a long-term presence in the most vulnerable areas, and the need to protect and restore the natural ecosystems. The Rebuilding Strategy includes 69 recommendations, many of which have already been adopted. They are divided into several policy priorities that were identified with the help of input from the Task Force's public engagement with local leaders and community groups. Many of the recommendations are directly linked to Sandy Supplemental funding. The Rebuilding Strategy also includes additional policy recommendations that will have a significant impact on how the region rebuilds, but that are not directly linked to Sandy Supplemental spending. Finally, in recognition of the increased risk the region and the nation face from extreme weather events, the Rebuilding Strategy includes recommendations that, if implemented, will improve our ability to withstand and recover effectively from future flood-related disasters. The Task Force recommendations include:

- Promoting Resilient Rebuilding, Based on Current and Future Risk, Through Innovative Ideas by:
  - Giving governments and residents the best available data and information on current and future risks to facilitate good decision making for recovery and planning – for example, by creating and making widely-available a Sea Level Rise projection tool.
  - Leveraging the Rebuild by Design competition to deliver innovative, resilient rebuilding ideas to the Sandy-impacted region.
  - Prioritizing the engagement of vulnerable populations on issues of risk and resilience.
- Ensuring a Regionally Coordinated, Resilient Approach to Infrastructure Investment by:
  - Helping communities work together to be better prepared at a lower cost for the risks associated with a changing climate.
  - Making the electrical grid smarter and more flexible, and protecting the liquid fuel supply chain to better prepare them for future storms and other threats.
  - Helping to develop a resilient power strategy for telephone and internet communication systems and equipment, so that our ability to communicate when it's most necessary is less vulnerable to disaster.
  - Providing a forum to coordinate and discuss large-scale, regional infrastructure projects and map the connections and interdependencies between them, saving money and getting better results for all levels of government.
  - Establishing guidelines to ensure those projects are situated and built to withstand the impacts of existing risks and future climate change, in the region, and across the country.
  - Assisting States and localities to optimize Sandy recovery infrastructure funding and leverage non-federal resources to help build critical infrastructure assets that are resilient to current and future risks.
- Providing Families Safe, Affordable Housing Options and Protecting Homeowners by:
  - Helping disaster victims to be able to stay in their homes by allowing homeowners to quickly make emergency repairs.
  - Preventing responsible homeowners from being forced out of their homes due to short-term financial hardship while recovering from disaster by creating nationally-consistent mortgage policies.
  - Making housing units – both individual and multi-family – more sustainable and resilient through smart recovery steps including elevating above flood risk and increased energy efficiency.
  - Communicating to State and local governments, residents, and workers consistent guidance on how to remediate indoor environmental pollutants such as mold.
- Supporting Small Businesses and Revitalizing Local Economies by:
  - Making it easier for small businesses to access Federal contracts for Hurricane Sandy rebuilding.

- Creating specialized skills training programs to support Sandy rebuilding including training opportunities for low income individuals and other vulnerable populations.
- Developing a one-stop shop online for everything related to small businesses and recovery.
- Improving the process for accessing critical disaster recovery loans and other resources; and increasing SBA's unsecured disaster loan limits and expediting the disbursement of small dollar loans.
- Addressing Insurance Challenges, Understanding, and Accessibility by:
  - Working with Congress on the affordability challenges posed by reforms to the National Flood Insurance Program (NFIP) so that responsible homeowners aren't priced out of their homes.
  - Encouraging homeowners and other policy-holders to take steps to mitigate future risks, such as elevating their homes and businesses above flood levels, which will not only protect against the next storm but also make their flood insurance premiums more affordable.
  - Streamlining payouts to homeowners and other policy-holders in the wake of a disaster.
- Building Local Governments' Capacity to Plan for Long-Term Rebuilding and Prepare for Future Disasters by:
  - Supporting regional planning efforts underway in New York and New Jersey to create and implement locally-created and federally funded strategies for rebuilding and strengthening their communities against future extreme weather.
  - Funding Local Disaster Recovery Manager positions in communities in the Sandy-impacted region and taking additional steps to prepare for future disasters.

These innovative strategies, along with the additional recommendations detailed in the report, can help the Sandy-affected region rebuild and serve as a model for every community in the country that faces greater risk from extreme weather.

President Obama's Climate Action Plan laid out a series of responsible and common sense steps to reduce carbon pollution and prepare communities for the impacts of a changing climate that are already being felt across the nation. That plan was informed by lessons from the Sandy recovery process, as well as several of the policies and principles developed by the Hurricane Sandy Rebuilding Task Force.

To date, the response to and recovery from this storm has been a testament to the unique spirit, strength, and will of the American people.

The recovery also highlights fundamental American virtues: we do not leave any communities to pick up the pieces by themselves, we harness American ingenuity, and we give all communities the tools they need to make sure that when we rebuild, we build back stronger and smarter.

# INTRODUCTION

Hurricane Sandy made landfall in New Jersey and New York on October 29, 2012. The results were tragic and devastating. The office towers of Lower Manhattan were left powerless and dark. Miles of rail lines were twisted and torn apart. Beach towns from New Jersey to Rhode Island were buried beneath mountains of debris. Millions of lives were upended. Most tragically, more than one hundred people lost their lives.

During the storm and in the days following, the President directed his Cabinet to lean forward, cut red tape, and get resources to survivors as well as state and local governments. At the peak of the response, the Federal Government mobilized more than 17,000 volunteers in the affected areas,[5] and more than $200 million in Federal services and resources were provided to address immediate recovery needs.[6]

The President recognized that, in addition to the immediate aid response, it was vital to have a Cabinet- level team focused on long-term rebuilding, working closely with the Federal Emergency Management Agency (FEMA) and the organizations put in place by the National Disaster Recovery Framework (NDRF) (see sidebar on page 32) to remove obstacles to resilient rebuilding and promote the long-term sustainability of communities and ecosystems.

In response to the crisis, and because of the scope of the impact and the need for the highest level of coordination for recovery, President Obama created the Hurricane Sandy Rebuilding Task Force (the Task Force) in December of 2012, and designated the Secretary of Housing and Urban Development (HUD), Shaun Donovan, as Chair. The additional members were the heads of twenty-three executive department agencies and offices.

The President, along with the support of State and local leaders, fought for much-needed Federal funds to aid the victims of the storm and provide needed resources for a successful recovery. Their efforts led to the Disaster Relief Appropriations Act, 2013 (Sandy Supplemental), which was passed by Congress and signed into law in January 2013, providing about $50 billion in funding to support rebuilding. Thus far, these dollars have provided support to hundreds of thousands of people and businesses in the affected region. Looking ahead, the Task Force's principal goal, which is set forth in this Rebuilding Strategy, has been to establish guidelines for the investment of the Federal funds made available for recovery and set the region on the path to building back smarter and stronger as part of a more resilient Nation.

The Task Force quickly established offices in New York, New Jersey, and Washington D.C., to facilitate engagement with State and local officials and other stakeholders. Additionally, the Task Force created an Advisory Group which included local elected leaders from the five states hardest hit by Sandy –Connecticut, Maryland, New Jersey, New York, and Rhode Island – to inform the Task Force's operation and help guide the Rebuilding Strategy.

Task Force members assigned staff with a wide range of talent, skills, and experience from their agencies to develop a viable Rebuilding Strategy. The Task Force organized many multi-disciplinary teams (e.g., engineers, financial analysts, grant managers, urban planners, data system specialists, etc.) to study the critical inter-relationships of complicated states, communities, and systems. These teams built on, and incorporated contributions from, existing Federal, State, and local efforts to develop the Rebuilding Strategy.

The Rebuilding Strategy includes 69 recommendations, across several policy areas, that are designed to align funding with local rebuilding priorities, eliminate barriers to recovery while ensuring effectiveness and accountability, coordinate across levels of government, facilitate a region-wide approach to rebuilding, and promote resilient rebuilding so that the region will be better able to withstand the impacts of existing risks and future climate change.

The Rebuilding Strategy is in alignment with President Obama's Climate Action Plan, released in June 2013. Both the strategy and the Climate Action Plan are designed to strengthen communities against future extreme weather and other climate impacts. For example, building on the implementation of the government-wide Flood Risk Reduction Standard initiated by the Task Force in the Sandy-affected region (discussed in more detail on page 44), the President's Climate Action Plan calls for agencies to update flood risk reduction standards for all federally funded projects nationwide. Further, the work of the Task Force emphasized the importance of incorporating and addressing the region's emerging risks resulting from rising sea levels into recovery planning, requiring region-wide, government-wide coordination.

These recommendations are the result of a community-based, locally driven process. They reflect months of outreach to State and local elected officials; tribal officials; non-governmental organizations (NGOs); non-profit organizations; representatives from the private sector; academics, think tanks and other science and policy experts; and other community organizations, particularly those serving vulnerable populations. Indeed a key function of the Task Force was to bring all of these players to the table to ensure their efforts are coordinated, that particular attention is paid to already disadvantaged and struggling communities, and that they are helping each other as they help themselves.

The Rebuilding Strategy is designed to be used by all of these actors, all of whose efforts will be critical to the successful rebuilding of the region and strengthening of the Nation.

## BACKGROUND ON THE REGION, THE STORM, AND THE RECOVERY

### Sandy's Reach

Hurricane Sandy affected twenty-four states across the northeastern and mid-Atlantic United States.[7] The Federal Government made major disaster declarations in New Jersey, New York, Connecticut, Rhode Island, Delaware, Maryland, Virginia, West Virginia, New Hampshire, Massachusetts, Pennsylvania, Ohio, and the District of Columbia.[8] Much of the destruction inflicted by Hurricane Sandy centered in the densely populated coastal areas of New Jersey and the New York metropolitan area.[9]

#### New Jersey and the New York Metropolitan Area

New Jersey is the most densely populated state in the nation and predominantly urban or suburban. The areas that sustained the most damage were the small- to medium-sized suburban beach communities along New Jersey's 137 miles of Atlantic Ocean coastline, with populations that swell during the summer tourism months; an additional 104 miles of shore along the Delaware Bay that consist of more rural and economically challenged towns; and the northern urban and suburban areas, such as Hoboken, Jersey City, Newark, Moonachie, and Little Ferry.[10] New Jersey's shoreline is intensely developed and includes year-round residents, several urban centers including Atlantic City, and a significant number of seasonal residences and facilities related to the multi-billion dollar per year tourism industry.[11]

With a total population of about 19 million, the New York metropolitan area is the largest metropolitan area in the U.S. and one of the largest in the world.[12] New York's recognized metropolitan area includes the five boroughs of New York City, Long Island, Southeastern New York State, Northern New Jersey, and Southwestern Connecticut. The region includes some of the wealthiest suburbs and poorest urban centers in the nation.

The New York metropolitan area is the largest economic engine in the nation, contributing 9.5 percent of the nation's gross domestic product (GDP).[13] At its center is the country's largest city, New York City, comprised of five boroughs, all of which sustained damage from the storm. Sandy wreaked havoc on the City and its expansive 520-mile shoreline.[14] To the east of the City is Long Island, the largest island in the contiguous United States. The 118-mile[15] island is composed of two counties, Nassau and Suffolk, which have a combined population of over 2.8 million people,[16] more populous than 16 states.[17]

As a center for many industries, including finance, international trade, biotechnology, media and entertainment, and tourism, New Jersey and the New York metropolitan area comprise one of the most important economic regions in the world. A diverse array of industries and businesses of all sizes create the regional economy. Sandy-affected counties are home to many prolific small businesses, and these Sandy-affected counties normally generate 90 percent of New Jersey's gross state product (GSP) and 70 percent of New York's GSP.[18] Additionally, in New York and New Jersey, small businesses are disproportionately located in coastal towns, and 77 percent of the States' small businesses are located in counties where Hurricane Sandy caused damage.[19] This density of commercial activity increases the regional economy's vulnerability to storms.

Commercial activity is highly dependent on the region's infrastructure. Even before Hurricane Sandy, significant infrastructure in the region was in need of repair due to chronic underfunding. According to a 2013 study by the American Society of Civil Engineers, many of New York State's bridges, the majority of its roads, and its wastewater and drinking water infrastructure are badly in need of investment and repair.[20] New Jersey faces similar conditions.[21]

The region's relatively expensive and unusually low-inventory housing market raised different challenges than those experienced in disasters such as Hurricanes Katrina, Ike, and Rita. Affordable, temporary housing units close to Sandy-affected neighborhoods were in short supply. This forced Federal, State, and local authorities to employ an array of policy tools to provide displaced individuals with places to stay.

Sandy also followed a protracted foreclosure crisis that affected much of the region and threatened to destabilize the market by causing mortgagors struggling to recover from the storm to fall behind on their payments. Owners who were able to weather the economic downturn and remain current on their mortgages were suddenly faced with the three-fold burden of not only making monthly payments, but also paying for repairs to their damaged homes and for temporary places to stay while repairs were being completed.

Finally, despite the vulnerability of the region to coastal and other flooding, the penetration of flood insurance in the region is extremely low. A February 2013 report on the National Flood Insurance Program (NFIP) estimated 15 to 25 percent of properties in Special Flood Hazard Areas (SFHA)[22] in the Northeast were insured for flood losses.[23] Specifically, just before Sandy hit, only 38,785 residential and business policies were insured in New York City out of more than 300,000 housing units and 23,400 businesses damaged by Hurricane Sandy's storm surge and inundation.[24] According to a May 2013 New York Federal Reserve Bank survey of small businesses across New Jersey, New York, and Southern Connecticut, only eight percent of respondents whose firms suffered damage had flood insurance.[25]

### *The Storm and Its Impact*

Hurricane Sandy made landfall near Brigantine, NJ at approximately 7:30 pm on October 29, 2012.[26] After barreling across the shores of Jamaica and Cuba, the storm transitioned back and forth between hurricane and tropical storm strength over the Atlantic before merging with a winter storm and crashing into the East Coast. Its strong winds, historic storm surges, heavy rain, and snowfall resulted in overwhelming destruction up and down the East Coast with effects felt as far west as Wisconsin.[27] At nearly the same time, communities in West Virginia and northwestern Maryland faced blizzard conditions that dumped as much as three feet of snow on some areas.[28]

Hurricane Sandy is the second costliest hurricane in the nation's history.[29] According to the National Oceanic and Atmospheric Administration's (NOAA) National Hurricane Center, Sandy was the largest storm of its kind to hit the East Coast.[30] The size and strength of the storm affected a variety of sectors throughout the region.

### Hurricane Sandy by the Numbers

| \$65 BILLION in damages and economic loss | |
|---|---|
| 200,000 | Small business closures due to damage or power outages |
| 2 million | Working days lost |
| \$58 million | In damages to the recreational fishing sector |
| 100 million | Gallons of raw sewage released in Hewlett Bay 2 days after Sandy |
| 70 | National Parks impacted |
| **At least 159 FATALITIES caused by Hurricane Sandy** | |
| 72 | U.S. fatalities directly caused by the storm |
| 87 | U.S. fatalities caused by circumstances indirectly associated with the storm |
| **8.5 MILLION customers left without power** | |
| 48,000 | Number of trees removed or trimmed to restore power in New Jersey |
| \$1 billion | Estimated cost of power and gas line repairs in New Jersey |
| **650,000 HOMES damaged or destroyed** | |
| 6,477 | Storm survivors in shelters at the peak of the disaster |
| 43% | Portion of those registered for FEMA assistance that were renters |
| 64% | Portion of renter registrants from NYC that were low-income |
| 67% | Portion of renter registrants from NJ that were low-income |
| **Portion of workers who commute using public transportation in the Tri-state area: 30.5 PERCENT** | |
| 8 | Flooded tunnels |
| 42 minutes | Average commute time in Brooklyn before Sandy |
| 86 minutes | Average commute time in Brooklyn after Sandy |
| **25 PERCENT of cell sites out of service in 10 STATES** | |
| 6 | Number of NYC hospitals closed because of the storm |
| 26 | Number of NYC residential care facilities closed because of the storm |

| 10 | Number of NYC hospitals that stayed open despite flooding or power outages |
|---|---|
| 8% | Portion of all N.Y.C. hospital beds that were unavailable after Sandy |
| 2 | Number of NJ hospitals evacuated because of the storm |
| 12 | Number of NJ residential care facilities closed because of the storm |
| **25 PERCENT of cell sites out of service in 10 STATES** | |
| 1,408 | Number of reported patients evacuated |
| 100% | Portion of all open NJ hospitals that utilized their emergency generators for any given time |
| **Hurricane Sandy's size at landfall: 1.8 MILLION SQUARE MILES** | |
| 3 | Peak storm Category in Caribbean |
| 14 feet | Peak height of storm surge in New York City |
| 32.3 feet | Peak wave height recorded off the coast of Monmouth County, NJ |
| 26 feet | Previous wave height record in that location, set during Hurricane Irene |
| 36 inches | Maximum snowfall recorded (Richwood, WV and Wolf Laurel My., NC) |
| 12.83 inches | Maximum rainfall recorded (Bellevue, MD) |
| 65 knots | Maximum sustained wind speed recorded (Great Gull Island, NY) |
| 83 knots | Maximum wind gust recorded (Eaton's Neck, NY) |
| **Disasters or emergencies declared in 13 STATES** | |
| CT DC DE MA MD NH NJ NY PA RI VA WV | States with emergency declarations |
| CT DC DE MA MD NH NJ NY OH PA RI VA WV | States with Major Disaster Declarations |

Sources:

National Hurricane Center, "Tropical Cyclone Report: Hurricane Sandy," 02/12/2013

National Climatic Data Center, "Billion-Dollar Weather/Climate Disasters," 2013

The Hartford 2013 Small Business Pulse: Storm Sandy, 2013

Climate Central, "Sewage Overflows from Hurricane Sandy," April 2013

National Park Service, "Status of National Parks Affected by Hurricane Sandy," 12/05/2012

New York University's Furman Center for Real Estate and Urban Policy,

"Sandy's Effects on Housing in New York City," March 2013

Enterprise Community Partners, Inc., "FEMA Assistance Analysis," March 2013

Federal Transit Authority, Hearing on Recovering from Superstorm Sandy: Rebuilding our Infrastructure, 12/20/2012

Rudin Center for Transportation NYU Wagner Graduate School of Public Service,

"Transportation During and After Hurricane Sandy," 11/2012

David Turetsky, Chief, Public Safety & Homeland Security Bureau, Federal Communications Commission, Remarks NENA

2013 Conference & Expo Charlotte, NC, 06/18/2013

New York City Special Initiative for Resilient Rebuilding, "PlaNYC: A Stronger, More Resilient New York," 06/11/2013

U.S. Census Bureau, "Commuting in the United States: 2009, American Community Survey Reports," 09/2011.

HHS analysis of State and industry data

NASA, "NASA Satellites Capture Hurricane Sandy's Massive Size," 10/30/2013

FEMA, "6 Months Report: Superstorm sandy from Pre-Disaster to Recovery," 04/25/2013

FEMA, "Disaster Declarations for 2012"

FEMA, "Disaster Declarations for 2013"

## Infrastructure

The damage from Hurricane Sandy to physical infrastructure in New York, New Jersey, and other impacted states is measured in tens of billions of dollars.[31] Separate from physical damage, EQECAT, a catastrophe risk modeling company, estimates the region lost between $30 billion and $50 billion in economic activity due to extensive power outages, liquid fuel shortages, and near-total shutdown of the region's transportation system.[32]

### Energy

Following Hurricane Sandy, power outages impacted approximately 8.5 million customers, including businesses and services, affecting millions more people.[33] [34] Additionally, breaks in natural gas lines caused fires in some locations, resulting in the destruction of many residences.[35] Access to gasoline and diesel fuel in New York City and northern New Jersey was severely impaired following Sandy. This was largely caused by flooding damage to major terminals and docks in the Arthur Kill area of New Jersey. These fuel shortages delayed first responders and other response and recovery officials. As a result, portable generators sat unused and lines at fueling stations were long and problematic while consumers struggled to identify which gas stations had power and were operational.

### Communications

The storm disrupted telecommunications and data access to millions of people and hundreds of thousands of businesses, paralyzing the greater New York Metropolitan economy. At the peak of the storm, tracking by the Federal Communications Commission (FCC) revealed that approximately 25 percent of cell sites across all or part of 10 states and Washington, D.C. were out of service.[36]

### Green Infrastructure

Storm surge associated with Hurricane Sandy caused dune and beach erosion, island breaching, and transport and deposition of sediment inland (i.e., overwash) in coastal communities from New England to Florida. Coastal flooding also caused significant erosion to existing natural infrastructure, inundation of wetland habitats, removal of or erosion to coastal dunes, destruction of coastal lakes, and new inlet creation.

### Transportation

Hurricane Sandy was the worst disaster for public transit systems (e.g., bus, subway, commuter rail) in the nation's history. On October 30, 2012, the morning after the storm made landfall, more than half of the nation's daily transit riders were without service.[37] New York City's subway system was shut down on October 28, in advance of the storm, and remained closed through November 1.[38] During that time, the City experienced traffic gridlock, and those who were able to get to work experienced commutes of up to several hours.[39] Seawater breached many critical infrastructure systems, flowing into the Hugh L. Carey (Brooklyn-Battery) Tunnel, flooding eight of the New York City Subway tunnels, and damaging a variety of other transportation systems in the region.[40]

## Average Commute Times by Home Region and Mode of Transportation. Pre Sandy Compared against November 1-2, 2012[41]

Due to the flooding of a major electrical substation in Kearny, NJ and Amtrak's tunnels connecting New York and New Jersey under the Hudson River, passenger train service was suspended for nearly a week in parts of the Northeast Corridor and full service was not restored until three weeks later on November 16.[42] The 100-year-old tunnels provide the only direct intercity and freight rail access from New Jersey to Manhattan.[43]

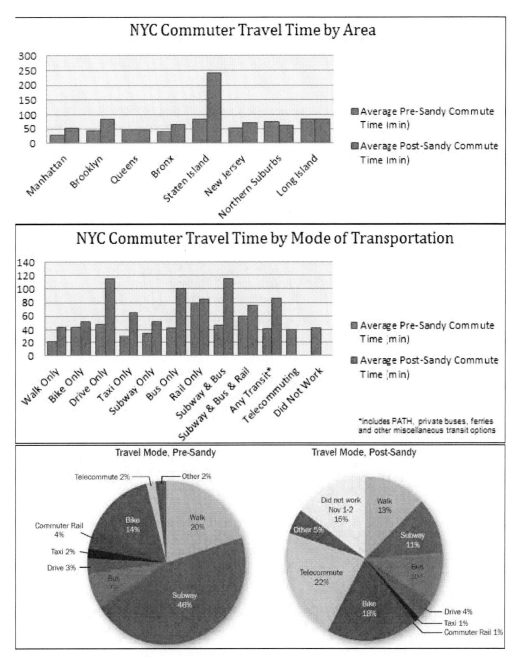

### *Stormwater Management and Drinking Water and Wastewater Treatment Systems*

Floodwaters, massive storm runoff, wind damage, and loss of electricity combined to cause wastewater treatment plants up and down the mid-Atlantic coast to fail.[44] These failures sent billions of gallons of raw and partially treated sewage into the region's waterways, impacting public health, aquatic habitats, and resources.[45]

The threat of contaminated flood waters entering groundwater aquifers, pipes, and wells that supply drinking water to much of the region also caused concern for public health. Many drinking water utilities experienced power loss, which disrupted their ability to provide safe water. Public health authorities in New York and New Jersey had to issue dozens of "boil water" advisories for customers from Nassau to Ulster counties in New York and from Atlantic to Sussex counties in New Jersey.[46] The advisories were eventually lifted after the water showed no contamination and there were no ill effects as a result of the threats.

### *Public Medical Facilities and Schools*

New York City-area hospitals and medical facilities, including the New York City Health and Hospitals Corporation facilities, were severely impacted by Hurricane Sandy; Bellevue Medical Center and Coney Island Hospitals, for example, were all flooded and eventually shut down due to the storm. In many places, there was extensive damage to mechanical, electrical, research, and medical equipment, much of which was located on lower floors or below grade to allow easier servicing and delivery of large equipment.[47]

In New Jersey, many health care facilities were severely impacted by Hurricane Sandy, including hospitals, Emergency Medical Service providers, Federally Qualified Health Centers, local health departments, vital statistics offices, home healthcare agencies, rehabilitation hospitals, dialysis centers, and long-term care facilities. Hospitals alone reported an initial estimated $68 million in damages; [48] Hudson County was hit hardest and closed some of its hospitals.[49]

In New Jersey, Hurricane Sandy disrupted schools, forcing many to close for more than a week following the storm. Schools took different approaches for temporary solutions immediately after the storm. These approaches included remaining closed until they were fully operational and temporarily providing instruction to students at alternate sites. In the case of Lincoln Park, schools opened for half a day a week after the storm – without electricity, working boilers, or lunch service.[50] A total of 13 schools across Bergen, Cape May, Hudson, Monmouth, and Ocean counties closed for longer periods of time primarily due to structural or utility damage.[51] Likewise, several school districts in the Rockaways and Nassau County (East Rockaways Union Free School Districts, Island Park Schools, Long Beach City Schools), as well as the New York City Department of Education/School Construction Authority, were damaged, with repairs in the State expected to be approximately $340 million.[52]

# Housing

Hurricane Sandy left its trace on hundreds of thousands of homes in communities across New York, New Jersey, and Connecticut. As a result, workers could not return to their jobs, children were separated from their schools, elderly and disabled residents were unable to receive essential care, vulnerable populations experienced environmental and public health challenges, and neighbors were torn from their communities and deprived of their support networks.

## Small Business

Hurricane Sandy devastated small businesses throughout the affected region. Flooding damaged inventories, machinery, and other structures; high winds and falling trees caused structural damage; and failure of power, water, telecommunications, and fuel infrastructure shut businesses down for days, if not weeks. Some small businesses still remain closed today and may never reopen. Supply chains, including small business suppliers,[53] were disrupted as well. Some sectors were disproportionately impacted, according to findings in a Department of Commerce study, particularly the travel and tourism industry in New Jersey. The report projects a measurable decline in tourism demand in 2013 that will have ripple effects throughout the state and across other industries.[54] Additionally, the recreational and commercial fishing industry, comprised largely of small businesses, depends heavily on coastal infrastructure and healthy coastal habitats and ecosystems, all of which were severely impacted by Hurricane Sandy.[55]

## Insurance

Private insurance companies will pay an estimated $18.8 billion to their policyholders in claims related to Sandy, compared to $48.7 billion in claims related to Hurricane Katrina and $25.6 billion related to Hurricane Andrew in 1992.[56] In addition, as of April 30, 2013, NFIP, administered by FEMA, had paid $6.7 billion in claims related to Sandy compared to $16.2 billion related to Katrina and $169 million related to Andrew.[57]

## A National Response

On October 26, three days before Hurricane Sandy made landfall in New York and New Jersey, State, Federal, and non-governmental organizations were working in the region to anticipate the storm's impact and prepare an effective disaster response. That day, the President held the first of 15 Sandy- related conferences and briefings, convening with representatives from FEMA, NOAA's National Hurricane Center, and the U.S. Department of Homeland Security (DHS) to discuss ongoing preparations for the storm. The day before the storm made landfall, the President approved emergency declarations under the Robert T. Stafford Act (Stafford Act) for New York, Maryland, New Jersey, Connecticut, Massachusetts, and the District of Columbia, making Federal support available to save lives, protect property, and enhance public health and safety. Also, before Sandy's landfall, 1,500 FEMA personnel were deployed along the East Coast to support preparedness and response operations.[59]

**Sandy Claims Paid by Type[58]**

| Homeowner & Residential Property | Claims (#) | Value ($) |
|---|---|---|
| New York | 501,447 | $2.1 billion |
| New Jersey | 328,946 | $1.56 billion |
| **Auto** | | |
| New York | 109,833 | $1.5 billion |
| New Jersey | 54,642 | $530 million |
| **Residential Flood (NFIP)** | | |
| New York | 54,894 | $3.2 billion |
| New Jersey | 70,787 | $3.1 billion |
| Rest of the region | 11,428 | $270 million |
| **Commercial Flood (NFIP)** | | |
| | 1,933 | $241 million |
| | 3075 | $315 million |
| | 792 | $43 million |
| **Commercial property** | | |
| New York | 30,817 | $1.33 billion |
| New Jersey | 39,870 | $1.2 billion |

Through the storm and in the days following, the President directed his Cabinet to lean forward, cut red tape, and get resources to the survivors and State and local governments. Additional emergency declarations were approved in Delaware, Pennsylvania, Rhode Island, Virginia, and West Virginia, while major disaster declarations were issued in New York, New Jersey, and Connecticut. At the peak of the response, the Federal Government mobilized more than 17,000 volunteers in the affected areas[60] and provided more than $200 million in Federal services and resources to address immediate recovery needs.[61] Within four weeks of the disaster, 450,000 applicants registered for assistance from FEMA and more than 4,700 applicants received shelter.[62]

## Recovery Progress

In total, the Sandy Supplemental appropriated about $50 billion in new budget authority for recovery efforts related to Hurricane Sandy and other major disasters in Fiscal Years (FY) 2012 and 2013. Congress provided an additional $9.7 billion in new borrowing authority to NFIP. Of that funding, approximately $18 billion is planned for expenditure on infrastructure systems, $1 billion for economic programs, $1 billion for natural and cultural resources, $800 million for Federal asset restoration, $750 million for health and social services, $300 million for program support and research, and $28 million for oversight.[63] Just more than $26 billion includes flexible funding programs at DHS for FEMA and at HUD for the Community Development Block Grant – Disaster Recovery (CDBG-DR) program, which will be deployed to address diverse, regional, unmet needs.

By July 1, 2013, 17 Federal agencies had announced more than $22 billion in funds to help the region affected by Hurricane Sandy rebuild. As of June 30, 2013, $9.18 billion had been obligated, representing 19.13 percent of total funding appropriated for the recovery. Of the $9.18 billion obligated by Federal agencies, more than $4 billion has been outlayed.

The three departments with the largest portion of recovery funds are HUD, the Department of Transportation (DOT), and DHS, with $15.2 billion, $12.4 billion, and $11.5 billion in funding authority, respectively. DHS has outlayed $3.9 billion, approximately 34 percent of the agency's total appropriation, for Sandy recovery, amounting to the largest proportion of funds outlayed by any agency.

---

## A NEW PREPAREDNESS DIRECTIVE AND A NEW RECOVERY FRAMEWORK

Hurricane Sandy marked the first full implementation of the NDRF in a large-scale disaster. The NDRF is one of the five integrated national frameworks required by Presidential Policy Directive-8: National Preparedness (PPD-8) and stemmed from the Post-Katrina Emergency Management Reform Act. This directive, issued by President Obama on March 30, 2011, is focused on "strengthening the security and resilience of the United States through systematic preparation for the threats that pose the greatest risk to the security of the Nation, including acts of terrorism, cyber-attacks, pandemics, and catastrophic natural disasters."[65]

The NDRF lays out pre- and post-disaster planning activities for disaster recovery, provides an interagency coordination structure, and defines roles and responsibilities for all who contribute to the disaster recovery. The NDRF defines disaster recovery as:

"Those capabilities necessary to assist communities affected by an incident to recover effectively, including, but not limited to, rebuilding infrastructure systems; providing adequate interim and long- term housing for survivors; restoring health, social, and community services; promoting economic development; and restoring natural and cultural resources."[66]

Creation of the NDRF was driven by the recognition that planning for long-term recovery must begin even as response activities are underway and must incorporate a wide array of stakeholders, including all levels of government, the private and non-profit sectors, emergency management and community development professionals, and disaster recovery practitioners. Recovery activities are divided into six areas (defined as Recovery Support Functions (RSFs)[67] to facilitate the identification, coordination, and delivery of Federal assistance needed to supplement recovery resources and efforts by State, local, and Tribal governments as well as private and non-profit sectors.

As a result, planning for long-term recovery from Sandy began at almost the same time as the response. We know from past disasters that planning for long-term rebuilding must begin even as response and initial, short-term recovery activities are underway.

This new framework for coordinating Federal assistance for recovery directed an influx of recovery-specific Federal personnel into the Sandy-affected region. The implementation of the NDRF meant that community recovery would be enhanced by instituting Federal Disaster Recovery Coordinators (FDRCs) and activating RSFs which focused on identifying recovery challenges, improving information sharing, leveraging existing resources, and providing technical assistance through Joint Field Offices (JFOs) in the region.

> The NDRF has significantly advanced the Federal Government's approach to disaster recovery in the United States. With the direction in the President's Climate Action Plan, recovery efforts will consider risks posed by sea level rise and climate change, resulting in a more resilient nation.

The largest portion of HUD's allocation is for the CDBG-DR program, a critical post-disaster funding source that provides grantees the discretion to address unmet housing, infrastructure, economic development, and other needs after other Federal, State, local, and Tribal resources have been exhausted.

Overall, Federal agencies have outlayed $2.93 billion in New York, $1.06 billion in New Jersey, and approximately $360 million across other states as of June 30, 2013.[64] The Federal Government has effectively partnered with states to make substantial progress in the recovery effort following Hurricane Sandy. In addition to the accomplishments achieved in partnership with the Task Force, which are described throughout this Rebuilding Strategy, selected projects and recovery activities initiated by Task Force member agencies are included in Appendix IV.

While significant progress has been made in helping residents, business owners, and communities get back on their feet, there is still far more work to do. As this Rebuilding Strategy emphasizes, decision makers must work to ensure this funding is spent in a way that not only rebuilds the communities impacted by Hurricane Sandy but also makes them stronger and more resilient to future storms.

## Facing a Growing Threat

Sandy and other recent disasters underscore the nation's vulnerability to extreme weather events under current climate conditions. Last year alone, there were 11 different weather and climate disaster events with estimated losses exceeding $1 billion each across the United States. Taken together, these 11 events resulted in more than $110 billion in estimated damages.[68] While scientific evidence does not yet tell us definitively whether storms like Sandy are growing more common, evidence indicates climate change is already altering environmental conditions in a way that suggests there may be changes in the frequency, intensity, duration, and timing of future extreme meteorological events, which may lead to unprecedented extreme weather events.[69]

Specifically, sea level rise due to ocean warming and ice melting will increase the risk of more severe inundation for any given coastal storm. Global sea level rise has been increasing over recent decades and is expected to continue beyond the end of this century, impacting millions of Americans living in coastal areas. These projections of increased risk cannot be overlooked in the development of hazard mitigation and recovery plans for the future (see Appendix V for more detailed discussion of sources of future risk), given that rebuilding after severe storms and other weather events costs taxpayers billions of dollars a year.

Countless examples from the Gulf Coast, the Jersey Shore, and other storm-struck areas demonstrate how non-structural hazard mitigation measures make communities more resilient to extreme weather events. Coastal homes that were elevated or had stronger roofs and beach communities with natural buffers or zoning, such as setbacks for the most vulnerable areas, fared better than their neighbors without similar hazard mitigation.[70]

No single solution or set of actions can anticipate every threat, but decision makers at all levels must recognize that climate change and the resulting increase in risks from extreme weather have eliminated the option of simply building back to outdated standards and expecting better outcomes after the next extreme event. There is clear evidence at the national level that investments made to mitigate risk have achieved significant benefits. For instance, the Multihazard Mitigation Council estimated that, on average, for every dollar invested by FEMA in hazard mitigation, the country receives at least $4 dollars in benefits.[71]

Whether homeowners are reinforcing their foundation or city planners are rerouting roads away from flood-prone areas, hazard mitigation measures can take on many forms. As noted earlier, the President's Climate Action Plan highlights the need for communities to prepare for the risks of climate change and outlines a series of steps the Federal Government will undertake to help communities understand and mitigate those risks. The President's plan directs agencies to remove barriers to local climate-resilient investments and create a centralized "toolkit" with information needed by state, local, and private sector leaders.

For communities to protect themselves from future risks, it is also necessary for them to have access to the most up-to-date, scientifically-sound information about the risks. The President's Climate Action Plan calls on the Federal Government to provide such information to communities and the Task Force focused on this direction in the Sandy-affected region.

Since FEMA had not updated flood maps of New Jersey and New York City in more than 25 years,[72] it was difficult for local planners to effectively understand and address current and future risks posed by climate change, urbanization, and other factors. Consequently, FEMA issued updated Advisory Base Flood Elevation (ABFE) maps in the immediate aftermath of the storm, and the Administration released a sea level rise tool designed to provide communities in the Sandy-affected region with timely information on how various scenarios of sea level rise would be expected to impact them.[73]

## Science and Technology Supporting Resilience

Science is at the heart of invention and the drive to improve our lives. Throughout U.S. history, science and technology have facilitated major economic and cultural shifts. These impacts are ever-present and are increasingly driving decisions in all aspects of our technology-based society. Science and technology can provide key capabilities for the response and rebuilding process, and scientific processes can help to inform our investments to rebuild more resilient communities. Overall, science needs to be an integrated part of post-disaster response and recovery efforts.

### *Investing in Better Science and Technology for Better Informed Decisions*
Although good science is necessary for supporting good decision making, it is not always sufficient. Science acts as evidence does in a court case; sometimes it needs to be explained or translated for particular applications the same way legal strategies are translated by lawyers to help others understand. New scientific knowledge, applied appropriately, can dramatically reduce risks U.S. citizens face and provide major economic opportunities. As a nation we

have made significant investments in science for this reason, and it is incumbent upon us to use science and technology to help communities and leaders make sound decisions about our future investments.

Recent trends and scientific evidence about how the atmosphere and oceans will respond to a warmer climate indicate an increasing likelihood of severe coastal storms; consequently, the costs to respond to extreme events of this type are expected to escalate. In order to reduce recurring costs and disruption to lives and communities resulting from dynamic environmental changes, we should wisely apply the lessons learned in this rebuilding process towards disaster risk reduction strategies.

Although current scientific knowledge does not generally provide a single, clear answer to complicated questions involved with rebuilding, evidence-based information, risk-based analysis, and robust cost- benefit analyses can help us to invest more wisely in future hazard mitigation. To improve community resilience, decision makers and scientists must take into consideration new paradigms, understanding complexities and interdependencies in natural and human systems, facilitating the training of scientists and decision makers on how to turn data into actionable information, and incorporating technological solutions and future research and development to meet resilience needs. Addressing these priority areas will also help us prepare for disaster responses that best meet community needs and capabilities.

## The Importance of Science in Rebuilding Efforts

The goals and processes of rebuilding require decision makers to routinely make complex decisions under uncertain and rapidly changing conditions, including responding to immediate needs while anticipating future risk. Effective response, recovery, restoration, and rebuilding in the aftermath of Hurricane Sandy required significant scientific input. As storms grow stronger and more frequent, more lives and economic investments are put at risk. At the same time, science and technology are uncovering new ways to reduce risks. In a region as unique and diverse as the one affected by Hurricane Sandy, scientific study helps us understand interdependencies, identify weak links and methods to strengthen them, and devise systems approaches to increase resilience. Likewise, better use of available scientific information and models can lead to better decision making in advance of the next major event.

## Scientific Data Sharing for Disaster Resilience

Federal agencies collected and disseminated vast quantities of scientific data that aided Hurricane Sandy preparation, response, and recovery. Interagency data sharing has been central to this process. Before the storm, the National Hurricane Center worked with FEMA to deliver Geographical Information System (GIS)-ready storm surge depth grids and forecasts. After the storm, FEMA, state, and local emergency managers used storm surge data and aerial imagery to guide evacuations, monitor local conditions, assess damages, and allocate response resources. Multi-agency coordination of post- storm data collection on hurricane-induced coastal changes ensured cost-effective coverage of the entire Sandy-affected region. NOAA collected data on changes to the New York Harbor, which enabled marine traffic to restart more quickly. The U.S. Army Corps of Engineers (USACE) is using U.S. Geological Survey (USGS) LiDAR data to assess alternatives for rebuilding projects on Fire Island. All these data will improve forecasting models and vulnerability assessments, allowing us to be better prepared for future storm events.

### *Hurricane Sandy Science Coordination Working Group*

Many of the agencies participating in the Task Force are engaged in scientific activities aimed at expanding knowledge of the Sandy-affected region and determining what steps can be taken to ensure that our coastal communities are more resilient to future risks. In order to best utilize the varied and extensive expertise of the Task Force member agencies, the White House Office of Science and Technology Policy (OSTP) established and chaired a Science Coordinating Group to work with the Task Force to provide support in policy development, facilitate interagency collaboration, and ensure the quality of information presented. The working group was formed drawing upon the existing scientific coordination bodies, including the National Science and Technology Council[74] and its various interagency subcommittees. Through the Science Coordination Group, the Task Force was able to capitalize on existing expertise to ensure the best available science was used to inform its policy recommendations.

### *DOI Strategic Sciences Group*

Former Secretary Salazar established the Department of Interior (DOI) Strategic Sciences Group (SSG) by Secretarial Order in 2012 to provide science-based assessments and interdisciplinary scenarios of environmental crises affecting Departmental resources. Based on an approach developed during the Deepwater Horizon oil spill, the SSG rapidly assembles teams of scientists and provides the scenario results to Departmental leadership to support decision-making. The Secretary deployed the SSG to develop scenarios of Hurricane Sandy's environmental, economic, and social impacts and potential interventions to improve resilience of the region in the face of future storms. The SSG briefed Task Force representatives, DOI leadership, White House staff, and officials in the affected region. The scenarios developed by the SSG are now the basis of criteria for selecting over $300 million in projects for Hurricane Sandy mitigation, $100 million of which will fund an external competition. A full technical report is in preparation.

## A Regional Approach to Resilience

Natural disasters do not respect State or local boundaries, thus rebuilding plans cannot be bound by jurisdictional lines. The scope of the damage from Hurricane Sandy escalated challenges associated with recovery. As communities began to recover, it was clear that, historically, too little consideration was given to inherent interdependencies – whether between multiple states, neighboring counties, or seaside towns. A series of uncoordinated hazard mitigation measures may yield unintended consequences and could ultimately decrease resilience in the long-term. Major rebuilding decisions made by community leaders should not be considered in isolation. Similarly, communities must be aware of vulnerabilities associated with common resources. If a major power plant for Community A is located in Community B and disaster strikes the latter, both communities will be forced to recognize their interdependencies and ideally work together to limit future impacts.

In order to make efficient investments that mitigate risk effectively and increase the resilience of a region, capital planning decisions must address shared local and regional goals, take into account interdependencies between human and natural systems, and result from a collaborative process. New protective technologies to mitigate regional risk must be incorporated into existing systems, such as technology that protects mass transit systems from flooding or resilient electric grid developments that counter the cascading effects of power surges during a disaster.

## Definitions

*More Detail on the Task Force's Definitions is Located in Appendix II*

Sustainability: Sustainability is the creation and maintenance of conditions under which humans and nature can exist in productive harmony, and fulfill the social, economic and other requirements of present and future generations. Sustainability involves providing for the long-term viability of the people and economy of the region and its natural ecosystems, which requires consideration of the risks posed by a changing climate, the practicality of maintaining a long-term presence in the most vulnerable areas, and the need to protect and restore the natural ecosystems.

**Resilience:** The ability to prepare for and adapt to changing conditions and withstand and recover rapidly from disruptions.

**Risk Assessment and Risk Management:** Risk assessment is evaluating and prioritizing known risks and their effects; risk management is making a decision and setting policy based on that knowledge.

**Hazard Mitigation:** An effort using non-structural measures to reduce loss of life and property by lessening the impact of a major storm.

**Vulnerable Populations:** Groups of people especially at risk to impacts of a major storm due to their location or because they are overburdened and lack resources or have less access to services.

## LONG-TERM PLAN FOR REBUILDING

President Obama directed the Task Force to establish "a long-term rebuilding plan that includes input from State, local, and Tribal officials and is supported by Federal agencies, which is informed by an assessment of current vulnerabilities to extreme weather events and seeks to mitigate future risks." The rebuilding plan will help drive regional coordination and make communities more resilient to future storms.

The plan will guide Sandy Supplemental spending and help align Federal, State and local policies to achieve several goals that are important to the long-term rebuilding of the region, in the most economically efficient ways possible. Those goals are:

- Promoting Resilient Rebuilding through Innovative Ideas and a Thorough Understanding of Current and Future Risk
- Ensuring a Regionally Coordinated, Resilient Approach to Infrastructure Investment
- Restoring and Strengthening Homes and Providing Families with Safe, Affordable Housing Options

- Supporting Small Businesses and Revitalizing Local Economies
- Addressing Insurance Challenges, Understanding, and Affordability
- Building State and Local Capacity to Plan for and Implement Long-Term Recovery and Rebuilding
- Improving Data Sharing Between Federal, State, and Local Officials

## PROMOTING RESILIENT REBUILDING THROUGH INNOVATIVE IDEAS AND A THOROUGH UNDERSTANDING OF CURRENT AND FUTURE RISK

It is increasingly important to take advantage of the latest data and technology to measure and manage risk. Flood risk maps need to incorporate what scientists know about the pace and impact of climate change on sea level and other environmental factors. At the same time, the demographics of at-risk communities—which change quickly and dramatically due to rapid urbanization and shifting work patterns—must be understood. In the Sandy region and across the country, communities once thought to be safe from risk are now beginning to recognize they face greater vulnerability to extreme weather and other natural disasters than previously imagined. Further, disadvantaged communities must account for higher risks due to their proximity to other environmental and health challenges.

It is vital that science-based tools and the best available data are used to better anticipate community vulnerabilities for future disasters and to adopt measures that will reduce future human, economic, and environmental costs.

Both science and technology are critical to an effective recovery. Investments now will last for decades, meaning current construction must be completed to standards that anticipate future conditions and risks. Technology can help mitigate future risks, for example, by protecting mass transit systems from the effects of flooding. Similarly, "islanding" sections of an electric grid may counter the cascading effects of a power surge during a disaster. Mapping software can help planners understand the complexities of regional interdependencies and turn scientific data into timely and actionable information.

Only with an accurate understanding of current and future risk and vulnerability can the effectiveness of hazard mitigation efforts be judged. This critical information ensures not only that good investment decisions are made, but also that insurance systems reflect reality and encourage responsible behavior and resilience.

A robust recovery must use good data and good science to support good decision making. Utilizing such information will ensure that decisions are well-informed and incorporate goals that are both clearly defined and realistic. Evidence-based information, risk-based analysis, and robust cost-benefit analyses could help governments, businesses, and homeowners better invest in measures that increase resilience on the national, regional, and local levels.

### Coastal Vulnerability, Storm Surge, and Flooding

Hurricane Sandy reminded us how vulnerable our coastal communities are to flooding and erosion. While many communities that lacked flood risk reduction measures suffered during the storm, the Task Force saw examples of hazard mitigation efforts that helped protect communities from excessive harm. To encourage these kinds of successful hazard mitigation efforts, the Task Force pursued two specific initiatives to enhance the quality of information used to assess risk: the first is focused on determining current risk, and the second is designed to help decision makers assess future risks.

In particular, the Task Force focused on helping communities make informed decisions to mitigate future disaster risk by helping those in the region carrying out rebuilding efforts understand and appreciate both current and future risk.


## Incorporating Projections of Current and Future Risk

### *Challenge and Goal*

Even a moderate amount of sea level rise will increase the flooding that coastal storm events cause. Recent research on the Atlantic coast demonstrates that the probability of coastal erosion increases with higher rates of sea level rise.[75] Flood risk, however, varies in different circumstances and depends on factors such as the design life of particular investments, the size of the planning area, and the willingness of the community to accept a higher or lower probability of impacts.

When determining the level of acceptable risk-tolerance, decision makers must assess the potential for catastrophic loss of life, damage to infrastructure, interruption to local economy, and threats to ecosystem functions. In addition, these decision makers must consider issues of perceived fairness and the voluntary nature of risks. Finally, the decision makers must take into account human vulnerability and the adaptive capacity of a system or community to respond successfully to a coastal flooding event, including adjustments to behavior, resources, and technologies. Considerations of risk vary considerably among and within coastal communities. While this remains an active area of research and public debate, it is nonetheless important to consider when discussing resilient recovery and planning.

The Task Force has worked to ensure that the decisions being made with regard to coastal planning, management, and risk assessment in the aftermath of Hurricane Sandy include in-depth analysis of both current and future conditions, especially related to future sea level. These actions will help identify and evaluate resilient rebuilding options that will mitigate the risks extreme weather poses.

**1. RECOMMENDATION:** Facilitate the incorporation of future risk assessment, such as sea level rise, into rebuilding efforts with the development of a sea level rise tool.

Recognizing the need to better publicize existing datasets and the development of regionalized climate-related decision support tools, the Federal Government introduced a suite of future flood risk tools to ensure that decision makers can minimize risk to the greatest degree possible.[76] FEMA, the White House Council on Environmental Quality (CEQ), the U.S. Global Change Research Program (USGCRP), NOAA, and USACE came together to combine various datasets and sources of expertise to produce tools accessible to local decision makers. These tools include an interactive web-based map and a sea level rise calculator with localized data. The mapping tool combines peer-reviewed global sea level rise scenarios with existing FEMA maps to project where 100-year floodplain boundaries are expected to be in the future. The sea level rise calculator allows the user to project future 100-

year flood elevations resulting from relative (i.e. regional) sea level rise. These tools will help local planners, floodplain managers, engineers, and others identify risks and safeguard long-term investments in the region.

President Obama announced in his Climate Action Plan that such sea level rise tools are part of a broader climate resilience toolkit that Federal agencies are developing. Adopting these tools will provide recovery planners with knowledge to better inform rebuilding efforts in the aftermath of Hurricane Sandy. These tools and related products that Federal agencies are developing with State and local partners will help coastal communities, both inside and outside the Sandy-affected region, incorporate more comprehensive flood risk information into their decision making.

Owner
**Leads**: *NOAA, USACE, FEMA, CEQ, USGCRP*
**Supporting Agencies:** *DOI*
Status
Recommendation adopted: Currently available for projects funded by the Sandy Supplemental and will be applicable to future disaster recovery efforts in the region.

**2. RECOMMENDATION:** Develop a minimum flood risk reduction standard for major Federal investment that takes into account data on current and future flood risk.

On April 4, 2013, HUD Secretary Shaun Donovan joined then DOT Secretary Ray LaHood to announce a minimum flood risk reduction standard that protects investments in Sandy-affected communities. This minimum flood risk standard addresses the increased flood risk that results from rising sea levels, more intense storms, increased urbanization in floodplains, and other factors. This standard, which is in line with standards that many State and local jurisdictions have adopted, requires all major rebuilding projects that rely on Sandy-related Federal funding to be elevated or otherwise flood-proofed according to the best available FEMA guidance plus one additional foot of freeboard. Where State or local building codes or standards already require minimum elevations, the higher of the competing minimums apply.

Additionally, per Executive Order 13514: "Federal Leadership in Environmental, Energy, and Economic Performance," Federal departments and agencies are currently required to consider and address how climate change affects their missions, programs, and operations. Executive Order 13514 led to the development of Federal Climate Change Adaptation plans for each agency. In addition, on June 25, 2013, President Obama's Climate Action Plan directed agencies to expand the application of this flood standard nationwide and update their flood-risk reduction standards for Federally-funded projects to reflect a consistent approach that accounts for sea level rise and other factors affecting flood risk.

Owner
**Lead:** *Task Force*
Status
Recommendation adopted: Currently applicable to projects funded by the Sandy Supplemental and will be applicable to future disaster recovery efforts in the region. Through the implementation of the President's Climate Action Plan, NSS will coordinate a policy

effort to update flood risk reduction standards for Federally-funded projects beyond the Sandy-affected region.

## Promoting Resilience through Innovation

On June 20, 2013, the Task Force launched Rebuild by Design, a multi-stage, regional design competition aimed at promoting resilience through innovation for the Sandy-affected region. The goal of the competition is two-fold: promote innovation by developing regionally-scalable yet locally-contextual solutions that increase resilience in the region, and implement selected proposals with both public and private funding dedicated to this effort.

### *Challenge and Goal*

The process of recovering from Hurricane Sandy has already produced valuable knowledge that will help the region rebuild in a way that makes the region more resilient in future storms; however, much more can be done to enhance understanding of the region and its interdependencies, as well as the ways in which investments can be targeted to best mitigate risk.

In the past, Federal agencies, in partnership with the private sector and philanthropies, have successfully used incentive prizes and challenges as tools to spur innovation and solve tough problems. Incentive prizes establish ambitious goals and bring a variety of approaches and perspectives to bear on a problem.[77] Since its launch in 2010, http://www.challenge.gov, an online platform for Federal Government-sponsored competitions, has featured more than 250 prize competitions offered by over 50 Federal departments and agencies. The figures below depict the added benefits of offering prizes.[78]

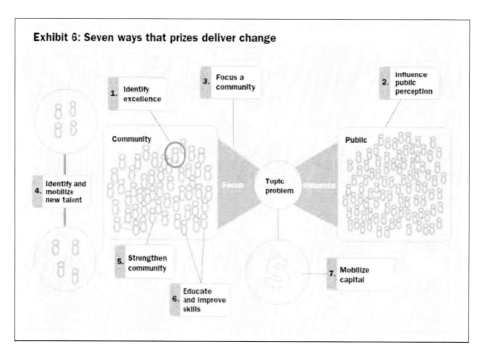

**Exhibit 6: Seven ways that prizes deliver change**

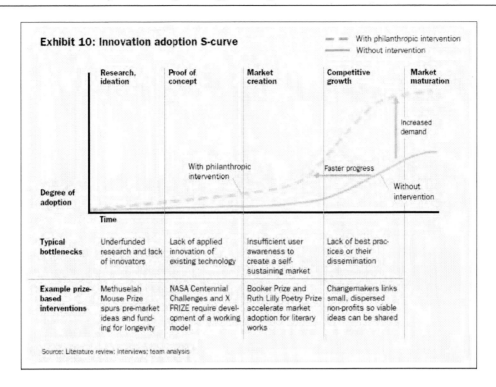

Exhibit 10: Innovation adoption S-curve

The Task Force is building upon these past successes to harness the innovation of interdisciplinary teams, foster regionalism and resilience, build the capacity of local communities to plan for the next storm, and attract long-term sustainable economic development in the Sandy-affected region.

**3. RECOMMENDATION:** Create a design competition to develop innovative resilient design solutions that address the Sandy-affected region's most pressing vulnerabilities.

The Task Force launched Rebuild by Design to promote resilience for the Sandy-affected region. With a region-wide focus, this competition will help provide solutions to problems that are too large or too complex for individual towns to solve themselves. Design solutions are expected to range in scope and in scale, from large-scale urban and multi-functional green infrastructure to small-scale distributed flood protection measures and resilient residential structures, for example. The competition process will also lead to increased understanding of regional interdependencies, thus fostering coordination and resilience at both the local and national levels. Competition participants will develop projects in consultation with existing and potential future CDBG-DR grantees to address recovery needs in the region. Winning designs may be supported by CDBG-DR funds. To the extent practicable, additional supplemental funding from relevant Federal programs will also be leveraged to support winning designs. Philanthropic organizations, including The Rockefeller Foundation, are supporting the design competition process and contributing to the prize pool.

The Rebuild by Design competition process is structured in four stages:

1) Request for qualifications and selection of five to ten teams (June – July 2013).
2) Analysis of the region through a participatory collaborative process and identification of design opportunities (August – October 2013).
3) Development of site-specific design solutions in collaboration with State/local government partners and other stakeholders (November 2013 – February 2014).
4) Design development of winning solutions and implementation of winning design solutions (March 2014 – TBD).

The competition will bring world-class expertise to multiple levels of government across the Sandy-affected region by engaging a diverse set of experts: engineers, architects, urban designers, community builders, artists, and ecologists are just some of the many professionals that could comprise the interdisciplinary teams, which will create innovative proposals for resilient rebuilding.

A jury will judge the designs at a date to be determined in 2014.

HUD will, in collaboration with philanthropic organizations, evaluate the Rebuild by Design competition process using the process of this competition as an inspiration, and research the possibilities of applying 'regional resilience by design' in other regions across the nation.

Owner
*Lead*: *HUD*
Status
Recommendation adopted: Competition currently underway to identify projects to be funded by the Sandy Supplemental. Similar competitions could be utilized for future disaster recovery efforts in the region and nationwide.

# ENSURING A REGIONALLY COORDINATED, RESILIENT APPROACH TO INFRASTRUCTURE INVESTMENT

The damage from Hurricane Sandy to physical infrastructure in New York, New Jersey, and other impacted states is measured in the tens of billions of dollars, but the impact of that damage on the people of the region goes well beyond the financial cost. For example, the failure of hospitals and health facilities due to disasters carries a high cost in terms of both lives and economic resources. Infrastructure systems are more than just physical assets; they create the framework that allows people to be safe and comfortable in their homes, the movement of goods and people, individuals to communicate with one another, and for society and communities to function.

The two overarching infrastructure-related goals of the Task Force were to ensure all Federal actions, policies, and resources work together to foster a quick and effective recovery from Hurricane Sandy and to encourage investment in systems and assets that ensures the region is better prepared to both withstand and recover from future disasters. This chapter describes the Task Force's recommendations and policy initiatives across the entire spectrum of infrastructure types as well as in specific segments of the infrastructure area.

## Infrastructure Resilience Guidelines

### *Challenge and Goal*

Many of the agencies involved in the unified Sandy recovery effort have done extensive work studying the effects of climate change on structures, administered pilot programs to analyze adaptation efforts, and revised building practices to incorporate modern standards; however, early meetings of the Task Force revealed that Federal agencies lacked a consistent approach to building resilience. There was also a lack of common understanding and language observed at the State and local levels. Executive Order 13632 charged the Task Force with identifying and working "to remove obstacles to resilient rebuilding in a manner that addresses existing and future risks and vulnerabilities and promotes the long-term sustainability of communities and ecosystems."[79] The Task Force concluded that agencies involved in the Sandy recovery effort should develop and adopt clear and consistent standards to guide resilient rebuilding. To that end, the Task Force created and led an interagency working group that developed a set of shared Federal resilience guidelines to govern Sandy-related infrastructure investment. To the extent feasible and allowable by law and regulation, these guidelines will apply to all infrastructure construction, including projects performed by Federal agencies and their contractors, as well as by State and local entities utilizing Federal funding.

This work resulted in the Infrastructure Resilience Guidelines (Guidelines). The Guidelines will lead to decisions that better protect communities and ensure wise investment of scarce public resources by setting criteria for investment and by helping align projects with national policy goals. The seven guidelines below represent the shared understanding of the Federal agencies involved in Sandy rebuilding and are being applied to Sandy recovery, as described in the policy initiatives in this chapter.

### Comprehensive Analysis

Use comprehensive, forward-looking, and science-based analysis when selecting, prioritizing, implementing, and maintaining infrastructure investments. When making investment decisions, the Federal Government should consider a broad range of information and best available data including projected future risks from climate change and other sources, anticipated impacts, and costs and benefits of alternative investment strategies (e.g., gray and green infrastructure options). Project design and selection processes will, to the extent allowable and appropriate, include an assessment of the following criteria:

- Public health and safety impacts (e.g., injury, illness, loss of life, impacts to hospitals and healthcare facilities, and psychological impacts).
- Direct and indirect economic impacts (e.g., the financial and opportunity cost of losing infrastructure functions and services following a disaster).
- Social impacts (e.g., community, regional, and governance impacts).

- Environmental impacts (e.g., sustainability considerations, impacts to natural and restored ecosystems, externalities, and environmental justice issues).
- Cascading impacts and interdependencies within and across communities and infrastructure sectors.
- Changes to climate and development patterns that could affect the project or surrounding communities.
- Inherent risk and uncertainty (in the analyses performed and due to future conditions).
- Monetization of the impacts – both the costs and the benefits – of alternative investment strategies.

The assessments should, wherever possible, include both quantitative and qualitative measures. These assessments must also be timely, so as to not delay the recovery of the region.

**Transparent and Inclusive Decision Processes**

Select projects using transparent, consistent, and inclusive processes. Apply a multi-criteria decision analysis – including a cost-benefit analysis – or other structured evaluation in Federal infrastructure funding selection and administration processes. Wherever practical and feasible, provide information broadly with clear, non-technical explanations of issues and proposed solutions. Share decision criteria, evaluation processes, and findings with all project stakeholders and interested parties to ensure transparency and inclusion. Include measures that will advance the engagement of vulnerable and overburdened populations.

**Regional Resilience**

Work collaboratively with partners across all levels of governance (i.e., Federal, State, regional, local, Tribal, territorial) and the private sector to promote a regional and cross-jurisdictional approach to resilience in which neighboring communities and states come together to: identify interdependencies among and across geography and infrastructure systems; compound individual investments towards shared goals; foster leadership; build capacity; and share information and best practices on infrastructure resilience.

A more detailed discussion of this approach as applied in the Sandy recovery is found in the Regional Infrastructure Resilience Coordination discussion in the next section.

**Long-Term Efficacy and Fiscal Sustainability**

For all infrastructure programs, agencies should require a plan to monitor and evaluate the efficacy and sustainability of the implemented project, taking particular account of changing environmental conditions such as sea level rise or changing development patterns using risk management tools (see Risk Assessment and Risk Management in Appendix II) as well as changing funding sources. Periodic evaluation of effectiveness and fiscal sustainability is essential to ensure that the Federal, State, and local agencies involved in funding infrastructure projects continue to be able to provide funding as needed, as well as to reflect any future changes in the Federal role in funding. In addition, periodic evaluation also allows improvements to existing infrastructure based on new, enhanced scientific understanding of risk or the development of more resilient technological solutions. Fiscal sustainability is important, for example, to ensure that funding both for operations (when required) and for maintaining the asset to a state of good repair is programmed and available to the entity operating the asset.

### Environmentally Sustainable and Innovative Solutions

Ensure that Federal infrastructure investments align with the commitment expressed in the President's Climate Action Plan and achieve operational resilience while also supporting Federal goals to promote innovation, sustainability, reduced environmental and public health impacts, and opportunities to leverage natural systems. Federal partners should collaborate to enhance their ability to adequately capture the entire value of green infrastructure and environmental factors when selecting infrastructure investments, including the compounding value of linked or proximate projects.

### Targeted Financial Incentives

Implement meaningful financial incentives and/or funding requirements to promote the incorporation of resilience and risk mitigation into infrastructure projects. Consistent with the President's Climate Action Plan, this should include removing barriers to using Federal funding/ programs to support climate-resilient investments, and encouraging and supporting the integration of climate-related risks into project design through agency grants, technical assistance, and other programs.

### Adherence to Resilience Performance Standards

Collaborate with State, local, Tribal, and territorial governments, as well as private stakeholders, to facilitate the development of resilience performance standards for infrastructure and use these performance standards when selecting infrastructure investments. Performance standards might include criteria for how strong of a storm systems should be able to withstand and how long different types of customers (e.g., hospitals, transit systems, gas stations) can be without power.

**4. RECOMMENDATION:** Apply Infrastructure Resilience Guidelines to all Federal infrastructure investments and projects for Sandy recovery.

The Task Force and the interagency infrastructure working group have already made substantial progress in implementing many of the Guidelines in the ongoing Sandy recovery efforts. The regional coordination workshops, described in the Regional Infrastructure Resilience Coordination section, brought together key officials from multiple states and localities. In addition, on June 20, 2013, the Task Force announced the Rebuild by Design competition, discussed in detail the previous chapter. Rebuild by Design attracted world-class talent to promote development of innovative projects that promote resilience as part of Sandy recovery. While much progress has been made, ongoing efforts are required to fully implement the Guidelines for Sandy-related recovery efforts, such as the next allocation of HUD, DOT, and DOI funding. The Recovery Support Framework Leadership Group (RSFLG) and Mitigation Framework Leadership Group (MitFLG) will oversee this effort, which will be conducted as part of the regional coordination effort discussed in the next section and done in coordination with the implementation of the President's Climate Action Plan.

Owner

*Leads: RSFLG and MitFLG*

*Supporting Agencies: HUD, FEMA, DOT, USACE, Environmental Protection Agency (EPA), DOI, U.S. Department of Energy (DOE), National Institute of Standards and Technology (NIST), NOAA, General Services Administration (GSA), and U.S. Department of Agriculture (USDA)*

Status

Recommendation adopted: Currently available for projects funded by the Sandy Supplemental and will, to the extent allowable by law and regulation, be applicable to future disaster recovery efforts in the region.

**5. RECOMMENDATION:** Consider applying the Infrastructure Resilience Guidelines nationally

The Task Force recommends that DHS' National Protection and Programs Directorate, under the policy leadership of the White House National Security Staff (NSS), support an interagency process to assess the value and feasibility of expanding the use of the Guidelines beyond the Sandy recovery efforts. These Guidelines represent the agreed upon consensus of Federal stakeholders regarding the goals and core elements of a successful Federal infrastructure resilience policy in the Sandy recovery. The Guidelines are consistent with executive guidance on resilience, including the goals outlined in the President's Climate Action Plan for supporting climate-resilient investments, the strategic imperatives in Presidential Policy Directive (PPD-21) corresponding to the development of a national strategy for critical infrastructure resilience, and the goal to strengthen security and resilience through national preparedness, as articulated in PPD-8. As such, adherence to the Guidelines may be beneficial beyond the Sandy recovery for both Federal agencies and potentially infrastructure owners and operators in building the next generation of resilient infrastructure. This effort should be coordinated with the efforts underway to implement the similar provisions of the President's Climate Action Plan and PPD-21.

Owner

*Lead: NSS and DHS*

*Supporting: CEQ, OMB, NIST, DOT, HUD, FEMA, DOE*

Status

Recommendation in process: This recommendation has been referred to the White House-led Interagency Policy Committee responsible for infrastructure resilience policy.

## Regional Infrastructure Resilience Coordination

### Challenge and Goal

A regional focus is important to making infrastructure investment decisions and building with resilience, given the regional impact of large disasters and the interconnectedness of local economies. Decisions about infrastructure in the New York – New Jersey metropolitan area impact tens of millions of people in multiple states as well as the largest local government in the country. Were these infrastructure systems to fail, there would be a cascading effect on both the region and the nation as a whole, as more wealth is created in this area than in any other metropolitan area in the United States.[80] Research also suggests that decision makers need more comprehensive discussion and coordination of the interrelated effects of the systems to effectively plan for future disasters.[81] These investment and building decisions should be coordinated and planned ahead of the disaster, not made ad hoc during the crisis.

Examples from Sandy that illustrate the need for regional coordination of resilience investments were seen in many instances. The storm's impact on fuel terminals in New Jersey and on pipelines caused a severe problem of fuel availability in New York City. A hospital is only functional when access routes to the facility are open and when availability of water, power, and telecommunications allow continuity of operations and the ability to absorb the additional demand for medical care. Similarly, removing sand from one location in the region to rebuild beaches in another location could weaken coastal protection in the source location, and/or impact local fisheries and tourism. Addressing such vulnerabilities will require the cooperation of New Jersey, New York City, and New York State, as well as private sector owners and operators.

The overall goal of adopting a regional approach is to promote better decision making, create more efficient and effective projects, and to avoid unintended impacts. For State and local stakeholders, the benefits include the ability to design more effective projects with knowledge of other linked investments, as well as the identification of opportunity projects – those ideas that were not previously proposed because they did not become apparent until other projects were considered. From the Federal perspective, this process lowers the risk of unplanned redundancies or gaps in resilience and spreads the Federal investment over the largest area in a coordinated, efficient, and equitable manner. These efforts are also aligned with the call for coordination in the NDRF, the National Mitigation Framework, the National Ocean Policy Implementation Plan, and the President's Climate Action Plan. The failure to coordinate an investment of this magnitude can result not only in wasted tax dollars, but also in increased vulnerability to the region and the nation as a whole.

**6. RECOMMENDATION:** Federal, State, and local agencies should continue to coordinate Sandy recovery infrastructure resilience projects.

The Task Force worked to ensure that both the natural and built infrastructure decisions for Sandy recovery consider other projects, assets, and dependencies across both the geographic region and the different types of infrastructure systems. The Task Force initiated this regional coordination effort by hosting a workshop to identify the dependencies between initially proposed infrastructure projects in the region and to discuss how to ensure awareness of these dependencies in the project development, design, and review process. This workshop, held on July 11, 2013, convened a group of technical experts from the Federal, State, and local agencies that are sponsoring or funding major infrastructure projects in New York and New Jersey. A broad sampling of proposed and potential (i.e., under study or not yet formally proposed) projects were mapped on a GIS and discussed in terms of scope, purpose, and interaction with other existing or planned projects. The Task Force collected these data and incorporated them into the GIS. The maps included projects that may be considered under grant funding from agencies such as DOT, FEMA, EPA, and HUD as well as projects to be directly contracted by agencies such as USACE and the National Park Service (NPS).

Following this workshop and through the rest of 2013, project sponsors, funding agencies, and reviewing agencies will meet in smaller groups to discuss the projects. These discussions will focus on how the projects impact or benefit other projects or systems, the opportunities identified for new or revised projects, and how to incorporate new technology and new approaches (e.g., nature-based systems) into projects. An example of this is a working group facilitated by the Task Force on flood protection issues related to "Hospital Row" on the east side of Manhattan. This effort is bringing together New York City, New York State, FEMA, USACE, the Departments of Veterans Affairs (VA), Health and Human Services (HHS), and HUD. Additionally, a small working group is looking at issues related to the resilience of the liquid fuels supply chain in New York and New Jersey. When beneficial, additional, larger workshops or meetings will be held to discuss specific projects or broader issues, and funding may be provided to assist in mapping and planning. The scope of the coordination will also be expanded to include projects in Connecticut as well as other States, if determined to impact projects in other parts of the region.

Owner
*Coordinating Agency: HUD*
*Supporting Agencies: DHS, USACE, DOT, EPA, DOE, USDA, DOI, U.S. Department of Commerce (DOC), U.S. Department of Labor (DOL), GSA, HHS, VA*
Status
Recommendation adopted: Currently available for projects funded by the Sandy Supplemental and will be applicable to future disaster recovery efforts in the region.

**7. RECOMMENDATION:** Institutionalize regional approaches to resilience planning in the NDRF and the National Mitigation Framework.

The NDRF and the National Mitigation Framework have broad mandates to support regional cooperation and coordination. One example of these mandates implemented is the regional cooperation supporting recovery from the 2012 drought. The Task Force recommends that RSFLG and MitFLG consider how to best incorporate regional infrastructure resilience into their respective frameworks.

Owner
*Leads: RSFLG and MitFLG*
Status
Recommended in process: Recommended for implementation in future projects funded by the Sandy Supplemental and applicable to resilient rebuilding following disasters nationwide.

## Federal Review and Permitting

Federal review and permitting responsibilities are authorized and assigned by Congress to multiple Federal agencies. These agencies seek to ensure that a project's potential impacts on safety, security, the environment, public health, and community resources are considered and that adverse effects are avoided, minimized, and mitigated throughout the project planning process. These responsibilities also include efforts to ensure that low-income and minority communities do not bear a disproportionate share of the impacts of any given project and that recipients of Federal funds comply with nondiscrimination laws, including Title VI of the Civil Rights Act of 1964,82 which prohibit discrimination, both intentional and unintentional based on race, color, national origin (including limited English proficiency), age, sex, and disability in any program or activity receiving federal assistance.[83] These efforts also align with the President's Climate Action Plan and Executive Order 12898 to identify innovative ways to help the most vulnerable communities prepare for and recover from the impacts of climate change.

Federal review and permitting is especially important for complex infrastructure projects. The President made development and repair of the nation's infrastructure a top priority of his Administration. Executive Order 13604, signed in March 2012, charged the Office of Management and Budget (OMB) and CEQ with managing a government-wide effort to increase the efficiency of the permitting and review process for complex infrastructure projects, while driving better outcomes for communities and the environment.[84] A steering committee established to lead this effort focused on 50 infrastructure projects of national or regional significance,[85] including three in the region that Hurricane Sandy eventually hit: the Tappan Zee Bridge, the Bayonne Bridge, and the deepening of the New York Harbor. Deliberate coordination among senior Federal agency leadership early in the review process for these 50 projects, as well as the engagement and dedication of staff teams throughout each agency, resulted in time savings estimates ranging from several months to several years, depending upon the project's scale, complexity, and stage of Federal review.[86]

### Challenge and Goal

Federal, State, and local officials expressed concern about potential delays of Sandy rebuilding projects caused by permitting and review activities. An estimated $20 billion of the nearly $50 billion allocated in the Sandy Supplemental for the region's recovery will be used on infrastructure projects.[87] Additionally, funds for housing as well as natural and cultural resources could total in the billions of dollars. All of the resulting projects are likely to require some form of Federal review or permitting. There are approximately 40 different permit and review processes among the Federal agencies, and the time required to ensure that projects comply with existing laws and regulations can range anywhere from two weeks to four years.[88]

It is clear that these required safeguards, addressed in the review process, are both necessary and worthwhile. They exist to ensure that approved projects do not jeopardize the Federal government's ability to fulfill Federal trust responsibilities, and to avoid, minimize, and mitigate any detrimental impacts when necessary to surrounding communities and the environment. However, when permits related to disaster recovery are not prioritized for review and those reviews are not effectively coordinated among the Federal agencies, project timelines can be delayed considerably, resulting in increased costs. The review process for potential Sandy recovery projects are also inherently complex, given their broad scope and the vast natural and cultural resources they can potentially impact. Given this complexity and the number of stakeholders involved in review, when not prioritized or effectively coordinated, these projects may be the most hindered by any such delays.[89]

Experiences from previous disasters, such as Hurricane Katrina, further illustrate concerns about the efficacy of Federal review and permitting systems. One post-Katrina report highlighted the fact that "quick action could not occur" because "agencies followed procedures that required extensive, time- consuming processes." The report explained that the slow recovery of important infrastructure, like hospitals, might be a factor in slowing the return of displaced residents.[90]

As a result of these challenges, Congress included two provisions in the Sandy Supplemental to address this issue. First, the Sandy Supplemental directed the President to establish an expedited and unified interagency review process for disasters by July 29, 2014. A steering group, composed of FEMA, DHS, the Advisory Council on Historic Preservation (ACHP) and CEQ, is guiding this effort. A unified Federal review can enhance the ability of the Federal environmental and historic preservation review process to inform and expedite disaster recovery decisions for grant applicants and other potential beneficiaries of disaster assistance, enhance consistency in the review process across Federal agencies, and assist agencies in better leveraging their resources and tools. Secondly, Congress included a provision that allows HUD and its grantees to adopt environmental reviews performed by FEMA or any Federal agency when the HUD grantee is providing additional assistance to actions performed under specific sections of the Stafford Act.[91]

The Task Force also sought to ensure that the Federal review and permitting processes for Sandy recovery and hazard mitigation projects are well-coordinated and prioritized, so that they can be delivered as efficiently and effectively as possible.

**8. RECOMMENDATION:** Establish a Sandy Regional Infrastructure Permitting and Review Team that leverages the Executive Order 13604 framework for Sandy projects.

The Task Force has been able to build upon the foundational success of the work of the Steering Committee, which Executive Order 13604 established.[92] The Task Force believes that the best practices and tools already developed through that effort will ensure that the most complex Sandy projects are delivered as efficiently as possible. Best practices will be applied to: those Sandy-funded infrastructure projects that involve multiple Federal, State, local or Tribal permits or reviews; those involving a multi-step, complex Federal review process, which require heightened project management and transparency; or projects that are otherwise particularly costly.

Another component of the infrastructure initiative driven by Executive Order 13604 was the establishment of regional teams to ensure that Federal and State permitting officials have an open channel of communication about projects once projects are selected. To build on this effort, the Task Force worked with OMB, CEQ, and Task Force partner agencies to develop a parallel Sandy Regional Infrastructure Team, which is responsible for facilitating early and ongoing coordination, prompt identification and resolution of issues, and alignment of Federal and state processes where appropriate. The regional team, which would provide regular reports to the Infrastructure Steering Committee, includes appropriate points of contact from OMB, CEQ, and agency headquarters, as well as senior representatives from the Federal agencies with responsibility for the permitting and review of Sandy projects, and relevant State permitting and review agencies. The first meetings of the agencies engaged in developing the regional team charter and protocols are scheduled for August and September 2013. The continued efforts of this interagency team, led by HUD, will ensure that, as the region rebuilds, the permitting and review of complex infrastructure projects are coordinated and delivered as quickly as possible.

Owner
*Lead: HUD*
Status
Recommendation adopted: Currently available for projects funded by the Sandy Supplemental and could be applicable to future disaster recovery efforts in the region.

**9. RECOMMENDATION:** Leverage the Executive Order 13604 framework to identify opportunities to expedite and improve other types of review processes through programmatic agreement or consultation where appropriate.

Beyond the long-term, OMB-, and CEQ-led efforts on infrastructure permitting and the interagency unified Federal review effort, agencies also identified two State-focused solutions in Sandy recovery that will immediately inform the work of improving and expediting the permitting and review processes. These can and should be replicated in other contexts.

First, to expedite the review of housing recovery projects in New Jersey, FEMA and HUD recognized that one Federal review would be sufficient for both agencies. This coordinated effort will avoid the delay that sequential and redundant reviews of housing projects could otherwise cause. The agencies are pursuing similar approaches with the State of New York and New York City.

Second was FEMA's work on historic preservation agreements in New Jersey. Based on an innovative programmatic agreement that FEMA and ACHP developed in the 1990s, FEMA worked with the New Jersey State Historic Preservation Officer (SHPO), New Jersey State Office of Emergency Management, ACHP, and four Tribes to develop an agreement that would meet State-specific needs, agency review requirements, and promote historic preservation awareness.[93] This agreement satisfied historic preservation compliance responsibilities by significantly accelerating the timeframe for FEMA consultation with SHPO, exempting small- scale projects from further review, and establishing treatment measures to resolve adverse effects to historic properties. Additionally, HUD, FEMA, and ACHP developed an addendum to the FEMA agreement that allows the New Jersey Department of Community Affairs to use the same terms and process to satisfy their compliance responsibilities for projects that only use CDBG-DR funds. FEMA also executed a counterpart historic preservation agreement for Sandy-related undertakings with the State of New York. Meanwhile, HUD grantees will leverage FEMA's agreement to satisfy their compliance responsibilities.

The Task Force recommends that additional agencies engage with ACHP to identify opportunities for these types of prototype agreements. Similarly, legally required environmental review processes can also be improved and completed in a more consistent and timely manner, through the use of programmatic consultations.

The negotiation process required of agencies, ACHP, and relevant SHPOs and Tribal Historic Preservation Officers can be lengthy and complex; however, potential efficiencies in the rebuilding effort warrant that agencies should pursue these agreements for as many programs and states as possible before disaster strikes. The Infrastructure Steering Committee has identified programmatic agreements as a best practice with the potential for expanded use for historic preservation requirements as well as other statutorily required environmental reviews. Additionally, the interagency group developing a Unified Review process for future disaster recovery efforts will also examine this issue. In the interim, the Task Force recommends that agencies begin to work with ACHP to determine which programs or undertakings could potentially be covered, as well as work to develop and implement the relevant program agreements. These agreements are expected to expedite the review and permitting process, so as to quickly and effectively rebuild the Sandy-impacted region.

Owner
**Lead:** *The Infrastructure Steering Committee established by Executive Order 13604*
Status
Recommendation adopted: To be implemented for future projects funded by the Sandy Supplemental and could be applicable to future disaster recovery efforts nationwide.

**10. RECOMMENDATION:** Disaster recovery efforts should account for the temporary staffing needs of Federal agencies and State and local governments who conduct reviews and permitting of Federal disaster recovery projects.

Recovery efforts should be structured to account for the need to ensure that all agencies have the capacity to effectively and expeditiously manage the process of administration, review, and permitting to complete projects without unnecessary delay. Decisions for all programs should account for the temporary increase in review and permitting activities required at Federal, State, and local levels.

Federal project and permitting agencies and recipients should plan for the temporary increase in review and permitting activities required post-disaster to ensure that disaster-impacted communities can rebuild efficiently and without unnecessary delays.

Owner
**Lead:** *OMB, CEQ*
Status
Recommendation in process: Recommended for implementation to enhance recovery efforts in future storms in the region and applicable to rebuilding following disasters nationwide.


## Infrastructure Finance

### Challenge and Goal

The damaging impact of Hurricane Sandy exposed vulnerabilities in the region's infrastructure to weather-related risk. In order to effectively address this risk it is not enough to bring existing assets to the pre-storm state: these long-lived assets must be rebuilt sustainably and resiliently in a way that reflects consideration of future risk. In order to rebuild damaged infrastructure and address vulnerabilities to future disasters, more than $20 billion is currently being targeted at infrastructure projects, and more funding will be made available as State and local officials finalize plans for FEMA and HUD programs, such as the hazard mitigation portion of Public Assistance and CDBG-DR.[94] The size and scope of the disaster, as well as the need to build back resiliently across many types of infrastructure systems in several jurisdictions, increased the need for ongoing Federal technical assistance to States and localities to help ensure that Federal infrastructure investments are optimized.

Even with the significant investment from the Federal Government for rebuilding in the Sandy-affected region, State governments do not have sufficient staff or financial resources to ensure all critical infrastructure assets can be rebuilt in a way that is resilient to both current and future risks. One way in which the States are looking at addressing this issue is by bringing private capital funding and financing into these projects.

**11. RECOMMENDATION:** Provide technical assistance to States and localities to help optimize Sandy recovery infrastructure funding, share best practices, leverage resources, advance sustainability, and meet the needs of vulnerable communities.

The alignment of Federal funding and increased leverage of non-Federal funds for infrastructure projects are important to the success of disaster recovery in the Sandy-affected region. To optimize the use of the various Federal funding programs to support infrastructure resilience projects, a grantee must be able to align and sequence the funds across different agency programs that support different modes of infrastructure as well as, potentially, across multiple jurisdictions. The Task Force worked with Federal agencies to ensure that State and local jurisdictions have a clear understanding of program eligibility requirements to align use of Federal funds to maximize resilience and other key infrastructure investment criteria described in the Guidelines.

The Task Force worked to help States understand the opportunities provided by leveraging resources, which may be used in future contexts to address need beyond assets that Sandy damaged. Leverage in this context refers to increasing the pool of available non-Federal funding to support additional Sandy recovery infrastructure projects today by: requiring impacted States and localities to match a percentage of Federal funding with State and local funding; use by States of loan repayment streams or a portion of Federal capitalization grants as collateral in order to borrow money from private, tax-exempt bond markets; or use by States of Federal grants to serve as an incentive, through use of a loan loss reserve or other credit-enhancement instrument, to attract other forms of private investment to support infrastructure projects. These actions can help States and localities increase resilience and the number of projects that can be funded, and thereby speed and enhance the recovery.

A number of existing Federal funding programs that help States and localities leverage Federal funding to expand the pool of capital available for infrastructure projects offer valuable lessons of how Federal financing programs can leverage resources, inform planning, and fund crucially needed infrastructure. For example, EPA's State Revolving Fund (SRF) programs provide grants to States to capitalize State loan funds, which States use to provide loans to communities to support infrastructure projects that protect water quality or provide safe drinking water.[95] In many States, including New York and New Jersey, State SRF program funds are used as collateral to issue tax-exempt bonds, the proceeds of which are subsequently lent at low interest rates to localities to support the development of wastewater and drinking water infrastructure.[96]

Both DOT's Transportation Infrastructure Finance and Innovation Act (TIFIA) and SRF programs provide technical assistance to States in evaluating the costs and benefits of using these programs to leverage private dollars for investment in infrastructure;[97] yet, these programs are sector-specific and therefore not optimally positioned to analyze and support infrastructure resilience improvements across sectors in the context of disaster response.

A multi-sector Federal infrastructure financing entity could complement and build on these programs' successes and enhance the ability of States and localities to coordinate planning and leverage resources for disaster recovery as well as more generally. President Obama, in his FY2014 Budget, requested that Congress create such an institution in the form of a National Infrastructure Bank. Under the President's proposal, the National Infrastructure Bank would be able to leverage private and public capital to support infrastructure projects of national and regional significance across a broad range of infrastructure sectors, including transportation, water, and energy.[98] The National Infrastructure Bank proposal has been included in the President's last four annual budget requests to Congress and has received bipartisan support, but has not yet been enacted by Congress.[99]

While the Task Force believes a National Infrastructure Bank is a more effective and efficient method of supporting State efforts to leverage non-Federal funds to address the funding gap for more resilient infrastructure investment, until Congress acts on the President's proposal, supporting States directly on State-based, multi-sector infrastructure programs is a valuable and appropriate role for the Federal Government. Thus, in the absence of being able to rely on a national entity to help optimize Federal investments in resilient infrastructure through the Sandy Supplemental, the Task Force worked with both New York and New Jersey to ensure that Federal funds were available to support the development or expansion of State programs that can leverage non-Federal funds for infrastructure projects in Sandy-affected areas.

- In New York, for example, the Task Force worked with HUD and the State to ensure that an initial allocation of $20 million in CDBG-DR funding is available to support the creation of a State infrastructure fund. The Task Force also worked to ensure that the framework for this fund incorporates the criteria outlined in the Infrastructure Resilience Guidelines. New York State is structuring this fund to facilitate the alignment of public spending at the Federal, State, and local government level and to leverage public funds to attract additional private funding for Sandy-affected infrastructure projects across multiple infrastructure sectors, including water, transportation, and energy. If successful, the fund may present one possible model for other jurisdictions that are seeking effective strategies for aligning and leveraging Federal funding to support disaster recovery.

- The Task Force has also worked with HUD, DOE, and the States of New York and New Jersey to ensure that $30 million CDBG-DR funding is available to support financing targeted at improving the resilience of energy infrastructure in Sandy-affected areas. More specifically, New York is pursing the establishment of a "Green Bank" Resilience Retrofit program, and New Jersey is considering an energy finance program. The programs in New York and New Jersey are exploring the financing of energy resilience- oriented activities that target important infrastructure facilities, including, but not limited to, smart grid technologies as well as distributed and resilient energy generation assets, such as Combined Heat and Power (CHP), microgrids, solar, fuel cells, and energy storage. These efforts would allow both States to evaluate a loan loss reserve in stimulating private investment in necessary energy infrastructure improvements and repair in Sandy-affected areas.

Owner
**Leads:** *HUD, DOT, DOE, EPA*
Status
Recommendation adopted: Currently available for projects funded by the Sandy Supplemental and will be applicable to future disaster recovery efforts in the region.

## Energy Infrastructure

### Challenge and Goal

Extensive power outages during Sandy affected millions of residents and resulted in substantial economic loss to communities.[100] Despite the size and power of Hurricane Sandy, this was not inevitable: resilient energy solutions could have helped limit power outages. In addition, improvements in and hardening of, the liquid fuel supply chain would have prevented some of the most visible impacts of the storm.

One of the biggest problems with the liquid petroleum (i.e., gasoline and diesel fuel), supply chain after Hurricane Sandy was flooding damage to major terminals and docks in the Arthur Kill area of New Jersey, as described earlier.

As shortages accumulated, consumers struggled to find gas stations that were functional. The lack of shared priorities among different groups of critical officials and service providers led to shortages and a general lack of information and coordination. Immediately after the storm, the White House Office of Science and Technology Policy (OSTP), FEMA, and DOE worked together to use technology to help inform the public which gas stations were open and had fuel and power from a backup generator. In spite of these efforts, many people struggled to get accurate and timely information about available fuel sources.

To prevent shortages in future disasters, the Task Force worked to ensure that critical infrastructure such as hospitals, transportation systems, drinking water and wastewater treatment plants, and public facilities, as well as industrial economic engines such as refineries, office buildings, data centers, and manufacturing facilities, become more energy resilient as a result of investments made by the Federal government during the Sandy recovery. Additionally, the Task Force encourages the alignment of investments in the Nation's energy infrastructure with the goal of improved resilience and the national policy initiatives regarding climate change, transparency, and innovative technology deployment. Most energy infrastructure is privately owned and operated, which means that resilience investment will come about only through close cooperation between the Federal and State governments and the private sector.

**12. RECOMMENDATION:** Ensure that Sandy recovery energy investments are resilient.

The Task Force and DOE provided technical assistance to New York and New Jersey to help them evaluate and develop pilot projects, financial mechanisms, and policy and market development tools and to generally promote cost effective investments in resilient energy generation and storage using Sandy recovery funds. The Task Force and DOE are also helping the states explore ways to use fees paid by utility customers and other revenue streams to help finance energy resilience for infrastructure. The region, assisted by the

Federal Government, will launch programs later this year using public-private partnerships to lower project costs and increase the value of energy resilient infrastructure. Through these and other measures, New York and New Jersey have embraced the opportunity to provide national leadership in energy resilience.

Specifically, in New Jersey, DOE and the Task Force worked in partnership with the State to review critical facilities and energy infrastructure and to develop a State-wide solution for resilient energy infrastructure. The State is considering an energy finance program and exploring how facilities funded by the program could serve as primary hubs for microgrids, distributed generation, smart grid technologies, and energy storage. The analysis began with a mapping of all relevant systems and needs in the State for a qualitative and quantitative analysis of requirements for a resilient state-wide system. This effort will complement previous efforts performed under DOE grants for energy assurance plans. DOE and the State also reviewed various deployment models designed to lower the cost of capital financing and leverage private sector expertise and capital through public-private partnership. This review also included exploration of financing structures such as loan loss reserves, revolving loan funds, and other credit enhancement mechanisms that are designed to magnify the impact of scarce public dollars. With assistance from DOE, the State is also exploring ways to create markets that value energy reliability. These innovative structures have the potential to unlock value from resilience beyond what is reaped in the event of a disaster.

In Bergen County, N.J., the public utility authority used a biogas-powered CHP system to keep its sewage treatment facilities working during and after the storm.[101]

---

### SUCCESSFUL IMPLEMENTATION OF CHP SYSTEMS DURING AND AFTER HURRICANE SANDY

CHP is an efficient and clean approach to generating electric power and useful thermal energy from a single fuel source -- eliminating the need for a separate on-site boiler or furnace and purchased electricity. College campuses such as Princeton University, Stony Brook University, New York University, and the College of New Jersey, used CHP to keep the lights (and the heat) on both during the storm and in the days and weeks that followed.[102] South Oaks Hospital on Long Island and Connecticut's Danbury Hospital used CHP to keep medical facilities online when the local electrical grids failed.[103][104] Commercial buildings and even residential communities like Co-op City in Bronx County, N.Y. showed the enormous resilience of CHP during Sandy.[105]

---

In New York, the Task Force, HUD, and DOE are providing funding and technical assistance to support the planning and implementation of resilient energy communities using microgrid and other distributed generation and storage technologies through the Green Bank Resilience Retrofit program. Connecticut is also pursuing projects with microgrids and CHP systems through a solicitation process that was started in the State prior to Sandy. In response to requests from stakeholders and Members of Congress, the Task Force worked with HUD, DOE, and EPA to develop guidance relating to the use of disaster funding in the Sandy Supplemental to support CHP technologies. Lessons learned from Hurricane Sandy will be considered to ensure that our power systems across the country are more resilient to disaster.

This summer, the Task Force along with DOE, New York Governor's Office, New Jersey Governor's Office of Recovery and Rebuilding, and Connecticut Governor's Office, are participating in a discussion of innovative finance, policy, and market development approaches to energy resilience. All of these issues are aligned with the goal of "building stronger and safer communities and infrastructure" as set forth in the President's Climate Action Plan.

Owner
*Leads: DOE, HUD, FEMA, EPA*
Status
Recommendation adopted: Currently available for projects funded by the Sandy Supplemental and will, to the extent allowable by law and regulation, be applicable to future disaster recovery efforts in the region as well as future disaster recovery efforts nationwide.

**13. RECOMMENDATION:** Mitigate future impacts to the liquid fuels supply chain like those experienced during the Sandy recovery.

The Task Force, in partnership with DOE, worked with State and local officials in New York and New Jersey as well as with other Federal agencies and industry partners to find ways to improve the resilience of the fuel supply chain during and following disasters in the region. All aspects of the supply chain were considered and the outcome of those discussions was a consensus that disruptions to the supply chain are caused by a number of separate, but often related issues.

The issues raised in these discussions included:

- Physical impacts to key distribution facilities and infrastructure (e.g., marine terminals, refinery, pipelines, storage facilities).
- Electric power outages at retail filling stations and important transportation-related infrastructure (e.g., pipelines, refineries, marine terminals, storage facilities).
- Public awareness of which retail locations were open and had fuel available.

Additionally, local safety rules for backup generators, including limiting the amount of fuel storage (e.g., a 72-hour supply), and requiring larger volumes of fuel for backup generators to be stored in basement locations, impaired energy resilience or created additional unsafe situations following Sandy.[106] For example, Bellevue Hospital Center moved their generators from the first floor to a safer location on the 13th floor prior to Sandy; but because the fuel was still stored at ground level and the pumps which supplied the fuel to the generators were submerged, hospital staff created a human chain to move the fuel by hand up 13 floors to keep life-safety power operating and their patients safe for another two days. New York City and other jurisdictions are reviewing these requirements to determine if new rules can be developed to maintain safety while increasing resilience. Lessons learned from Hurricane Sandy will be considered to ensure that our fuel delivery systems across the country are more resilient to disaster.

Owner
**Leads:** *DOE, FEMA, HUD*
Status
Recommendation adopted: Currently available for projects funded by the Sandy Supplemental and will, to the extent allowable by law and regulation, be applicable to future disaster recovery efforts in the region as well as future disaster recovery efforts nationwide.

**14. RECOMMENDATION:** Encourage Federal and State cooperation to improve electric grid policies and standards.

States should work with DOE and the Institute of Electrical and Electronic Engineers to develop a new approach for electric grid operations. The new approach would define policies and technical requirements for how to incorporate smart grid technology, microgrids, building controls, and distributed generation, including CHP, with two-way flow networks into the grid. This approach would ensure that problems can be isolated, surviving generation can be optimally dispatched (with priority to essential services), and that degradation can be graceful and not catastrophic. This approach would allow building controls to provide a minimal level of service such as basic lights and refrigeration during emergencies. States should also review DOE's new report, "U.S. Energy Sector Vulnerabilities to Climate Change and Extreme Weather,"[107] which assesses vulnerabilities that would be helpful in developing a new approach for electric grid operations. Improvements need to include addressing damage to power generation and medium to long-term alternatives to power sources if critical power generation facilities are damaged or destroyed.

Owner
**Lead:** *DOE* Status
Recommendation adopted: To be implemented for future projects funded by the Sandy Supplemental and could be applicable to future disaster recovery efforts nationwide.

**15. RECOMMENDATION:** Mobilize the private sector and non-profit community to develop innovative solutions that support and integrate whole community efforts for disaster relief.

OSTP and FEMA, with the support of DOE and other Federal agencies, will convene an all-day brainstorm with whole community partners, such as technologists, entrepreneurs, designers, philanthropists and local and state officials at the White House to develop innovative solutions to support how disaster survivors respond to and recover from disasters. These solutions will empower disaster survivors and enhance the ability of first responders as well as Federal, State, and local officials to conduct response and recovery activities. All efforts will support and integrate whole community efforts to better prevent, protect, mitigate, respond to, and recover from disasters.

Owner
**Lead:** *OSTP and FEMA, in coordination with DOE, and other Federal agencies*
Status
Recommendation adopted: Brainstorm currently scheduled for the end of August.

**16. RECOMMENDATION:** Develop a resilient power strategy for wireless and data communications infrastructure and consumer equipment.

DOE and the National Telecommunications Information Administration (NTIA, part of DOC), should work with FCC to promote a programmatic approach to ensure that cellular towers (antennas), data centers, and other critical communications infrastructure are able to function regardless of the status of the electrical grid. In addition, encouraging stored power (i.e., batteries) for consumer level broadband equipment, through funding or other means, will improve impacted individuals' ability to seek information, help with recovery needs, communicate with family members, and even work from home when transportation or business facilities are significantly compromised.

Owner
*Leads: DOE and NTIA*
Status
Recommendation in process: Under consideration for implementation for future recovery efforts.


## Transportation Infrastructure

### Challenge and Goal
Sandy caused damages directly (from the wind and water) and indirectly (loss of power) to the region's transportation infrastructure. More than half of the nation's total daily trips on public transportation systems occur within the Sandy-affected region. The day after the storm, nearly all of the region's systems were shut down due to flooding, wind damage, or loss of power, further complicating the rebuilding effort.

Adding to the difficulty of restoring transit in the region was the fact that the Federal Transit Administration (FTA), the Federal agency responsible for supporting the recovery of transit, was unfunded for this purpose and had no rules and regulations in place to allocate funding once Congress made an appropriation. In 2012, Congress authorized, but did not immediately fund an emergency relief program for public transit.[108] In addition, DOT was working diligently to implement several provisions in the law that had short implementation deadlines. The transit emergency relief program authorized in the law was not one of the programs with a statutory implementation deadline, so it was prioritized behind the programs Congress required in the statue to be implemented quickly. The Federal Highway Administration's (FHWA) Transportation Emergency Relief program, covering roadways, bridges, and tunnels, had successfully been used prior to Hurricane Sandy, but was also in need of funding to be able to respond to immediate needs after the storm. Ultimately, Congress appropriated over $12 billion to the two programs in the Sandy Supplemental.

On March 29, 2013, FTA issued an interim final rule to direct the transit emergency relief program to ensure that Sandy funds were quickly but appropriately allocated to repair projects in the region. This regulation sets forth the general program requirements for funds expended under the program. Due to some structural differences between the highway and transit programs at DOT, the highway emergency relief program rules are different. The transit rules are more reflective of the overall policy goals of rebuilding more resiliently and ensuring that all investments align with national policy goals such as flood risk management and climate change adaptation. The Task Force's goal is to align both programs with current national policy goals and lessons learned from the Hurricane Sandy recovery efforts.

**17. RECOMMENDATION:** Expedite flow of Sandy transportation funding to needed repairs.

The Task Force and DOT worked closely with State transportation agencies and transit operators in the region to ensure that DOT efforts were coordinated with other agency efforts and aligned with national policy goals being developed by the Task Force.

Soon after the establishment of the Task Force in December 2012, Secretary Donovan, DOT Deputy Secretary Porcari, and FTA Administrator Peter Rogoff met with the heads of the major transit agencies in the region to make clear that once funding was appropriated by Congress, DOT would make it quickly available, but with tight reporting requirements and controls. With an assessor on the ground in the days immediately after the storm's impact, FTA worked closely with the large affected transit agencies to determine the extent of the damage, estimate the costs of needed repairs, and ensure that the design for the repair work improved the resilience of the systems against future storms.

Coordination between the FHWA and the States was initiated immediately after the storm, even before funding was available.

In addition, FEMA is funding, under its Public Assistance program, repairs to airports, port and harbor facilities, and other publicly owned transportation systems not covered by the FTA or FHWA emergency relief programs. Most of these assets were owned by the Port Authority of New York and New Jersey, which worked closely with FEMA to assess damages and estimate repair costs. To ensure FEMA and FTA did not provide duplication of funding to State and local transportation agencies, FEMA and the FTA signed a Memorandum of Understanding on March 25, 2013, clearly stating what types of projects would be funded by each agency.[109]

Other transportation systems, such as the intercity rail lines operated by Amtrak, and Federal assets at airports such as air traffic control towers and navigation systems, were funded or repaired by the Federal Railroad Administration (FRA) or the Federal Aviation Administration (FAA), respectively. In a unique partnership with NPS, the piers and docks on Liberty Island, which allow ferry access to the Statue of Liberty, were repaired by the Eastern Federal Lands division of FHWA.

As a result of its internal efforts to address the speed of recovery and the need for accuracy and accountability, FTA allocated $2 billion within the first 60 days of the authorization's enactment, and FHWA was able to release close to $500 million in emergency relief funds by March 2013. Real projects are now complete or currently underway, including restoration to Ocean Parkway, work to repair New Jersey Transit's Hoboken Terminal, efforts to reopen Route 154 in Old Saybrook, Connecticut and restoring tunnel lighting, track replacement, power cables, signals and communications equipment for the Greenpoint Tube in New York City.

Owner

**Lead:** *DOT* Status

Recommendation adopted: Currently available for projects funded by the Sandy Supplemental as well as future disasters in the Sandy-affected region.

**18. RECOMMENDATION:** Align Sandy transportation funding expenditures with national policy goals.

The Federal Flood Risk Reduction Standard announced by the Task Force (best available flood hazard data plus one foot of freeboard) applies to the rebuilding of structures that were substantially damaged and will be repaired or rebuilt with Federal funding. For example, DOT has adopted the flood risk reduction standard for all Sandy-related transportation repairs and resilience projects. FTA has included the Standard in its interim final rule for its emergency relief program.

The second allocation of public transportation emergency relief funds in response to Sandy that included $5.7 billion in funds for four of the area's most affected transit agencies, of which $1.3 billion will be used for locally prioritized projects to make transit systems more resilient to future disasters. FTA will also develop a competitive process for additional Sandy funding to identify and support larger, stand-alone resilience projects in the impacted region. The new resilience grants will be based in part on the successful Transportation Investment Generating Economic Recovery (TIGER) program, which was developed under the American Recovery and Reinvestment Act, 2009 (ARRA) to generate economic growth and environmental benefits for an entire region. FTA is taking the TIGER model and incorporating the Infrastructure Resilience Guidelines and other resilience components, including the goals of the President's Climate Action Plan, to develop a specific program for the Sandy-affected region. The overall goal of the new program is to ensure the region's public transit systems can continue to serve their critical function in the face of future disasters and the impacts of climate change.

Owner

**Lead:** *DOT*

Status

Recommendation adopted: Currently available for projects funded by the Sandy Supplemental and will be applicable to future disaster recovery efforts in the region.

# Green Infrastructure

## *Challenge and Goal*

For the purposes of this Rebuilding Strategy, green infrastructure is defined as the integration of natural systems and processes, or engineered systems that mimic natural systems and processes, into investments in resilient infrastructure.[110] Green infrastructure takes advantage of the services and natural defenses provided by land and water systems such as wetlands, natural areas, vegetated sand dunes, and forests, while contributing to the health and quality of life of America's communities.

At the scale of a neighborhood or community, green infrastructure may refer to stormwater management systems that mimic nature by soaking up and storing water or to the patchwork of natural areas that provides habitat, flood protection, cleaner air, and cleaner water to communities (noting that some jurisdictions are experimenting with implementing green infrastructure stormwater management systems on a citywide or watershed basis). On a larger scale, there are a variety of ways in which humans are trying to prevent the flooding of coastal environments by implementing green infrastructure.

Communities at increasing risk from coastal storms can use green infrastructure approaches that restore degraded or lost natural systems (e.g., wetlands and sand dunes ecosystems) and other shoreline areas to enhance storm protection and reap the many benefits that are provided by these systems. There is also quantitative evidence supporting the importance of protecting intact systems where they exist because these systems may provide some wave attenuation capability, particularly in low-energy storm surges.[111] Protecting, retaining, and enhancing these natural defenses should be considered as part of any coastal resilience strategy.

The Task Force worked to ensure that Sandy Supplemental funding for infrastructure is used to integrate these types of nature-based approaches, where appropriate and beneficial, into designs for recovery and hazard mitigation projects across the region. And that it was done in alignment with both the Infrastructure Resilience Guidelines and the President's Climate Action Plan.

## Successes in Hazard Mitigation through Green Infrastructure during Hurricane Sandy

Green infrastructure includes natural and/or restored features (e.g., wetlands or sand dune ecosystems), that incorporate the natural processes (e.g., flood protection, water filtration) that are recognized as integral to community, economic, and environmental resilience. These approaches have proven successful in other regions, and it appears they reduced flood damage where applied in the region impacted by Sandy.

During Sandy, an example of effective hazard mitigation through green infrastructure was demonstrated at the Alligator River National Wildlife Refuge in North Carolina. As part of a climate change adaptation project, oyster reefs were installed several years ago parallel to the Pamlico Sound shoreline near Point Peter Road and the canal that ends at the Sound. The oyster reefs absorbed some of the energy of storm-generated waves and decreased the amount of erosion at the end of Point Peter Road and along the shoreline adjacent to the road. The water control structure installed in the canal next to the road as part of this project likely slowed erosion by adapting the flow of storm flood waters from a channelized system to a sheet flow system which emulated natural processes.

**19. RECOMMENDATION:** Consider green infrastructure options in all Sandy infrastructure investments.

To ensure that Federal infrastructure investments are resilient while also supporting Federal goals to promote innovation, environmental sustainability, resilience, and climate adaptation, the Task Force developed a set of Guidelines for Federal infrastructure investment in Sandy recovery. Environmentally sustainable approaches will include consideration and integration of the following ecosystem services, including valuation where feasible and appropriate: (1) provision of habitat (coastal, inter-coastal, inland); (2) landscape conservation for the tourism, recreation, and aesthetic values on which economies depend; (3) watershed protection for clean drinking water and improved flood management; (4) threatened and endangered species conservation and restoration; and (5) other associated ecosystem services from which people derive benefits (e.g., aquaculture and recreational and commercial fishing). The Guidelines, discussed in more detail at the beginning of this chapter, are being applied by Federal agencies to grants, loans, Federal construction, and all other Federal infrastructure funding mechanisms supporting recovery in the Sandy-impacted region. Rather than just rebuilding damaged infrastructure to its pre-disaster standard, these Guidelines and other proposals within the Rebuilding Strategy, encourage construction of sustainable and resilient infrastructure built to better withstand future disasters.

Federal agencies funding and building infrastructure projects are leading the implementation of this recommendation in coordination with other Federal agencies with capabilities in natural science and State and local partners.

Owner
***Leads:*** *Agencies funding and building infrastructure projects (DOT, HUD, USACE, DOI, EPA, DHS, GSA, U.S. Department of Defense (DOD), HHS, VA)*
***Supporting Agencies:*** *CEQ, OSTP, NOAA, USDA*
Status
Recommendation adopted: Currently available for projects funded by the Sandy Supplemental and will be applicable to future disaster recovery efforts in the region as well as future disaster recovery efforts nationwide.

**20. RECOMMENDATION:** Improve the understanding and decision-making tools for green infrastructure through projects funded by the Sandy Supplemental.

The Task Force worked with Federal agencies to ensure that Sandy-affected States and local communities that are interested in pursuing green infrastructure solutions have access to Federal tools that can assist them in evaluating whether green infrastructure can be a beneficial component of their recovery strategy. Agencies such as EPA, USACE, NOAA, and DOI provide a range of tools to State and local partners, including modeling capabilities, decision support tools, case studies, and best management practices. The Task Force also worked with agencies and the private sector to leverage Federal funding programs, green infrastructure set asides, and other resources to mobilize private financing for natural infrastructure solutions. Continued progress will require a focus on developing and improving techniques and tools for measuring and predicting the effectiveness of natural infrastructure approaches, and on innovative uses of Federal and local funds to attract more private investments. The following examples are a sampling of how agency Sandy recovery efforts are providing valuable science- based information on how best to integrate natural systems in creating resilient infrastructure, communities, and economies.

NOAA is advancing the integration of green infrastructure into Sandy recovery and resilience efforts by providing financial support, information, tools, and services for coastal communities. With Sandy supplemental funding, NOAA will be releasing Coastal Resilient

Networks (known as CRest) grants to provide funding for advancing recovery efforts, with priorities that target resilient communities and coastlines, including promotion of natural shoreline restoration efforts.

NOAA, in partnership with USACE and other Federal agencies, is also supporting an economic assessment to analyze the relative levels of inundation protection and related benefits associated with shoreline rebuilding and restoration alternatives in the Sandy-affected region. This analysis will provide information on benefits and cost-effectiveness of different alternatives to inform recovery and resilience efforts. NOAA will also be revising and updating Environmental Sensitivity Index maps in areas affected by Sandy, which will provide important reference material for green infrastructure planning.[112] Finally, Sandy funding will support restoration and repair of a range of sensors and monitoring infrastructure damaged by the storm to inform modeling and predictive capabilities relative to sea level rise and flood surge. These efforts and related information, tools, and training will support assessments and implementation of natural systems to reduce impacts of storms and provide information and guidance on integrating natural (e.g., living shorelines and wetlands restoration) and nature-based (e.g., sand dune ecosystem creation) approaches to increase resilience of coastal ecosystems and communities.

As a part of its responsibilities for managing national parks and refuges along the nation's coasts, DOI is researching and monitoring the effectiveness of green infrastructure in their role in promoting coastal resilience. Within DOI, several agencies are using Sandy recovery funding or working in Sandy-affected areas to further the science and understanding of green infrastructure.

- USGS initiated efforts to provide communities with updated (post-storm) mapping of land and water features as well as real time data on stormwater levels to support model predictions of the surge of high water levels during storms and the impacts they have on coastal bays and estuaries.

- The Bureau of Ocean Energy Management has initiated projects involving data collection and resource identification, environmental assessment, environmental monitoring, and stakeholder support and outreach to be responsive to the need for sand resources for projects in Massachusetts, Rhode Island, New York, New Jersey, Delaware, Maryland, Virginia, North Carolina, South Carolina, and Florida.

- NPS is currently assessing the role of the coastal barriers in providing protection to shore communities and monitoring how quickly beaches and dunes recover from the erosional impacts of Sandy. In partnership with USGS, they are also monitoring the biological and physical response of a breach in the federal wilderness on Fire Island in New York. A large body of scientific data and information published over the past 50 years show that the influx of large amounts of sediment and water from the ocean into the bays, which result from breaching, are essential for the long-term maintenance of the barrier island and back-bay systems and their biologically diverse habitats and ecosystems.[113] Protecting these barrier island processes is an essential element in maintaining long- term resilience to the barrier and long-term protection to mainland communities.

- At the John H. Chafee National Wildlife Refuge in Rhode Island, the U.S. Fish and Wildlife Service is working with The Nature Conservancy to repair extensive shoreline erosion by using natural materials and "living shoreline" techniques, making this important salt marsh better able to withstand future storm impacts.

Several agencies are also collaborating to promote and study green infrastructure options. EPA and the USGS are partnering on a targeted pilot initiative to support the Task Force using an ecosystem services analytic framework. The pilot will build on recent scholarship seeking to quantify how retained natural ecosystems and habitats can serve to increase resilience by protecting coastal communities and ecosystems from flooding and storm damage, and will evaluate tradeoffs between retaining natural systems and enabling development.[114]

USACE has undertaken and is presently undertaking several actions to implement this recommendation in partnership with other stakeholders. The Sandy Supplemental requires a Comprehensive Study of the flood risks of vulnerable coastal populations in areas that were affected by Hurricane Sandy. Tools are also being developed to identify opportunities to coordinate navigation dredging and regional sediment management programs to promote a robust coastal landscape that provides a full range of economic, environmental, and risk reduction services.

Dredging actions undertaken as a part of the Sandy Supplemental are currently utilizing nature-based approaches which support the development of nature-based features through the beneficial use of dredged material (i.e., consistent with USACE's Engineering With Nature research). Coordination with State and local authorities on these projects in New Jersey and Rhode Island are providing opportunities for innovations in dredging operations that will nourish eroded beaches and near-shore habitats, construct wetlands, and restore island habitats that were damaged during Sandy.

Owner
**Leads:** *DOI, NOAA, USACE, EPA, USDA*
Status
Recommendation adopted: Currently available for projects funded by the Sandy Supplemental and will be applicable to future disaster recovery efforts nationwide.

**21. RECOMMENDATION:** Create opportunities for innovations in green infrastructure technology and design using Sandy funding, particularly in vulnerable communities.

The Sandy Supplemental included $570 million in funding for capitalization grants to EPA SRF programs ($475 million for wastewater treatment and $95 million for drinking water), which primarily provides localities with low-interest financing to support renovations and improvements designed to enhance resilience and to mitigate against flood risk in the Sandy- affected region. In recent months, EPA has worked closely with New York and New Jersey to develop guidelines, issued May 2013, on eligible uses of the these funds, which include both green infrastructure stormwater management systems, such as permeable pavement and green roofs, and natural storm surge prevention systems, such as sand dune ecosystems, tidal wetlands, and natural berms or levees, as well as supporting efforts in vulnerable communities.

To help build coastal resilience, DOI is launching a $100 million competitive grant program using funding provided for Sandy recovery to foster partnerships and promote resilient natural systems while enhancing green spaces and wildlife habitat in needed areas along the Sandy landscape. An additional $242 million from the Sandy Supplemental will be allocated to support projects for coastal restoration and resilience at DOI assets, including national parks, refuges, and Tribal lands across the region. Through the lessons learned by implementing these projects and monitoring their future success at enhancing resilience and protecting communities, DOI intends to build knowledge to better prepare the Federal Government and local communities as they prepare for future storms.

One more innovative way the Task Force is creating opportunities for green infrastructure is the regional design competition, Rebuild by Design, described in more detail on page 47. While green alternatives are encouraged in all focus areas, the ecological and water body network focus area of the competition specifically requests concepts that address the interdependencies between the natural and built environments.

Owner
**Leads:** *DOI, EPA, HUD*
Status
Recommendation adopted: To be implemented for future projects funded by the Sandy Supplemental.

**22. RECOMMENDATION:** Develop a consistent approach to valuing the benefits of green approaches to infrastructure development and develop tools, data, and best practices to advance the broad integration of green infrastructure.

Research suggests that green as well as gray infrastructure, and the integration of the two, can reduce the risk of fatalities and property loss in vulnerable coastal communities and provide significant additional measurable benefits.[115] However, more work is needed to develop short- and long-term benefit-cost analysis and science-based decision criteria for reducing the risk of flooding through these systems. CEQ should convene relevant parties from across government to develop a consistent, science-based approach for evaluating the value and performance of nature-based defenses for coastal protection, stormwater management, building design, and environmental compliance mitigation requirements, and to develop a clearinghouse of tools, data, and best practices for integrating green infrastructure and Low Impact Development in urban coastal areas into all applicable Federal investments. This work should make use of several ongoing efforts such as: the USACE Comprehensive Study; DOI's competitive grant program for coastal habitat restoration; EPA's existing body of research and experience with stormwater-related green infrastructure; the Infrastructure Systems Rebuilding Principles developed by NOAA and USACE to promote a unified strategy for activities in coastal restoration; work to implement the President's Climate Action Plan; and various existing research efforts underway or funded by agencies such as USACE, NOAA, DOI, USDA, and EPA. This effort should focus on developing, and making publicly available, a set of tools and data to assist States and local communities in understanding and replicating best practices across regions, and in evaluating the full value of green investments, including the positive external effects on addressing climate change and other threats, and investigating market-based approaches to ecosystem services to capture the full value of green infrastructure investments. This effort should include engagement of coastal and community decision makers to help identify information needs and evaluate methodologies.

In addition to efforts to provide tools, information, and best practices for valuing and deploying green infrastructure and natural defenses, agencies should examine how to improve and better leverage incentives for green infrastructure deployment, and work to remove unnecessary barriers.

Owner
*Lead: CEQ*
*Supporting Agencies: OSTP, EPA, NOAA, DOI, USACE, USDA*
Status
Recommendation in process: Recommended for implementation for future projects funded by the Sandy Supplemental and coordinated with implementation of the President's Climate Action Plan.

## Water Infrastructure

### *Challenge and Goal*

Water is one of the most basic and essential resources on the planet. The management of water requires a broad range of systems and facilities to ensure that we have enough where we need it and not too much where we do not want it. Whether it involves flood risk reduction, stormwater or wastewater management, or ensuring clean and available drinking water, the resilience of complex water infrastructure is critical to the health of individuals and the viability of communities. One common theme impacting the development of water infrastructure is the emphasis on maintaining the delicate ecological balance required to preserve this crucial natural resource. As was discussed in the previous section on green infrastructure, using natural systems or building infrastructure which mimics nature is an important way to maintain this balance. The integration of gray and green types of infrastructure is important in managing water because it furthers the national policy goals of environmental sustainability, working to mitigate the impacts of climate change, and adaptation to the impacts of rising sea levels and more intense storms.

Hurricane Sandy overwhelmed, compromised, and in some cases destroyed much of the region's water infrastructure. Beaches were washed onto roads, houses, rivers, and even across barrier islands. Flood walls were breached and overtopped and stormwater systems were inundated. The flooding and loss of power caused wastewater and drinking water systems to fail, impacting hundreds of thousands of people and causing untold ecological damages to waterways and sensitive habitats.

The Task Force worked to ensure that water infrastructure repaired, built, or improved as part of the Sandy recovery addresses the national policy goals of resilience, sustainability, and climate change adaptation.

**23. RECOMMENDATION:** Ensure Sandy recovery water infrastructure investments are timely, resilient, sustainable, and effective.

In the area of stormwater management, EPA has been leading efforts to incorporate natural systems into infrastructure for many years. EPA's programs provide technical assistance and training, modeling tools, research, partnership opportunities, and further encourage the use of green systems to manage wet weather through the permitting and regulatory processes under the Clean Water Act. These projects promote resilience and ecosystem benefits, and they have been proven to reduce flooding risk from stormwater. EPA has been providing this support to the State and local agencies throughout the Sandy recovery process.

The repair of wastewater and drinking water facilities damaged by Sandy is being addressed, in large part, by FEMA under the Public Assistance program. FEMA will spend more than a billion dollars on repairs to these facilities and improvements to ensure they are prepared for threats posed by future sea level rise and other impacts of climate change. FEMA's programs can fund resilience mitigation as part of a repair project or separately as part of the Hazard Mitigation Grant Program (HMGP). HMGP funds are prioritized by the States and the total amount of funding is based on a percentage of funds approved to repair damage within the State. DOE and the Task Force provided New York and New Jersey technical assistance to identify critical projects and develop strategies to help them maximize the impact of HMGP funding.

Using Sandy Supplemental funding provided to the New York and New Jersey SRFs, EPA and the States will work to ensure impacted drinking water and wastewater systems are more resilient. The States develop project plans and submit their plans to EPA for review and for public comment. EPA allows, and strongly encourages, the use of green infrastructure as part of these project plans, but ultimately the States are responsible for project selection. New York and New Jersey are also considering financing programs that leverage CDBG-DR funding to attract private capital to support resilient energy investments to protect the water infrastructure. DOE and EPA have been providing technical assistance to help the States evaluate the energy and water nexus and explore public-private partnerships to make these water facilities more energy efficient and resilient.[116]

The Sandy Supplemental also authorized and appropriated funds for USACE to undertake a Comprehensive Study of the flood risks of vulnerable coastal populations in areas that were affected by Hurricane Sandy within the boundaries of the North Atlantic Division of USACE. The Sandy Supplemental further requires the "evaluation of the performance of existing projects constructed by USACE and impacted by Hurricane Sandy for the purposes of determining their effectiveness and making recommendations for improvements thereto."

The Comprehensive Study will be a broad, conceptual, examination of the best ideas and approaches to reducing the vulnerability to major storms over time in a way that is sustainable over the long-term both for the natural coastal ecosystem and for communities given expected changes in sea level rise, extreme weather events, and other impacts of climate change. The study will include economic analyses and will also investigate how more emphasis on naturally occurring features and processes might contribute to a reduction in the flood and coastal storm risks. The study will also evaluate the performance of green infrastructure, such as ecosystems, during Hurricane Sandy and investigate the potential for risk reduction measures for back-bay communities. The Comprehensive Study will be aligned with the President's Climate Action Plan, the Infrastructure Resilience Guidelines, and the Infrastructure Systems Rebuilding Principles jointly developed with NOAA. USACE will proceed collaboratively in partnership with Federal, State, tribal, and local officials, with participation and input from the public, academia, NGOs, and the private sector.

Owner

**Leads:** *USACE, EPA, NOAA, HUD, DOI, FEMA, DOE*

Status

Recommendation adopted: Currently available for projects funded by the Sandy Supplemental and will be applicable to future disaster recovery efforts in the region.

**24. RECOMMENDATION:** Ensure Sandy recovery water infrastructure projects are coordinated with other infrastructure investments.

Much of the extensive damage to infrastructure across the region was caused by flooding from storm surge and from the loss of electrical power, which also resulted from flooding. As described above, the Task Force has initiated a process to ensure that infrastructure resilience projects are considered in the context of other projects in the region, which may have some dependencies or linkages across geography or type of infrastructure. The regional coordination effort is described at the beginning of this chapter. EPA, FEMA, DOI, HUD, and USACE are the main agencies funding water projects and will be responsible for participating in the regional coordination efforts along with DOE who will provide best practices and technical assistance capabilities for energy resilience projects to protect water infrastructure from vulnerabilities in the grid.

Owner

**Leads:** *HUD, EPA*

**Supporting Agencies**: *USACE, EPA, NOAA, DOI, FEMA, DOE*

Status

Recommendation adopted: Currently available for projects funded by the Sandy Supplemental and will be applicable to future disaster recovery efforts in the region.

# Building Codes

## *Challenge and Goal*

Using disaster-resistant local building codes is the most effective method to ensure new and rebuilt structures are designed and constructed to a more resilient standard. The adoption and enforcement of building codes happens at both the State and municipal levels; but, a consortium of experts, practitioners, and stakeholders from both the public and private sector—under the auspices of the non- profit International Code Council (ICC)—develop the consensus model codes. The ICC is an association whose mission includes developing model codes and standards used to ensure the safety, sustainability, and consistency of buildings and other engineered structures. The membership of the ICC includes approximately 50,000 Federal, State, and local code enforcement and fire officials, as well as architects, engineers, and other construction professionals and manufacturers. The ICC publishes the International Codes (I-Codes), which all fifty states and the District of Columbia have adopted.[117]

Additionally, the I-Codes are referenced in construction guidelines of some corporations and are used by many Federal agencies. One of the I-Codes used for commercial construction is the International Building Code (IBC). The I-Codes are published on a three-year cycle, with the most current version of the IBC being the 2012 version (published in April 2012).

The International Residential Code (IRC) is a stand-alone code that covers regulations for one- and two-family dwellings and townhouses.

While the IBC and IRC have been adopted in the States most impacted by Sandy, the most current version of the model building codes (2012) have only been adopted in Rhode Island and Maryland: New Jersey has adopted the 2009 version, New York the 2006 version, and Connecticut the 2003 version. Both New York and New Jersey, however, are currently in the process of adopting the current editions of the codes.

**25. RECOMMENDATION:** States and localities should adopt and enforce the most current version of the IBC and the IRC.

Use of the most current code ensures that buildings and other structures incorporate the latest science, advances in technology, and lessons learned. These codes help ensure that more resilient structures are built and that communities are better protected from all types of hazards and disasters. The codes are models and should be reviewed to ensure all local issues and geographic vulnerabilities are addressed in the final code that the jurisdiction adopts. In most cases, States and municipalities add specific requirements or increase the standards, but in some cases they have removed or weakened key provisions of the model codes. State and localities should be careful when considering changes to the model codes during the adoption process to ensure that they do not compromise the level of resilience and safety that these standards afford.

In some States, a complex regulatory review process delays the adoption of the most current codes. As noted above, the review process is important to ensure local issues and requirements are included in the adopted code, but it is also important to adopt the new versions of the codes as quickly as possible to provide the most current science and thinking on resilience into all new and rebuilt structures. Finally, much like the advisory base flood elevation mapping that FEMA released, the current version of the model codes can be adopted by private sector owners when building or improving structures, as a way to ensure their building provides the highest level of safety, resilience, and sustainability even if the local codes do not yet require some of these standards. Building to these standards not only will reduce risk, but also could, in turn, lead to lower insurance rates and maintenance costs.

Owner
*Lead*: MitFLG as a coordinating entity
Status
Recommendation in process: Recommended for implementation for future projects funded by the Sandy Supplemental and applicable to resilient rebuilding following disasters nationwide. This recommendation has been referred to the MitFLG for coordination.

# RESTORING AND STRENGTHENING HOMES AND PROVIDING FAMILIES WITH SAFE, AFFORDABLE HOUSING OPTIONS

From the public housing projects in Queens and Brooklyn that remained for days without light and heat to the beach front towns along the Jersey shore where surging tides plowed houses from their foundations and left them buried in sand, the storm upended tens of thousands of lives across the New York and New Jersey region. Sandy rendered individual homes and entire neighborhoods uninhabitable and, in some cases, unrecognizable.

Because the region has a high population density, relatively expensive housing market, and low housing inventory, responding to the housing needs of affected residents raised challenges different from those faced in disasters such as Katrina, Ike, and Rita. Affordable, temporary housing units in close proximity to storm-affected neighborhoods were in short supply, which forced Federal, State and local authorities to employ an array of policy tools to provide displaced individuals with a place to stay. Some of these tools had been used in past disasters, but many were significantly adapted or developed in real time to respond to Sandy.

## Shelter-in-Place Initiatives

### Challenge and Goal

In the immediate aftermath of the storm, agencies charged with response and recovery faced the daunting task of finding short-term housing for tens of thousands of people with damaged homes. Quickly rehabilitating salvageable homes became an essential response activity, especially given the high cost and scarcity of temporary housing in the Sandy-affected areas. FEMA assistance allowed those without alternatives to temporarily relocate to hotels, but few expected these programs to sufficiently cover every eligible household.

**26. RECOMMENDATION:** For future disasters that affect high-density and high cost areas, shelter-in-place programs like New York City's Rapid Repair and FEMA's Sheltering and Temporary Essential Power (STEP) programs should be implemented to reduce the number of people displaced from their homes that would otherwise require short-term housing. Evaluate the effectiveness of STEP and compare outcomes to other forms of temporary emergency sheltering implemented in response to Sandy. In addition, evaluate the New York, New Jersey, and New York City implementation of sheltering in place programs.

In New York City, thousands of households were able to take advantage of the City's newly developed Rapid Repair program. This program funded temporary emergency repairs, which permitted homeowners to quickly restore their dwellings to a level of habitability. This allowed temporary units to be available for those who needed them and prevented families from having to relocate.[118] Rapid Repair is an adaptation of FEMA's STEP program. STEP is a new pilot program that provides homeowners with a maximum of $10,000 per unit to complete necessary and essential repairs to their primary residences, including the restoration of power, heat, and hot water, as well as temporary exterior repairs.[119] New York City worked with FEMA to adapt STEP so that the program would be compatible with the City's particular needs, including the City's specific permitting requirements.

In New Jersey, the State requested implementation of the existing shelter in place options, Blue Roof and Rapid Temporary Repair, immediately after the disaster. FEMA later made STEP available in Atlantic, Cape May, Middlesex, Monmouth, and Ocean Counties; however, the program was only used in the town of Sea Bright, with very mixed results.[120]

Programs like STEP and NYC Rapid Repairs reduced the need for emergency shelter.[121] The Task Force recommends that FEMA study STEP and NYC Rapid Repairs to evaluate their success, determine whether and to what extent such programs should be eligible and/or improved for future disasters, and, as appropriate, strengthen and scale the program to ensure that it is replicable in diverse communities nationwide.

Owner
*Lead: FEMA*
Status
Recommendation in process: FEMA has already begun a review and analysis of its shelter in place programs. This review will include examining the potential of expanding the STEP program nationwide.

## Community Development Block Grant – Disaster Recovery

*Challenge and Goal*
As State and local governments in the hardest hit areas of the region confronted the enormity of the task ahead of them, they depended on the Federal government to fund numerous projects, including costly rehabilitation programs for damaged homes and the elevation of houses that sat in the floodplain. To provide State and local governments with the funding and flexibility they needed to finance unmet recovery needs, Congress appropriated over $15 billion for the CDBG-DR program to fund recovery from Sandy and other eligible disasters. Allocating these CDBG-DR funds quickly and effectively was the responsibility of HUD, as was providing appropriate standards and guidance for grantees.

**27. RECOMMENDATION:** HUD should expedite future allocations from the remaining CDBG- DR funds for Sandy recovery and other eligible disasters, as well as other allocations (if appropriated) for future disasters. HUD should continue to provide consistent and appropriate standards for the use of CDBG-DR funding. In addition, HUD should encourage grantees to use toolkits and other existing resources to expedite program implementation.

The Task Force worked with HUD to expedite CDBG-DR allocations and to ensure that appropriate standards guided the use of these funds. Under the CDBG-DR program, funds are allocated to affected State and local government grantees based on objective determinations of need. Eligible recipients (potential grantees) then submit action plans, which detail how the eligible recipients would use funds and how they would meet the objectives of the CDBG-DR program. These objectives focus on assisting low-and moderate-income (LMI) populations, providing affordable and workforce housing, promoting sustainable and resilient rebuilding, and assisting those who are most vulnerable to disasters.

---

### GREEN BUILDING STANDARDS

To encourage sustainable building practices in the storm-affected region, HUD is requiring CDBG-DR grantees to adopt green building standards for replacement and new construction of residential housing.

Although even prior to Sandy there was significant interest in these types of standards in the region, some state and local jurisdictions either had not previously applied any energy efficiency standards or had applied inconsistent standards. Through the CDBG-DR Notice, HUD provided a menu of standards that could be applied uniformly across each jurisdiction. These standards not only promote greater energy efficiency, but also improve long-term affordability by reducing utility costs. This marks the first time that a CDBG-DR allocation has included such standards.

After Sandy, HUD made its first CDBG-DR allocation in record time— just eight days from when Congress appropriated funds— which allowed money to flow as quickly as possible to grantees once their action plans were submitted and approved. New York State's plan dedicated $838 million for housing programs,[122] New Jersey's provided $1.16 billion,[123] and New York City's allocated $648 million.[124] In all three instances, plans focused on the rebuilding or rehabilitation of single family and multifamily buildings, while also including resilience and mitigation measures. All three action plans also addressed vulnerable populations, including the elderly and the disabled, and made funding available for mold remediation.

### HUD Programs in a Box

When responding to Sandy, all three of the primary grantees of disaster recovery funds (New York, New Jersey, and New York City) developed a significant number of CDBG-DR funded programs on their own. For example, these grantees established buyout programs, set up housing counseling services, and performed rehabilitation work in their jurisdictions. Not all CDBG-DR grantees have the capability or the institutional knowledge to develop these kinds of programs quickly after a disaster. For this reason, HUD developed tool kits, or "Programs in a Box," that grantees can readily utilize to speed program implementation. Grantees that receive future CDBG-DR allocations can use these toolkits for Sandy or future disasters. Sandy-affected grantees have already used these toolkits to establish housing counseling for residents that are experiencing financial hardship while repairing their homes. The housing counseling toolkit is most efficiently used when grantees use existing housing counselor networks (e.g., HUD- approved counselors).

Owner
**Lead:** *HUD*
Status
Recommendation adopted: Applies to grantees in the Sandy-affected region and will be applicable to future allocations of CDBG-DR in the region.


## CDBG-DR Funding for Public and Assisted Housing

### Challenge and Goal

A significant number of vulnerable residents found themselves in the storm's path, including substantial low-income,[125] elderly, and disabled populations, each of whom required special consideration from responders and policy makers. Many of these residents were either unable or unwilling to evacuate, and the special assistance that these residents required often took a long time to arrive. In particular, a significant concentration of New York City's public housing projects were located in mandatory evacuation zones, but for various reasons, many residents remained in their homes during the storm. As a result, many public housing residents became stranded without power and heat, in some cases for weeks. While cities developed and instituted evacuation plans, these plans failed to prepare for the eventuality that many people would not or could not evacuate. Stories of people using their gas stoves to stay warm and of elderly people unable to descend from high-rise apartments due to non-working elevators were common. In many of the multifamily housing projects throughout the region, generators, emergency boilers, and pumps would have prevented widespread hardship. Although public housing authorities might be expected to provide these kinds of emergency services, private landlords rarely have these kinds of capabilities. Public Housing Authorities (PHAs) and assisted housing managers used insurance money, funds from reserve accounts, and disbursements from FEMA's Public Assistance program to make some of their repairs and to restore units. Unfortunately, prior to Sandy, Federal funding was insufficient to obtain emergency resources that would have protected residents left behind after the storm.

The Task Force sought to ensure that public housing agencies and other assisted multifamily housing received funding for hazard mitigation as well as for rebuilding. This approach helps protect residents from facing the same problems in future disasters.

**28. RECOMMENDATION:** Require grantees to use CDBG-DR funding to support public and HUD-assisted multi-family housing, as well as subsidized and tax credit- assisted affordable housing with recovery and risk mitigation efforts.

Unlike prior disaster recovery efforts, the CDBG-DR Notice governing Sandy recovery funds included a model provision to focus the attention of grantees on HUD-assisted housing (public housing and multifamily) and their residents, a population that has not usually been a focus of CDBG spending. HUD Notice 78 FR 14329 (March 5, 2013) required grantees to identify how they will address the rehabilitation, mitigation, and new construction needs of each impacted PHA, as well as the multifamily assisted housing within their jurisdictions.

The State of New Jersey set aside $179.5 million from the first tranche of CDBG-DR funding to create new affordable housing units, as well as to restore damaged public housing, HUD- assisted multifamily developments, and other subsidized and tax-credit assisted housing. In addition, the State of New York provided $10 million to assist public housing units, and[126] New York City committed $120 million to design and construct improvements to public housing. The first phase of the City's plan includes the installation of permanent generators at 100 of the New York City Housing Authority's (NYCHA) most vulnerable buildings that were affected by the storm. Mitigation measures should address environmental exposures, including indoor, on-site, and off-site exposures.

Owner
*Lead: HUD*
Status
Recommendation adopted: Grantees are now using CDBG-DR funds provided in the Sandy Supplemental to assist public and HUD-assisted housing. It is HUD's intent to implement this requirement for CDBG-DR use in future disasters.

## Federal Housing Administration (FHA) and Federal Housing Finance Agency (FHFA) Mortgage Policy Alignment

### *Challenge and Goal*

Sandy came on the heels of a protracted foreclosure crisis that affected much of the region and threatened to destabilize the housing market by causing mortgagors struggling to recover from the storm to fall behind on their payments.[127] Owners who had been able to weather the economic downturn and remain current on their mortgages were suddenly faced with the three-fold burden of paying for their existing mortgage, financing repairs to their damaged homes, and renting a temporary place to live while those repairs were being completed. Beyond identifying shelter for displaced individuals, the Federal Government sought to stabilize housing markets by preventing foreclosures.

While Government Sponsored Enterprises (GSEs) had issued foreclosure moratoria in prior disasters, policies differed between the FHFA (which oversees the Federal National Mortgage Association (Fannie Mae) and the Federal Home Loan Mortgage Corporation (Freddie Mac)) and FHA (which is part of HUD). Previously, announcements were not coordinated and eligibility requirements varied among the different GSEs.

The Task Force sought to promote consistent standards to help homeowners recovering from disasters stay current on their Federally-backed mortgages.

**29. RECOMMENDATION:** Align the foreclosure prevention policies of FHA and FHFA – including policies on moratoria, forbearance, and refinancing.

In the aftermath of the storm, FHA and FHFA introduced consistent and coordinated policies to institute a moratorium on foreclosures of government-backed loans in disaster-affected areas. The alignment of these policies helped to minimize confusion for homeowners and mortgage servicers, and it prevents mortgage servicers from introducing arbitrary policies. The moratorium initially lasted through January 2013 and was later extended through April 2013. This marked the first time that FHA and FHFA had aligned their post-disaster moratorium policies. In addition, these two agencies also issued amended eviction policies to protect tenants.

FHA and FHFA offered those with Federally-backed mortgages a forbearance period of up to twelve months, the ability to modify their mortgages, and, in many cases, the opportunity to obtain streamlined mortgage refinancing through FHA's Streamline Refinance program. A forbearance period alone would have left borrowers owing a large lump sum to their lenders after twelve months, something most people could not afford after shouldering the cost of repairs and temporary housing. By working with lenders to offer modifications and the Streamline Refinance program, FHA and FHFA allowed homeowners to amortize the amount owed from the forbearance period and pay it off over several years. Many homeowners who refinanced using the Streamline Refinance program actually lowered their monthly payments by taking advantage of historically low interest rates. Typically, the savings from the reduced rate was more than enough to make up for arrears accrued following the disaster. Homeowners were eligible for the Streamline Refinance program as long as they were current on their mortgages when the storm hit and if the refinancing would not increase their payments. Registration was simplified by limiting the documentation requirement.

The Task Force played a central role in bringing FHFA and FHA together to align their policies with one another. This coordinated initiative will benefit not only those in Sandy-affected areas but also those eligible homeowners recovering from Hurricanes Irene and Lee. More significantly, perhaps, these policies have the potential to help an untold number of borrowers affected by future disasters who would otherwise find themselves unable to support their mortgages while attempting to recover. These policies give responsible homeowners the breathing room needed to remain in their homes after a disaster strikes.

Owner
**Lead**: *HUD*
Status
Recommendation adopted: Currently available for eligible homeowners with Federally-backed mortgages in the Sandy-affected region and applicable to future disaster recovery efforts as appropriate.


## Model Affordable Housing Programs

### Challenge and Goal
Due to the high cost of housing in the region and the limited supply of affordable units, State and local governments have struggled to maintain the local supply of affordable housing through the rebuilding process. Although Federal sources, such as CDBG-DR, provide recipients with funding that can be used to repair and rebuild lost or damaged affordable housing stock, State and local governments must often work with the non-profit and private sectors to form partnerships that leverage Federal funds.

**30. RECOMMENDATION:** HUD should explore ways to assist State and local governments to develop model affordable housing programs that leverage funding from the public, private, and philanthropic sectors for affordable housing development and preservation in Sandy-affected areas, as well as in other regions that could potentially be affected by future disasters.

The development of model affordable housing programs allows local recipients of Federal funds to increase their investment in neighborhoods recovering from the storm. For multifamily housing, one potential model to reduce the cost of development is a partnership that provides a secondary risk market through a securitization mechanism that allows state or local housing entities to make more loans.

Another model for distressed single-family loans is a partnership of the Federal Government, the State, and a local Community Development Financial Institution (CDFI), which is a non-profit lending institution certified by the Community Development Financial Institution Fund of the U.S. Department of the Treasury (Treasury). This model leverages private capital with State and Federal funds to purchase federally-distressed, single-family mortgages in the counties that were significantly impacted by Hurricane Sandy. This structure would allow a CDFI to work with HUD and the State to purchase pools of mortgage notes from FHA and then work with low- and moderate-income homeowners to help them retain their homes. It also creates opportunities to remediate vacant properties.

Both the single and multifamily models are community centered and create strong partnerships with regional organizations that specialize in financing projects to meet community needs. In addition, these partnerships encourage more resilient building practices and promote sustainable environmental and land use planning.

To ensure that Sandy-affected communities do not suffer a net loss of affordable or accessible housing after the storm, the Task Force has worked in both New York and New Jersey to develop programs that harness the power of the Federal, private, and non-profit sectors. By partnering with the Federal Government, States and local governments can finance development at lower interest rates, making development more feasible and increasing the number of units available to low- and moderate-income families. Governments can also partner with private entities to ensure that low- and moderate-income homeowners are able to remain in their homes.

Owner
*Lead: HUD*
Status
Recommendation underway, pending further action: Recommended implementation for future projects funded by the Sandy Supplemental and would be applicable to resilient rebuilding following disasters in the region. The risk sharing model proposal is currently under review by HUD and Treasury, and the single-family asset sale model proposal is currently under review by HUD.

## Model Certification Programs for Disaster Resilience (FORTIFIED/Resilience STAR)

### Challenge and Goal

For the past several years, builders seeking to improve energy efficiency and to develop sustainably have relied on certification programs and model codes such as ENERGY STAR and the U.S. Green Building Council's Leadership in Energy and Environmental Design (LEED) program. The implementation of green building measures saves homeowners money over the useful life of a building by lowering utility costs, in addition to minimizing harm to the environment. However, no certification program has achieved comparable success for the promotion of resilience and hazard mitigation against natural disasters. While some localities incorporate resilience into their building ordinances, many of the States at the greatest risk of catastrophic events have the least stringent codes. Minimum model building codes adopted by most States and municipalities address common safety concerns; yet, these minimum model building codes do not provide the necessary protections to help homes withstand catastrophic events.

The Task Force encouraged and promoted pilot programs that require buildings to incorporate resilience and hazard mitigation measures to determine whether these measures effectively protect structures from catastrophic events.

**31. RECOMMENDATION:** Encourage and promote the Insurance Institute for Business and Home Safety (IBHS) FORTIFIED home programs/ Resilience STAR development standards.

The IBHS, a non-profit research affiliate of the insurance industry, developed FORTIFIED, which provides practical, meaningful, hazard-focused solutions for new and existing structures throughout the United States. For example, FORTIFIED for Safer Living is a "code-plus" new construction program that helps homeowners and home builders create stronger, safer houses from the ground up. The program's standards, design guides, and third-party validation process are designed to reliably increase a home's resistance to the natural hazards that threaten the area where the house is located. These standards exceed the minimum life- safety requirements of local building codes. The IBHS FORTIFIED Home Hurricane program focuses on retrofitting existing homes to improve their hurricane resistance. This program also uses third-party validation and can be applied to new construction. In some states, including Alabama, Mississippi, and North Carolina, insurance incentives are mandated for homes built or retrofitted to FORTIFIED standards. In addition, the States of Louisiana and South Carolina may provide residual market premium credits for FORTIFIED for Safer Living homes.

After the FORTIFIED program was well-received by policymakers and insurers working on State- level recovery and rebuilding in the Sandy-affected region, the Task Force worked to bring FORTIFIED to a development in New Jersey as part of another pilot project that will begin in September.

DHS has also developed Resilience STAR, its own voluntary designation for homes designed and constructed to be resilient to natural disasters. An initial pilot will take place in a high-risk community, such as coastal Alabama, in partnership with FORTIFIED. An additional Resilience STAR pilot may be introduced in New York in the coming months as well.

As rebuilding proceeds in the Sandy-affected region, the wide spread use of these voluntary standards would promote building practices that reduce human suffering, property loss, and recovery time by incentivizing stakeholders to incorporate resilience into design and construction. These standards would not only make building occupants safer, but also may lower insurance rates. Costs to homeowners are marginal[128] and because this is a voluntary, consumer-driven program, there is no additional expense to government.

Owner
*Leads: DHS for Resilience STAR and Treasury/Federal Insurance Office (FIO) for IBHS FORTIFIED*
Status
Recommendation in process: Currently implemented for Sandy recovery projects and will be applicable to future disaster recovery efforts in the region as well as future disaster recovery efforts nationwide.

## CDFI Toolkits

### Challenge and Goal

State and local governments work with limited resources as they rebuild but they are often able to work with non-profits and private sector partners to leverage available funding. However, many State and local governments lack the capacity to identify opportunities and work with potential partners.

The Task Force seeks to help State and local grantees develop the capacity to leverage Federal disaster assistance.

**32. RECOMMENDATION:** Help identify opportunities for State and local housing programs to leverage funds and create public-private partnerships.

To help maximize Federal investment in State and local housing programs, the Task Force has been working with grantees to help them identify opportunities to leverage funds and develop public-private partnerships that attract financing for rebuilding activities. To encourage these partnerships, the Task Force, through HUD's Office of International and Philanthropic Innovation (OIPI), collaborated with the Opportunity Finance Network (OFN), one of the largest associations of CDFIs. Together, OIPI and OFN created the first ever master list of CDFIs for State and local governments looking to lend and leverage CDBG-DR funds with private and philanthropic funders. This master list, or "index," contains a comprehensive list of proven lenders that provide technical assistance and training and that already engage in housing, small business, or other types of community lending. The list identifies the type of lending each CDFI offers and whether the CDFI participates in a state small business program supported by Treasury's State Small Business Credit Initiative (SSBCI). As State and local units of government work with homeowners, renters, and small business owners to leverage CDBG-DR funding, the list will help quickly identify lenders and available financial resources that can assist in the rehabilitation and new construction of homes, rental buildings, and small businesses, as well as with risk mitigation activities.

Owner
*Lead*: HUD
Status
Recommendation adopted: Currently available for projects funded by the Sandy Supplemental and will be applicable to future disaster recovery efforts nationwide.

## Mold Remediation and Other Indoor Pollutants

### Challenge and Goal

One of the most common and intractable problems for many residents in the aftermath of the storm has been the persistence of mold. Mold is common after flooding and requires particular expertise to remediate, which can be costly for homeowners.

The Task Force is working to develop guidance and to encourage the use of best practices for home and rental owners seeking to remove mold after a disaster.

---

## HISTORIC PRESERVATION FUNDS AND TAX INCENTIVES

A significant percentage of the affected infrastructure, including housing, is listed on or eligible for the National Register of Historic Places. $50 million was appropriated by Congress from the Historic Preservation Fund to be allocated to tribal, state and local preservation grants to public and private owners of historic properties damaged by the storm, following the example of the successful Hurricane Katrina initiatives. The Historic Preservation Fund is available to homeowners as well as commercial property owners. The repairs must follow the Secretary of the Interior's Standards for Rehabilitation. In addition, the tax credits for historic preservation projects are available at the normal percentage of 20% for certified rehabilitation costs for commercial historic properties. The program is administered by the National Park Service and the IRS

---

**33. RECOMMENDATION:** FEMA, EPA, HUD, and HHS should issue consolidated guidance on remediation of indoor air pollutants (e.g. mold, lead, radon, and asbestos) that can pose health hazards for workers and residents in the Sandy-affected region. In addition, these agencies should recommend or establish region and housing stock specific toolkits related to indoor air pollutants for States and localities responding to disasters. Tribal, State, and local governments should include the remediation of these indoor environmental pollutants in their rebuilding construction/rehabilitation programs.

Although mold removal is not regulated like lead paint or asbestos abatement, several agencies, including EPA, HHS and its Centers for Disease Control and Prevention (CDC), the National Institutes of Health (NIH), National Institute of Environmental Health Sciences (NIEHS), DOL, and HUD each issued comprehensive guidance on remediation techniques for homeowners. In addition, HUD's Office of Healthy Homes and Lead Hazard Control (OHHLHC) has detailed staff to the JFOs in New York and New Jersey to provide information directly to the public about how to address mold, asbestos, and lead-based paint damage.

Owner
*Lead: HUD*
Status
Recommendation in process: Currently being implemented in the Sandy-affected region and will be applicable to future disaster recovery efforts in the region as well as future disaster recovery efforts nationwide.

## Convene Housing Partners to Integrate Plans and Facilitate Statutory, Regulatory, and Policy Changes to Improve the Delivery of Immediate, Interim, and Long-Term Housing in the Event of a Disaster

### Challenge and Goal

One of the most important and time-sensitive concerns for an individual or family recovering from a disaster is locating housing (temporary, interim, or long-term). For residents displaced for an extended period of time, the government often steps in and provides rental assistance. Over the last several major disasters, Federal agencies have used a variety of programs to provide housing, but many of these programs have raised challenges and concerns for both the Federal Government and for recipients. These challenges often stem from restrictive statutory provisions that limit the Federal Government's ability to respond to specific disaster scenarios, due to restrictions on how agencies, such as FEMA, can allocate responsibility to State and local governments.

The dense population and urban landscape of New York and New Jersey presented a unique housing challenge following Hurricane Sandy. Additionally, low vacancy rates limited the supply of housing that was available for displaced families, leading to high costs of the limited housing supply. The traditional housing alternatives and policies used in previous disasters were not feasible given these unique characteristics of the Sandy-affected region.

The housing challenges that arose after Hurricane Sandy revealed the need for flexible solutions that allow the Federal government to address the housing needs that arise from any particular disaster and enable agencies to adapt their policies to specific situations. The housing challenges in the aftermath of Sandy also raise the question of whether State governments should be given the opportunity to receive funding, given that the States may be better positioned to develop appropriate housing solutions.

The Task Force aims to ensure better coordination between Federal housing partners and to develop improved housing solutions, which give the Federal Government and States the flexibility to adapt to meet the specific needs that arise in a particular disaster.

**34. RECOMMENDATION:** Bring together the Housing RSF and Emergency Support Function six partner agencies to review and integrate existing housing plans, as well as existing statutes, regulations, and policies for potential changes (statutory, regulatory or policy) to improve the delivery of housing solutions for future disasters.

Owner
**Leads:** *HUD and FEMA*
Status
Recommendation underway, pending further action: The Task Force will work with HUD and FEMA to convene the partner agencies and establish goals and milestones.

## SUPPORTING SMALL BUSINESSES AND REVITALIZING LOCAL ECONOMIES

Small businesses are particularly vulnerable to disasters because they often have small profit margins and cannot sustain extended business interruption. They also typically lack adaptive business management models, tend to be underinsured, and, often, depend on generating revenues from customers and clients who have also been impacted by the disaster. Disasters amplify existing economic issues and launch long-term recovery trajectories for small businesses and entrepreneurs.[129]

The Task Force also recognizes the role small businesses play in recovery and rebuilding after a disaster. Small businesses, such as grocery stores, pharmacies, and gasoline stations, provide services in their communities. Furthermore, small business contractors may contribute to economic recovery by taking on government contracts for rebuilding and long-term resilience and hiring a local workforce to do the work.

There are more than 28 million small businesses in the United States. These firms create two of every three net new jobs and employ half of America's workforce.[130] Small businesses also increase equity and inclusion by providing opportunity to vulnerable populations. Of small businesses nationwide, nearly one-third (7.8 million) are owned by women and nearly one-fourth (6.1 million) are owned by minorities.[131] More than 60 percent of workers with a disability are employed by small businesses, and more than 60 percent of workers with less than a high school education are employed by small businesses.[132]

For these reasons, small businesses have been a major focus of recovery and rebuilding efforts from the Federal to the local levels since the moment Hurricane Sandy passed.

## Local Coordination and Communication of Information

### Challenge and Goal

After a disaster, small businesses need immediate, direct, and consistent communication about resources available to them. There are a number of organizations and entities at the local level that provide this communication. These entities should be well coordinated with the Federal agencies that can provide financial and other assistance.

In the aftermath of Sandy, the Task Force heard from frustrated small business owners that there were dramatic differences in the amount and quality of information provided by local and Federal government officials regarding financial and technical assistance, power outages, school and road closures, and other pieces of information. For some, this inconsistency created confusion and delayed recovery.

While Federal agencies post information about their own disaster recovery programs, they often do not reference resources provided by other agencies. As a result, small business owners must spend countless hours navigating numerous websites to find crucial information. Additionally, vulnerable populations and typically underserved communities do not always have ready access to needed information.

The following recommendations were developed with the goal of improving and institutionalizing local coordination, including the Economic RSF, as well as enhancing communication of information related to Hurricane Sandy recovery.

---

# EDA

DOC's Economic Development Administration (EDA), as Coordinating Agency for the Economic RSF, integrated the technical assistance resources of the Federal government with those initiatives of the States to reduce duplication of effort and promote more effective information sharing between all levels of government and the private sector. Efforts included train-the-trainer Access to Capital workshops, a tourism recovery peer-to- peer forum, and collaborative efforts between Federal and State governments with the private sector to enhance risk management.

---

**35. RECOMMENDATION:** Build a Disaster Preparedness and Operations Team (DPOT) focused on planning to help SBA district offices, including those in the Hurricane Sandy region, ensure clear and consistent guidance on how to access both local and Federal aid following a disaster.

SBA will further refine its existing coordination with local resource partners and economic agencies by building a DPOT to advise each of its 68 District Offices, including those in the Sandy-affected region. Prior to a disaster, SBA District Offices already work closely with their resource partners -- including Small Business Development Centers (SBDCs), Women's Business Centers (WBCs), and the SCORE Association -- and with local community officials and small businesses to develop working relationships and ensure clear and consistent guidance on how to access local and Federal aid following a disaster. SBA will further support these individual District Office led efforts with a headquarters based DPOT which will include disaster assistance marketing and outreach teams as well as appropriate representatives from SBA Headquarters. DPOT teams will support the District Offices in pre-disaster training and networking. They will also provide "reach-back" and deployable support to speed comprehensive small business economic recovery following a disaster. These additional coordination efforts will be incorporated into SBA's existing Disaster Preparedness and Recovery Plan. These new teambuilding efforts will help develop more effective small business support networks and will be structured to include vulnerable populations.

Owner
*Lead: SBA*
Status
Recommendation adopted: To be implemented for future projects funded by the Sandy Supplemental and will be applicable to future disaster recovery efforts in the region as well as future disaster recovery efforts nationwide.

---

# SBDCs

Small Business Development Centers (SBDCs) provide a vast array of technical assistance to small businesses and aspiring entrepreneurs through professional business advisors. Services provided by SBDCs help small businesses thrive. They include the development of business plans, manufacturing assistance, financial packaging and lending assistance, and procurement and contracting aid.[133]

Women's Business Centers (WBCs) represent a national network of nearly 100 educational centers designed to assist women in starting and growing small businesses.[134] Through the management and technical assistance provided by WBCs, entrepreneurs (especially women who are economically or socially disadvantaged) are offered comprehensive training and counseling on a variety of topics, in many languages, to help them start and grow their own businesses.

The SCORE Association is a non-profit association comprised of 12,000 volunteer business counselors throughout the U.S. and its territories.[135] SCORE members are trained to serve as counselors, advisors, and mentors to aspiring entrepreneurs and business owners. These services are offered at no fee as a community service.

**36. RECOMMENDATION:** Institute a "No Wrong Door" approach to federal information sharing after disasters by building on existing information platforms and cross-referencing Hurricane Sandy disaster recovery resources. Furthermore, measures should be taken to ensure that information about economic recovery from Hurricane Sandy is accessible to vulnerable populations.

A user-friendly tool that can allow users to specify their needs and effectively search and access all applicable program information, potentially including nonfederal resources, is needed. Platforms like Business USA, DisasterAssistance.gov, the National Disaster Recovery Program Database, and Max.gov are intended to share disaster recovery information from multiple sources. However, the sites are not all well linked and businesses, communities, and individuals may have to look at multiple sites to find the information and applications they need.

As an outgrowth of both the Sandy recovery efforts and the Administration's response to the 2012 Drought, the RSFLG is reviewing multiple databases that have been created with the objective of easing the search for specific federal and non-federal resources. In most instances, data presented still require significant drill down to find applicable information for specific issues. Additionally, linking the tool directly to primary sources so that data automatically update would ensure quick access to current data.

## Business USA

On October 28, 2011, the President issued a challenge to government agencies to, in the best interest of serving America's business community, think beyond their organizational boundaries and start thinking and acting more like the businesses they serve. He directed the creation of Business USA, a centralized, one-stop platform to make it easier than ever for businesses to access services to help them grow and hire. Federal agencies and local governments can *provide information and forms that can be linked to the existing "Seek Disaster Assistance" tool* (http://business.usa.gov/disaster-assistance) *on Business USA. In addition, Business USA provides call center, email, and chat features so any inquiries can be funneled to the appropriate agency or local authority.*

*Business USA* (http://www.business.usa.gov) *implements a "No* Wrong Door" approach for small businesses and exporters by using technology to quickly connect businesses to the services and information relevant to them, regardless of where the information is located.

The following agencies have pledged their commitment to making this site a one-stop shop for everything related to business in the Federal government: USDADOC, DOL, Treasury, VA, EPA, Equal Employment Opportunity Commission, Export-Import Bank of the United States, GSA, Overseas Private Investment Corporation, SBA, Trade and Development Agency, the White House, and the Internal Revenue Service (IRS).[136]

Owner
*Lead: RSFLG*
Status
Recommendation adopted: To be implemented for future projects funded by the Sandy Supplemental and will be applicable to future disaster recovery efforts in the region as well as future disaster recovery efforts nationwide.

**37. RECOMMENDATION:** Encourage HUD CDBG-DR grantees to address the needs of a broad range of affected small businesses, including through the provision of grant funds to community organizations that work closely with businesses whose needs might otherwise be unmet.

Community-based and economic development organizations are on the front lines when disaster hits. These organizations have close relationships with local businesses and knowledge of their communities' needs and assets. They also have networks of stakeholders that grantees can and should leverage to share information about available assistance. While these important organizations may have provided informal assistance after Sandy, they tend to be under- resourced in spite of the considerable value they have to add in short- and long-term rebuilding. HUD will issue guidance to encourage grantees consistent with this recommendation.

Owner
*Leads: HUD and Grantees*
Status
Recommendation adopted: Recommended for implementation for future projects funded by the Sandy Supplemental and would be applicable to resilient rebuilding following disasters in the region as well as resilient rebuilding following disasters nationwide.

## Access to Technical Assistance

### Challenge and Goal
Through its community engagement process, the Task Force learned that technical assistance in the form of business counseling was inconsistent or not easily accessible. Small business owners cited specific services needed in the short-term, such as completing loan applications, business planning, legal counseling, and assistance with landlord-tenant issues. In addition, businesses have asked for help with business continuity and risk management, marketing, and strategies to build resilience and mitigate losses from future disasters.

SBA sought and received ad hoc authority to expand recovery-related technical assistance efforts led by its network of resource partners at SBDCs, WBCs, and SCORE. The Sandy Supplemental made $19 million available for this purpose. The Task Force recognizes the need to increase the availability of technical assistance to help small businesses recover from Hurricane Sandy, as well as to fund small business incubators and accelerators that can provide start up and entrepreneurial assistance to new businesses and ensure economic growth and resilience.

**38. RECOMMENDATION:** Remove statutory barriers for SBA programs that provide additional technical assistance to small businesses before, during, and after a disaster.

Currently, there are limits on SBA's ability to provide technical assistance before and after disasters. The Task Force recommends taking the following steps to modify legislation that would benefit the Sandy-impacted region, as well as future disaster areas:

- Authorize permanent no-year authority and no-match funding, through a separate line item, for future SBA appropriations of disaster grants for SBDCs, WBCs, and SCORE serving a disaster area.
- Waive territorial limitations for SBDCs, WBCs, and SCORE in providing technical assistance after a disaster.

Owner
*Lead: SBA*
Status
Recommendation underway, pending further action: These activities are being implemented for the Sandy disaster area through funds and authority provided for these purposes in the Sandy Supplemental; permanent authority would require legislative action and would be applicable to recovery and resilient rebuilding following future disasters nationwide.

**39. RECOMMENDATION:** Provide SBA statutory authority to fund incubators and accelerators.

By providing SBA grant authority and no-match funding for incubators and accelerators, SBA would be able to work collaboratively with its resource partners to aid entrepreneurs, start- ups, and small businesses (including vulnerable populations) after a disaster by providing them mentorship, resources, and training. These companies will in turn contribute to economic growth and resilience in disaster-impacted regions.

Owner
*Lead: SBA*
Status
Recommendation submitted: Would be applicable to resilient rebuilding following disasters in the region and to resilient rebuilding following disasters nationwide.

## Access to Capital for Small Businesses

*Challenge and Goal*
After a disaster, while revenues are depressed, small businesses urgently need capital to offset disrupted cash flows, replace inventory, manage repairs, and retain employees. In the months and sometimes years following a disaster, small businesses that may be adapting their business model to a post-disaster, or rebuilding, economy need long-term working capital that will give them the flexibility they need to adapt. While grant and low-interest loan programs were made available by CDFIs within two months of the storm, these programs were few and far between and had limited funding. SBA loans filled much of the gap in needed loan financing. In addition, there are currently CDBG-DR funded grant and loan programs underway in the Hurricane Sandy region.

The Task Force found numerous challenges faced by small business owners trying to access financial assistance from Federal and local sources. Specific challenges to accessing

SBA's Disaster Loans included: a perception of excessive "red tape," leading to fewer applications submitted; mixed communication by governments and other entities, leading to discouragement from applying for SBA loans; confusion surrounding "duplication of benefits" rules; delays in the application process and rigorous application requirements; a limited array of loan products; and challenges specific to "micro" businesses owned and run by vulnerable populations that may not be engaged with more traditional associations and networks and may have limited abilities to complete the application process.

---

### SBA's DISASTER LOAN PROGRAM

SBA's Disaster Loan Program was, and is, the most consistent avenue of recovery for businesses after a disaster. Following the 2005 Gulf Coast hurricanes (Katrina, Rita, and Wilma), SBA experienced significant challenges meeting the demand for its disaster home and business loans. Since then, SBA has completely rebuilt its disaster operation, upgraded technology, reformed processes, and leveraged personnel to create a system far better able to handle major disasters and serve survivors. This is evidenced in the early recovery work from Sandy:

SBA's Disaster Electronic Loan Application (ELA) resulted in 55 percent of all Sandy disaster loan applications being in electronic form; this is up from 36 percent submitted via ELA in FY2012 and 27 percent in FY2011.[137] Average times between loan application submission and approval fell from 61 business days in FY2006 to 15 business days in FY2012 (inclusive of all SBA declared disasters in 2012).[138] This fiscal year, the average SBA response time has been 27 business days for the over 108,700 disaster loan applications for all recently declared disasters.[139] However, the average application processing time for businesses in Hurricane Sandy has been 42 days, suggesting that further improvements can be made to manage large catastrophic events.[140] The average approval rate for SBA disaster loans for Hurricane Sandy as of July 2013 was 53 percent (home 55 percent, business 41 percent); as of July 2013, SBA had approved 36,137 loans totaling $2.4 billion, with 32,194 home loans for $1.94 billion and 3,943 business loans for $448.3 million.[141]

---

The Task Force recognizes the importance of enhancing access to capital for small businesses impacted by Hurricane Sandy.

**40. RECOMMENDATION:** Institute new and innovative process improvements to SBA's Disaster Loan program.

Several steps can be taken to continue to make processing and approval times more efficient including:

- Developing a process of separate application tracks for business and home disaster loans.
- Establishing a process to expedite approval of disaster loan applications that meet minimum credit score and other specified eligibility requirements.

- Establishing a new training module for reserve disaster loan officers based on efficiencies and improvements identified in an analysis of the Hurricane Sandy response.

After a disaster, homeowners normally apply for loans faster than small businesses. Typically, small business owners first assess the economic damage to their businesses caused by disrupted supply chains, displaced consumers, structural damage, inventory loss, and a range of other complex factors. As a result, small businesses apply for disaster loans much later than homeowners and, if they are handled in the same processing tracks, usually face delays due to the large number of home loan applications filed ahead of them. SBA will address this problem by creating a separate track for small businesses, with the potential to improve processing times for both small business and home loans.

Expediting the approval of certain SBA disaster loan applications will make processing more efficient and, by determining which applications can be processed quickly and deploying staff accordingly, SBA can then dedicate more staff to potentially more time-consuming applications.

The establishment of a new training module builds upon continuous procedural improvements to the disaster loan program made by SBA since Hurricane Katrina and ensures that a trained reserve staff is in place for the next disaster.

Owner
*Lead: SBA*
Status
Recommendation adopted: To be implemented for future disaster recovery efforts in the region. This will also be applicable to future disaster recovery efforts nationwide.

**41. RECOMMENDATION:** Modify regulations to adopt an "alternative size standard" for small businesses for SBA's Economic Injury Disaster Loans similar to the standard for SBA business loan programs, to enable more businesses to qualify for loans.

Currently, to qualify for SBA Economic Injury Disaster Loans, a business is determined to be small based on either its revenues or number of employees. By offering an alternative size standard based on the same standards used for SBA's 7(a)/504 loan guarantees, more small businesses in need of capital after a disaster that do not have traditional sources of financing available to them could qualify for disaster loans.

Owner
*Lead: SBA*
Status
Recommendation adopted: To be implemented for future disaster recovery efforts in the region and will be applicable to future disaster recovery efforts nationwide.

**42. RECOMMENDATION:** Increase SBA's unsecured disaster loan limits and expedite the disbursement of small dollar loans.

Currently, SBA's limits on unsecured disaster loans, which do not require collateral, are $14,000 for physical damage and $5,000 for economic injury.[142] If the limits were raised to $25,000 for both physical and economic injury, more small businesses that may be impacted by future disasters would be provided with much-needed small dollar loans following a disaster. Additionally, to speed up the disbursement time of funds, SBA plans to create separate queues for unsecured and secured loans.

Owner
*Lead: SBA*
Status
Recommendation underway, pending further action: To be implemented for future disaster recovery efforts nationwide. This recommendation will require both statutory and regulatory changes.

**43. RECOMMENDATION:** Defer loan payments due to SBA from Microloan Intermediaries, when appropriate as determined by SBA Administrator, if a certain percent of the Intermediary's portfolio is made up of loans to micro- borrowers in major disaster areas, including the Hurricane Sandy region.

SBA provides funds to specially designated intermediary lenders, which are non-profit community-based organizations with experience in lending as well as management and technical assistance. These intermediaries administer SBA's Microloan program for eligible borrowers. SBA's Microloan program provides loans up to $50,000 to help small businesses and certain non-profit childcare centers start up and expand. The average microloan is about $13,000.[143] By deferring loan payments due to SBA when their borrowers are clearly having difficulty making payments, microloan intermediaries have more flexibility to defer small business microloans.

Owner
*Lead: SBA*
Status
Recommendation adopted: To be implemented for future disaster recovery efforts in the region and will be applicable to future disaster recovery efforts nationwide.

**44. RECOMMENDATION:** Encourage HUD CDBG-DR grantees and private sources to fund additional CDFI outreach and support to small businesses in vulnerable communities.

Treasury has encouraged and facilitated steps by grantees and other funders to support CDFIs. CDFIs have the ability to leverage significant private resources to support small businesses and reach vulnerable populations. The Task Force has also collaborated with HUD to create a CDFI index containing information about CDFIs that are active in the Sandy-affected region. The index is explained in the Housing chapter of this report on page 95.

Owner

**Lead:** *Treasury, in coordination with HUD*

Status

Recommendation adopted: Recommended for implementation for future projects funded by the Sandy Supplemental and would be applicable to resilient rebuilding following disasters in the region as well as resilient rebuilding following disasters nationwide.

**45. RECOMMENDATION:** Raise awareness that Treasury's SSBCI Program can be used for disaster recovery, including Hurricane Sandy recovery.

SSBCI provides States significant flexibility to build on successful models for State small business programs, including collateral support programs, Capital Access Programs, loan participation programs, and loan guarantee programs. In addition, many State and local governments have experience setting up temporary disaster assistance programs for small businesses immediately following a crisis. SSBCI allows States the flexibility to leverage SSBCI funding to help small businesses impacted by disasters rebuild their business stronger than before.

---

## SSBCI

The SSBCI was funded with $1.5 billion from the Small Business Jobs Act of 2010 to support State and local programs that provide lending to small businesses and small manufacturers that are creditworthy but are not getting the loans they need to expand and create jobs.[144] SSBCI is expected to help spur up to $15 billion in lending to small businesses, or a 10:1 leverage ratio on each federal dollar, by December 31, 2016.[145]

---

To support the work of the Task Force, Treasury used the annual conference of SSBCI state program managers held June 3-4, 2013 at the Dallas Federal Reserve Bank to promote the program's flexibility to provide capital to small businesses that are still recovering from Hurricane Sandy or last summer's historic drought.

Owner

**Lead:** *Treasury in coordination with the States*

Status

Recommendation adopted: Implementation underway for future disaster recovery efforts in the region and future disaster recovery efforts nationwide.

## Rebuilding Contracts

### *Challenge and Goal*

After a disaster, there are a number of contracting opportunities at the Federal, State, and local levels. These types of contracts are often well-suited for small businesses to perform; however, small businesses need access to these opportunities, as well as the skills and knowledge of how to compete and win the contracts. Following Sandy, key concerns that the small business community expressed to the Task Force about contracting included: difficulty finding information about available rebuilding contracts; a possible shortage of local contractors for certain work or with FEMA certification; difficulty for minority-owned small businesses to compete with better-capitalized businesses for contracts; a struggle to find opportunities related to long-term rebuilding; and difficulty determining which resources would be available to help small businesses maximize long-term rebuilding opportunities.

SBA Administrator Karen Mills and OMB's Office of Federal Procurement Policy Administrator Joe Jordan currently convene the White House Small Business Procurement Group on a quarterly basis to hold the 24 top-procuring Federal agencies accountable to meeting their small business contracting goals and to ensure best practices are disseminated throughout the government. At the June 26, 2013 meeting, which Task Force Executive Director Laurel Blatchford attended, Administrator Mills and Administrator Jordan asked agencies to maximize utilization of small businesses in Sandy-related disaster contracts. Presently, the statutory goal for prime contracts to small businesses is set at 23 percent. (There is no specific goal set for disaster recovery contracts.) As of July 2013, 27.1 percent of Sandy-related prime contract[146] dollars obligated in the Federal Procurement Database System went to small business, exhibiting a strong Federal commitment to small business contracting.[147] Of note, 13.6 percent of Sandy-related prime contract dollars obligated in the Federal Procurement Database System went to local New York and New Jersey businesses of all sizes.[148]

---

## THE SBA ACT

The Small Business Act stipulates that all small businesses have the maximum practicable opportunity to provide goods and services to the Federal Government. Congress, in furtherance of that policy, enacted various small business goals for Federal procurement. SBA is responsible for the management and oversight of the small business procurement process across the Federal Government. SBA works with Federal agencies to negotiate small business prime and subcontracting goals to ensure that small businesses have the maximum practicable opportunity to provide goods and services to the Federal Government.

Furthermore, the goal negotiation seeks to ensure that the Federal Government meets the 23 percent statutory goal to small businesses, 5 percent to women-owned small businesses, 5 percent to small disadvantaged businesses, 3 percent to service disabled veteran-owned small businesses, and 3 percent to certified Historically Underutilized Business Zone (HUBZone) small businesses.[149]

---

Several recommendations are designed to continue making progress on increasing small business[149] contracting for Hurricane Sandy rebuilding and long- term resilience with an emphasis on utilizing local business capacity. By involving local businesses in recovery efforts, communities can keep revenues local, create local jobs, and help minority and disadvantaged businesses recover.

**46. RECOMMENDATION:** Create opportunities and tools to increase access for small businesses to rebuild their businesses and participate in Hurricane Sandy rebuilding.

SBA has or is implementing multiple activities supporting this recommendation:

- On August 7, 2013, SBA and other Task Force agencies collaborated on the Hurricane Sandy Small Business Recovery and Matchmaking Summit in Newark, N.J. The event educated more than 400 affected small businesses about local and Federal resources and connecting them with government and global corporate buyers. Modeled after SBA's American Supplier Initiative, this event was designed to increase the number of small businesses in the corporate and Federal supply chains, equip small businesses with the tools to be effective suppliers, and build lasting relationships between small businesses and government and global corporate buyers.

- Responding to the need to ensure that small businesses have a one-stop source to identify not only Federal contracting opportunities related to Hurricane Sandy but also State and local contracting opportunities, SBA expanded its existing Sandy website (http://www.sba.gov/Sandy) to include contracting opportunities for small businesses at the Federal, State, and local levels. This effort centralizes and improves the communication of information about contracts; thus, addressing a concern that small businesses in the Sandy-affected region expressed to the Task Force.

- The Task Force and SBA identified the need for increased training for contracting officers on special regulations that apply to disaster response-related contracts (e.g., set-asides that can be used for local and small businesses). SBA will develop an online webinar series to provide this training, which will be available on an ongoing basis on SBA's "Government Contracting Classroom" (http://www.sba.gov/gcclassroom).

Owner
*Lead: SBA*
Status
Recommendation adopted: Implementation underway or completed for disaster recovery efforts in the region. The contracting officer training will also benefit future disaster recovery efforts nationwide.

**47. RECOMMENDATION:** Make statutory changes to existing SBA initiatives to make it easier for small and local businesses to access Federal contracts for Hurricane Sandy rebuilding.

The changes below would directly impact small and local contractors' ability to receive Hurricane Sandy rebuilding contracts in years to come and impact future recoveries from disasters:

- Provide authority to SBA to reinstate as a Disaster Historically Underutilized Business Zone (HUBZone) for five years any HUBZone whose HUBZone designation expired in the preceding five years and is in a county with a Presidential Declared Disaster. This would give local firms based in those areas the ability to become HUBZone certified and obtain preference in Federal contracting dollars, helping to stimulate local economies.

- Upon the request of a certified 8(a) firm in a major declared disaster area, SBA will suspend the firm's participation in the nine-year 8(a) Business Development program for a one-year period while the firm recovers from the disaster to ensure the firm is able to take full advantage of the program, rather than being impacted by lack of capacity or contracting opportunities due to disaster-induced disruptions. During this suspension, the firm would not be eligible for 8(a) Business Development Program benefits, including set-asides; however, the firm would not "lose time" in the nine-year program due to the extenuating circumstances that the disaster created.

HUBZone and the 8(a) Business Development Program are two key programs SBA implemented to help small, disadvantaged businesses compete in the marketplace and gain preferential access to Federal procurement opportunities.

Owner
*Lead: SBA*
Status
Recommendation underway, pending further action: Recommended for implementation of future projects funded by the Sandy Supplemental and will be applicable to future disaster recovery efforts in the region and nationwide.


## Workforce Training and Employment Opportunities

### Challenge and Goal

The short-term workforce impacts of Hurricane Sandy were due to myriad challenges, including: disruptions of public transportation and road closures; electricity outages; gas leaks; limited childcare; and damages to personal residences. Many of the businesses that escaped physical damage from high winds or flooding sustained economic damage, such as business interruption or changes in clientele, and were unable to keep employees working. According to analysis from the Department of Commerce (DOC), changes in unemployment claims, payroll employment, and industrial production suggest that economic activity in the New York-New Jersey area almost fully resumed within a couple of months after the storm. Potential economic gains are likely to be realized over the next several years, according to DOC's analysis, if repair and construction needs, as presented by the states, are met.[150]

In order to meet those repair and construction needs, local governments will need to ramp up retraining and other workforce development programs necessary to help workers adapt to new trades. In addition, local workforce development institutions, both public and private, will need to adjust to prepare the local workforce for significant new opportunities that will come with large-scale infrastructure and resilience projects. Ideally, these organizations will be able to provide, in a relatively short amount of time, retraining opportunities to allow otherwise unemployed or underemployed residents gain access to the rebuilding boom.

---

## DOL's Registered Apprenticeship Program

Through DOL's Registered Apprenticeship program there are opportunities for local residents to help rebuild communities and receive on the job learning experiences. Pairing dislocated workers with Registered Apprenticeship sponsors/employers provides a benefit to both the worker and the employer: the worker will receive paid training, and the employer will receive a staff resource that could result in a permanent staff resource once the training period is completed.

---

And although falling unemployment numbers show progress,[151] they may not reflect underemployment and other disproportionate impacts in certain communities and industries. In Sandy's aftermath, those that were unemployed prior to the storm are having a difficult time finding employment, and individuals unemployed as a result of the storm might not have the skills needed to obtain employment in the recovery economy. In some cases, there is a readily available and qualified out-of-state population to do recovery-related work. In other cases, vulnerable populations fear being excluded from skills building and job placement opportunities, and significant barriers exist for low-skilled, limited English proficiency, minority, and disabled workers in learning about job opportunities and hiring processes.

Recommendations are designed to enhance job options and opportunities for local residents to participate in Hurricane Sandy rebuilding.

**48. RECOMMENDATION:** Promote best practices of local workforce agencies that are integrating disaster recovery and long-term Hurricane Sandy rebuilding into their ongoing efforts.

An example of a best practice is the Recovery Talent Network in New Jersey, established by the New Jersey Department of Labor and Workforce Development (LWD) and led by Ocean County College. The Recovery Talent Network will assess the overall workforce needs of Hurricane Sandy impacted employers in New Jersey and will work with educational institutions, workforce development organizations, and other stakeholders to develop new programs to connect unemployed individuals with employment opportunities.

DOL's Employment and Training Administration (ETA) regularly shares best practices with other States, including New Jersey's Talent Network efforts. ETA's regional office also will share best practices relating to Hurricane Sandy rebuilding with other States, including New York, at ETA's State Administrators' meeting, scheduled for August 5-6, 2013 and Business Services virtual meeting, scheduled for August 13-15, 2013.

LWD developed the concept of Talent Networks in 2010, starting with six networks built around six Garden State industry clusters that employ more than half of the workers in New Jersey and pay more than two-thirds of the wages earned in the State. Talent Networks enlist employers to identify the skills employers need in new employees to further the growth and operations of their businesses. In turn, the Talent Networks work closely with State workforce development agencies, educational institutions, and career and technical education schools to develop those skills in the workforce, improving employment possibilities and fueling the State's economic growth.

Owner

*Leads: DOL, in coordination with the States*

Status

Recommendation adopted: Implementation underway for future projects funded by the Sandy Supplemental and will be applicable to future disaster recovery efforts in the region and will be applicable to future disaster recovery efforts nationwide.

**49. RECOMMENDATION:** Encourage HUD CDBG-DR grantees, in complying with Section 3 regulations, to maximize efforts to create specialized skills training programs in the areas needed most for Sandy rebuilding, ranging from mold remediation and construction to ecosystem and habitat restoration, green infrastructure, and coastal engineering. Furthermore, the Task Force recommends that these training programs include low-income individuals and other vulnerable populations and create local Hurricane Sandy recovery jobs that pay wages and benefits at industry standards.

Section 3 is a provision of the Housing and Urban Development Act of 1968. The purpose of Section 3 is to ensure that employment and other economic opportunities generated by certain HUD financial assistance are directed—to the greatest extent feasible and in a manner consistent with existing Federal, State, and local laws and regulations—to low- and very low- income persons, particularly those who are recipients of HUD assistance for housing, and to business concerns that provide economic opportunities to low- and very low-income persons. The Task Force recognizes that providing job training, employment, and contract opportunities to low- or very-low income residents in connection with projects and activities in their neighborhoods is a key strategy for revitalizing communities. For example, these opportunities could be publicized widely at public housing facilities to increase participation of its residents, especially where there are HUD-funded projects at those facilities.

Owner

*Lead: HUD, in coordination with grantees*

Status

Recommendation adopted: To be implemented for future projects funded by the Sandy Supplemental and will be applicable to future disaster recovery efforts in the region and will be applicable to future disaster recovery efforts nationwide.

**50. RECOMMENDATION:** Pursuant to Executive Order 13502, executive agencies should be encouraged to consider Project Labor Agreements (PLAs) on large-scale construction projects in the Hurricane Sandy region in order to promote economy and efficiency in federal procurement.

President Obama's Executive Order 13502 encourages federal agencies to consider requiring the use of PLAs to promote the efficient and expeditious completion of federal construction projects. PLAs can provide structure and stability that may help agencies manage the challenges, posed by large-scale construction contracts, to efficient and timely procurement. PLAs can help ensure large scale federal construction projects are completed on time and on budget by:

- Providing a mechanism for coordinating wages, hours, work rules, and other terms of employment across the project.
- Creating structure and stability through the use of broad provisions for grievance and arbitration of any disputes that may arise on site, including procedures for resolving disputes among the construction crafts.
- Prohibiting work stoppages, slowdowns, or strikes for the duration of a project and obligating senior union management to use their best efforts to prevent any threats of disruption of work that might arise.
- Ensuring expeditious access to a well- trained, assured supply of skilled labor, even in remote areas where skilled labor would have otherwise been extremely difficult to find in a timely fashion.

---

### PROJECT LABOR AGREEMENTS

On February 6, 2009, President Obama issued Executive Order 13502: Use of PLAs for Federal Construction Projects under the Federal Property and Administrative Services Act [40 U.S.C. 101 et seq.] Pursuant to this order is the promotion of efficient procurement and completion of large scale Federal construction projects ($25 million and more) in an economical, efficient, and timely manner.

Under the Executive Order, a PLA is defined as a pre-hire collective bargaining agreement with one or more labor organizations [as defined in 29 U.S.C. 152 (5)]. Labor organizations in the construction industry maintain a permanent workforce that can predict labor costs while bidding on contracts. Further, these labor organizations are adept in managing multiple teams of construction craft workers at a single location. PLAs greatly reduce labor disputes -- with guarantees against strikes, lockouts, and similar job disruptions -- and uncertain craft work assignments.

---

The Sandy-affected region has traditionally utilized PLAs as an effective way to complete complex construction projects, taking advantage of a highly skilled permanent workforce and experienced contractors. In carrying out large-scale construction projects for Sandy rebuilding, federal agencies are reminded of their responsibilities under Executive Order 13502. To further support the goal of Executive Order 13502 in the region, and to ensure those impacted by Hurricane Sandy benefit from local federal construction projects, the Task Force also recommends encouraging the use of registered apprenticeship programs, developing community partnerships, and promoting the hiring of local workers.

Owner
*Coordinating Agency: DOL*
*Supporting Agencies: Agencies funding and building infrastructure projects (DOT, HUD, USACE, DOI, EPA, DHS, and GSA)*
Status
Recommendation adopted: To be implemented for future projects funded by the Sandy Supplemental and will be applicable to future disaster recovery efforts in the region.

# ADDRESSING INSURANCE CHALLENGES, UNDERSTANDING, AND AFFORDABILITY

When risks are known and disasters are imminent, individuals can take immediate precautions like boarding up windows when the forecast predicts high winds, seeking shelter during tornadoes, and clearing basements of valuables in the face of floods. Businesses can likewise prepare for disruption and, in some cases, plan to operate remotely. For risks less imminent and more difficult to predict, insurance can be an important line of defense against economic loss. In the absence of insurance, the cost of repairing damaged property is usually borne by the property/business owner or the Federal government through federal assistance and often has negative social consequences—disrupting lives and livelihoods.[152]

There are two approaches to reducing the cost of recovery from future disasters. The first is to mitigate and reduce risk by moving out of harm's way or hardening properties to better withstand flood or other hazards. The second is to insure property and transfer the risk. The Task Force is proposing initiatives to encourage investment in both hazard mitigation and insurance. For these approaches to be effective, individuals need to understand their risks, take steps to reduce risk, and invest in applicable insurance products that will adequately transfer their risk in the case of a disaster.

## Disbursement Delays

### *Challenge and Goal*

After Sandy, an enormous number of insurance claims were filed in the region. Specifically, in New York and New Jersey—as of June 2013, 830,000 homeowner, 165,000 auto, and 126,000 residential flood insurance claims had been filed. An additional 71,000 commercial property claims and 5,000 flood claims were also filed by businesses.[153] Given this incredible volume of claims, it is not surprising that many home and business owners were frustrated by the adjustment and inconsistent disbursement processes. Policy holders with mortgages faced a particular set of frustrations. For this group, insurance claim checks were sometimes issued jointly to the property owner and the property owner's mortgage provider. In certain cases, the claim proceeds were made available to the property owner immediately. In other cases, funds were held by banks and released in increments as repairs were completed. The amount of funds that can be released, as well as the manner in which they can be released, is generally established pursuant to regulations set by Fannie Mae, Freddie Mac, and FHA.

In the case of Sandy, the most common consumer complaint concerned banks and mortgage providers not processing insurance proceed checks in a timely manner. For example, in March 2013, four months after Hurricane Sandy, some banks were holding back 44 percent of Sandy insurance claims (compared to the industry average of 17 percent) amounting to 1,109 checks totaling nearly $41 million.[154] While banks often play an important role in ensuring appropriate use of disbursements for rehabilitation activities and may help property owners navigate the rebuilding process, the delays have been a source of great frustration in the region.

The Task Force's goal was to unify disbursement regulations, reduce confusion, and expedite the release of funds.

**51. RECOMMENDATION:** Establish Unified Insurance Disbursement Process.

One reason for the delayed disbursement of insurance funds described above is that Fannie Mae, Freddie Mac, FHA, and a multitude of private sector lenders had different policies for approving the release of insurance claim funds. To address this issue, the Task Force established a working group of lenders to review and propose unified policies and processes that could be adopted by the lenders and financial institutions. The policies are being worked on for future disasters and will be presented to FHFA and FHA for review and approval.

Owner
**Leads:** *Task Force, FHFA, FHA, Lenders*
Status
Recommendation adopted: Implementation underway for revised disbursement process for current Sandy recovery efforts that will be applicable to future disaster recovery efforts in the region as well as future disaster recovery efforts nationwide.


## Consumer Confusion

### Challenge and Goal
After Sandy, as after most other large hurricanes, many homeowners were surprised to learn what was and was not covered under their insurance policies. In particular, property owners were surprised to learn that their homeowners' policies did not cover floods. This was especially true for those property owners who did not live in FEMA-designated flood zones. Misunderstandings were compounded by confusion over whether damage was caused by flooding (covered only by flood insurance) or by wind and rain (covered by some, but not all, homeowners' policies).[155]

Businesses, likewise, were confused about what was covered and not covered by their commercial insurance policies. According to a survey conducted by the New York Federal Reserve Bank, only eight percent of small businesses that incurred damage related to Sandy had flood insurance.[156]

Another source of confusion and surprise for property owners affected by Sandy was that many had no previous knowledge they were at risk of flooding. As described earlier in the Rebuilding Strategy document, many flood maps for the region were out of date and greatly underrepresented the geographic areas at risk of flooding. FEMA identifies one percent probability flood event on its maps; flooding that exceeds the one percent event can and does happen. This can be catastrophic when property owners outside mapped flood zones are unaware of their risk and lack adequate insurance to protect their financial interests.

As a result, the Task Force has worked to highlight best practice consumer communication regarding property owners' risks, insurance coverage, and insurance policies, and has also worked to promote general disaster preparedness.

**52. RECOMMENDATION:** Support efforts to reduce consumer confusion regarding risk and insurance coverage while working to increase hazard preparedness.

To improve understanding of risks, FEMA has a process to keep flood maps updated. Map changes may have an impact on flood insurance rates. In March of 2009, Congress approved the Risk Mapping, Assessment, and Planning (Risk MAP) tool to update flood maps. Among the major objectives of Risk MAP is to ensure that 80 percent of the nation's flood hazards are current (meaning the flood hazard data is either new, recently updated, or deemed still valid). FEMA is required by law to review maps every five years to ensure individuals have up-to-date information about their flood risk.

To increase take up of flood insurance by individuals and businesses, the Task Force recommends leveraging the lessons learned from NFIP's FloodSmart marketing campaign in the 2004-2010 timeframe in ongoing outreach efforts. These include:

- Communicating both probabilities and consequences, including actionable information specific to the individual.
- Incorporating decision aids specific to the location and individual (e.g., the FloodSmart flood risk assessment tool for specific addresses) that provide premium and insurance agent information.
- Communicating sources and pathways of flooding.
- Encouraging individuals to assess the consequences of not carrying insurance on their individual financial situation.
- Leveraging windows, such as after flood events or when map revisions occur, when affected individuals are focused on insurance and flood risk and may be receptive to change.
- Utilizing "consumer-speak" to deliver an effective message that is relevant to consumers.[157]

As a result of the FloodSmart outreach campaign, there was an increase in number of people renewing their policies and, therefore, more flood insurance coverage in force in the 2003-2006 timeframe, highlighting the campaign's contribution to flood risk communication.[158]

The Task Force also sought to encourage individuals to prepare themselves for relevant hazards and supports FEMA's efforts in this area. Despite multiple campaigns and awareness efforts, a large percentage of Americans have not performed preparedness actions to increase their personal safety nor, as previously mentioned, do they understand their risk and insurance coverage, or lack thereof, should they be hit by a disaster or emergency. Effective campaigns encourage behavioral change by linking strategies with community-based action.

To this end, FEMA's Individual and Community Preparedness Division (ICPD) will launch America's PrepareAthon!, a nationwide, community-based campaign for action to increase emergency preparedness and community resilience and build understanding of risk and insurance. Though not yet officially launched, shortly after Hurricane Sandy, America's PrepareAthon!, in partnership with the Ready Campaign, the Ad Council, Al Roker and the Today Show, launched a public service announcement designed to inform citizens about preparing their homes for safety.[159]

Once launched, twice yearly, in the spring and fall, America's PrepareAthon! will highlight a "national day of action," on which millions of citizens can participate through drills, group discussions, and exercises to practice for local hazards. The Task Force strongly encourages using these days to also emphasize the value of insurance and educate potential consumers on available insurance products and hazard mitigation measures. The campaign is actionable, measurable, and informed by the latest scientific research to help increase the number of citizens who understand the hazards most likely to occur in their community; know the corresponding protective actions, hazard mitigation measures, and community plans; practice a real-time behavior to increase their preparedness; and contribute to increase community preparedness planning.

Owner
**Leads:** *FEMA and* Federal Insurance Office within the Department of the Treasury
Status
Recommendation adopted: Will be applicable to future disaster recovery efforts nationwide. The soft launch of America's PrepareAthon! is scheduled for September 5, 2013.

**53. RECOMMENDATION:** Improve National Flood Insurance Program (NFIP) policyholder awareness of factors that affect flood risk and insurance rating decisions.

Currently, policyholders have little access to NFIP resources or data that would provide detailed information on their property's vulnerability to flood hazards. Compounding the issue, the program lacks structure-specific elevation data for more than 1.5 million[160] structures in the floodplain that receive subsidized rates or non-elevation based rates, and the program is therefore incapable of calculating or communicating structure-specific risk for those policies.[161] This information is not available because these homes were constructed and a policy was issued before the community's flood insurance rate maps were issued.

As a result, many policyholders are largely unaware of the various factors that influence their assessed flood risk and corresponding insurance premiums. These policyholders are at a disadvantage in terms of taking steps to manage their existing risk. The factors that have the greatest influence on the program's current rating process are elevation and environmental conditions that affect the NFIP's designation of flood zones.[162]

To best address this challenge, the Task Force recommends that the NFIP provides structure- specific information and hazard mitigation suggestions for Sandy-impacted customers' annual premium bills. This will serve as a mechanism by which the program can stimulate individual demand for hazard mitigation measures and more effective hazard mitigation and floodplain management at the community level.

Owner
**Lead:** *FEMA*
Status
Recommendation adopted: FEMA has begun to implement for some policies. Will be applicable to those impacted by Sandy and policy holders nationwide.

## Actuarially Sound Rates

### Challenge and Goal

In the summer before Hurricane Sandy, Congress passed the Biggert-Waters Flood Insurance Reform Act of 2012 (BW12), reauthorizing the program through 2017 with significant reforms. Congress acted to make the NFIP rates more risk-based, reducing existing subsidies. As of March 2013, the NFIP owed the Treasury $24 billion, in part, due to the large losses from Katrina in 2005 and Sandy in 2012.[163]

Key provisions of the legislation require the NFIP to phase out subsidized and grandfathered rates so that policy premiums reflect true actuarial risk. One of the benefits of moving to actuarially sound rates is that property owners will have better information about the risks at hand and therefore will have better clarity on the potential payoffs of hazard mitigation and insurance. The reforms will mean premium rate increases for some, but not all, policyholders over time. The NFIP has already begun to implement the phase-out of some subsidies. Residents and business owners in the Sandy-affected region have expressed concern and uncertainty about how the changes will affect the cost of insuring their properties.

As the NFIP transitions toward full risk rates, there will be significant increases in premiums for some subsidized and grandfathered policies. Individuals whose properties are at risk of flooding may lack the resources to make prudent risk management and mitigation decisions, including those to relocate, mitigate, or purchase adequate insurance. BW12 authorized studies by FEMA, the National Academy of Sciences, and the Federal Insurance Office within the Department of the Treasury, to analyze: "methods to encourage/maintain participation in the NFIP, methods to educate consumers about the NFIP and flood risk, and methods for establishing an affordability framework for the NFIP... including the implications of affordability programs for the NFIP and the Federal budget." However, the study will not be done in the timeframe originally scoped in the law. Specifically, due to a dearth of data on structure-specific risks and policy holders' incomes, merely scoping the study is now expected to take 18-24 months.

Changes due to BW12 have and will continue to take effect. Specifically, as of January 1, 2013, policies on pre-FIRM subsidized second homes began to see price increases of up to 25 percent. Pre-FIRM subsidized businesses and repetitive loss properties will likely see increases beginning October 1, 2013. These rates will continue to increase by 25 percent per year until they reach their full actuarial rates. Also, beginning October 1, 2013, new pre-FIRM policies, lapsed pre-FIRM policies, and policies on pre-FIRM homes sold to new owners since July 6, 2012 will be immediately charged full actuarial rates. Beginning late 2014, those areas where a FIRM has been revised or updated on or after July 6, 2012, including both those recently mapped into the expanded flood plains and those whose rates do not reflect their property specific full-risk rate, will be phased into property-specific full risk rates over five years.

Many property owners do not clearly understand their flood risk and/or the ultimate cost of flood insurance (due to uncertainty about possible affordability measures being authorized). Property owners face hard choices in determining whether to remain in their properties.

Therefore, when considering a path toward recovery for the region, affordable insurance may be a limiting factor given the number of people living in the newly drawn flood plain and their ability to pay the projected higher rates. For New York City, the updated flood maps show almost double the number of residents living at risk: 398,000 people today as opposed to 218,000 based on the 1983 maps. The number of buildings in the floodplain has likewise almost doubled to 67,700 buildings today from 35,500 in 1983. Based on climate change estimates, this number is expected to grow to 88,700 buildings by the 2020s and 114,000 buildings by the 2050s for New York City.[164]

Owners of properties in the floodplain are at high risk of sustaining flood damage over the life of their mortgages. To provide financial protection against the risk of flooding, structures with federally backed mortgages are required to buy flood insurance. However, for those experiencing the phase-in of actual risk rates, or for those newly added to the NFIP-designated Special Hazard Flood Area or floodplain, the cost of flood insurance or significant increases to flood insurance policies may be an expense that they did not plan for when they bought their home or business. In addition, the cost of flood insurance may decrease the value of properties in floodplains as prospective buyers will factor flood insurance into the price of a flood-prone property.

Property owners in the floodplain who incurred damage during Sandy and accepted Federal monies (e.g., from FEMA, SBA, or HUD) will be required to purchase and maintain flood insurance. Those who are new policy holders may be required to pay actuarially sound rates immediately, rather than benefitting from subsidy phase-outs provided by the law for existing policy holders.

Based on initial analysis completed by the Task Force, the 100-year flood plain areas (including coastal V zones)[165] hold about 5.6 percent of the US population, of which 41.4% are Low to Median Income (LMI).[166] This emphasizes the importance of evaluating the affordability issue, per the requirements of the law. Property owners, be they owners of small businesses, homeowners, or landlords, may not be able to maintain the status quo if the cost of insuring their properties becomes overwhelming. Affordable housing units may become unaffordable.

To this point, New Jersey's CDBG-DR Action Plan reflects concerns that rising premiums will drive homeowners out of shore communities. For this reason, the State is providing a one-time payment of $10,000 to as many as 18,000 homeowners who can use it for any purpose, including payment of premiums if homeowners commit to stay in the community for a period of three years.[167]

**54. RECOMMENDATION:** Encourage increased hazard mitigation activities including elevation in order to protect property against future losses.

The National Institute for Building Safety's Multihazard Mitigation Council has estimated that for every dollar invested in hazard mitigation, a savings of four dollars is achieved.[168] Disaster survivors currently have access to post-disaster Hazard Mitigation Grant Funds in coordination with their state and local hazard mitigation plans to assist in taking protective mitigation actions against future events. Disaster survivors may also utilize CDBG-DR programs for elevating and for buy-outs to get people out of harm's way. In addition to elevating the structure, existing guidance from FEMA suggests property owners use good construction standards to mitigate risk including:

- Raising utilities or other mechanical devices above expected flood level.
- Wet floodproofing in a basement or in areas above and below ABFE.
- Using water resistant paints or other materials.
- Dry floodproofing non-residential structures by strengthening walls, sealing openings, or using waterproof compounds or plastic sheeting on walls to keep water out.[169]

As an example program, New York City is proposing to encourage existing structures in the floodplain to adopt flood resilience measures through an incentive program and targeted building requirements. Specifically, the program consists of two elements:

- A $1.2 billion incentive program, subject to available funding, will offer grants or, where appropriate, loans to building owners to help fund a percentage of the eligible costs of completing all or some of the recommended resilience measures; and
- A requirement for large buildings (i.e., those with 7 or more stories that are more than 300,000 square feet in size) to undertake flood protection measures by 2030.[170]

The Task Force supports and advocates for this use of CDBG funding.

Owner
*Lead: FEMA*
Status
Recommendation adopted: Currently available for projects funded by the Sandy Supplemental and will be applicable to future disaster recovery efforts in the region/will be applicable to future disaster recovery efforts nationwide.

**55. RECOMMENDATION:** Continue to assess actuarial soundness of decreasing premiums based on mitigation activities other than elevation.

The NFIP currently assesses a structure's general characteristics to determine actuarial rates by setting premiums that vary based on a number of factors, including the structure's flood zone, elevation, number of floors, construction, and occupancy, among other characteristics. As a result of BW12, many structures with basements that currently receive subsidies or grandfathered discounts will move to full-risk rates. Hurricane Sandy highlighted the fact that many urbanized areas have high concentrations of older row homes or brownstones, with basements, that are not easily elevated. Due to concern that full-risk premiums for these structures could make flood insurance premiums unaffordable, stakeholders affected by Sandy requested that FEMA consider partial mitigation credits to reduce premiums. In recognition of the anticipated premium increases and in consideration of the specific concerns from those in the impacted area, FEMA reevaluated the credit available under existing authorities to non- subsidized, undiscounted, basement rates to ensure adequate credit is given when electrical and mechanical equipment is elevated at or above the base flood elevation. These activities will significantly reduce the total claim payment, and will therefore result in rate reductions that reward homeowners for good mitigation practices.

The Task Force recommends FEMA work with New York City to communicate the benefits of mitigation activities other than elevation that would reduce risk and premiums.

Owner
**Lead:** *FEMA and NYC Mayor's Office of Long-Term Planning and Sustainability*
Status
Recommendation adopted: Revisions to the NFIP rate manual are underway.

**56. RECOMMENDATION:** Analyze affordability challenges of flood insurance and the impact on economically distressed households facing premium increases.

As the NFIP transitions toward full risk rates, as discussed above, there will be significant increases in premiums for some currently subsidized and grandfathered structures. Individuals whose properties are at risk of flooding may lack the resources to make prudent risk management and hazard mitigation decisions, including the decision to relocate, mitigate, or purchase adequate insurance.

The Administration highlighted this concern in its Statement of Administration Policy to the Senate NFIP reauthorization bill.[171] As previously mentioned, FEMA is charged by BW12 to complete a study with the National Academy of Sciences (NAS) to analyze the following: methods to encourage/maintain participation in the NFIP, methods to educate consumers about the NFIP and flood risk, and methods for establishing an affordability framework for the NFIP… including the implications of affordability programs for the NFIP and the Federal budget.

Accordingly, the Task Force agrees with the importance of studying and exploring affordability. Because there will be property owners who cannot bear the cost of flood insurance, more must be done to address the affordability issue. The Administration is committed to working with Congress on additional reforms to help economically distressed homeowners that strengthen the NFIP and are consistent with the President's Budget.

Owner
**Leads:** *FEMA, HUD, and FIO*
Status
Recommendation adopted: To be implemented for future disaster recovery efforts nationwide. FEMA is working with the National Academy of Sciences to initiate the affordability study.

## BUILDING STATE AND LOCAL CAPACITY TO PLAN FOR AND IMPLEMENT LONG-TERM RECOVERY AND REBUILDING

The scope and scale of Hurricane Sandy challenged the uneven capacities of State and local governments, which also faced differences in needs and readiness for disaster recovery. Many of the municipalities that experienced severe river flooding and the coastal towns along the New Jersey Shore and on Long Island are without full time planners, city managers, grants managers, engineers, and architects, and thus do not have the in-house capabilities to lead comprehensive, long-term recovery planning efforts on their own.

The NDRF includes the Community Planning and Capacity Building Recovery Support Function (CPCB RSF), coordinated by FEMA, to help communities address this challenge and coordinate the resources and expertise of supporting organizations to build local capacities and support local and regional planning efforts. The FDRCs for each state are responsible for managing and directing the RSFs in their respective states. At the national level, the RSFLG provides guidance and coordination for consistency among RSFs.

Planning for recovery from a catastrophic event like Sandy is a massive challenge for even the best prepared communities and it should not be postponed until the immediate response is complete. Recovery planning and decision-making take place under severe time constraints and deal with the rebuilding of multiple systems simultaneously. This effort involves stakeholders who have been traumatized and triggers funding sources not normally available. Successful recovery under such difficult circumstances depends on two critical factors: capacity building and planning.

Sandy revealed the necessity of improving hazard mitigation efforts to alter how vulnerable coastal areas of the densely populated northeast are occupied. Long-standing land use patterns have placed people, property, and infrastructure in locations that have significant risk of flooding and storm surge and that will become more vulnerable as sea level continues to rise. Municipalities need to build the capacity and expertise to take the steps necessary to reduce that risk. Hazard mitigation and risk reduction must be a primary goal of recovery efforts in the region even if fragmented land use authority and governance make this a difficult proposition.

- Capacity Building – Disaster recovery reveals the importance of having capabilities and capacity in the right place at the right time. This means ensuring that personnel have the appropriate skills and tools related to urban design and recovery planning, community and economic development, mapping and data analysis, stakeholder and civic engagement (including populations with limited English proficiency), environmental contamination assessment and response, engineering, land use planning, and building code expertise specific to disaster recovery and
- resilient rebuilding. In addition, all stakeholders must have an understanding of available Federal, State, and local disaster assistance programs and resources and the ability to manage largescale grants.
- Not all of the capacity to recover must be housed in local government agencies. Partnerships among various levels of government and with the private sector, academia, NGOs and philanthropic organizations should be available to address the full range of capacity needs. In addition to skilled personnel, it is necessary to develop disaster recovery tools, best practices for more resilient reconstruction, approaches to system upgrades that enhance the ability to withstand future impacts, coordinated management to ensure leveraging of multiple funding sources, and technical assistance for local recovery planning and capacity building. Additionally, prior to a disaster occurring, it is important to have baseline benchmarks and metrics of community and environmental health so that impacts from the disaster can be accurately identified.

- Recovery Planning – Effective recovery planning engages the community in order to reflect local values and address the needs of vulnerable populations. Local leaders should have funding and technical resources available to allow them to present citizens with plans reflective of the best available lessons and techniques from other jurisdictions and recovery efforts. State and Federal governments serve as partners in that effort, smoothing access to recovery funds that enable planning, community engagement, and the building of community capacity. Federal agencies serve to help State and local governments facilitate cross-sector partnerships, address the needs of low-income, minority, limited English proficient, and other vulnerable populations, and ensure that issues of regional and intergovernmental significance are adequately addressed in local planning processes. Effective recovery planning ensures that all populations, particularly disadvantaged populations, are meaningfully engaged in an open and inclusive citizen participation process.

Task Force community outreach efforts focused on understanding on-the-ground capacity and community planning challenges associated with recovery, assessing unmet needs, and removing obstacles to rebuilding in a manner that addresses existing and future risks and vulnerabilities. State and local challenges related to capacity centered on three main areas:

1. Support and resources for local recovery planning and management, including tools.
2. Enhancing the regional coordination necessary to adequately address large-scale, integrated solutions across jurisdictions.
3. Support and resources for building the capacity of and coordination among philanthropic and non-profit partners working on recovery.

The Task Force worked on the following initiatives in response to challenges identified on the ground and developed recommendations for actions that should be taken going forward.

## Building Local Capacity

### Challenge and Goal

Given the stresses on municipal budgets post-Sandy, most local governments lack the funding to fill the Local Disaster Recovery Manager (LDRM) positions that are strongly recommended by the NDRF. The primary role of these positions is to coordinate and manage the overall long-term recovery and redevelopment of a community, which includes the local administration and leveraging of multiple Federally-funded projects and programs.

Meeting requirements for staffing is a constant challenge in a post-disaster environment. Federal and State funding for LDRMs is currently an activity that is recommended within the NDRF and the role is key to ensuring that Federal funds for recovery are properly used. This problem is not unique to Sandy, but repeats itself after every major disaster in this Nation and presents what is perhaps the greatest barrier to successful recovery operations. Methods to fund these positions must be found, and Federal interagency coordination to confront this challenge represents a pressing need.

**57. RECOMMENDATION:** Work with States and local jurisdictions to consider funding strategies and raise awareness about the need to fill LDRM positions.

As part of the Sandy recovery, HUD should encourage States and local government grantees to dedicate adequate CDBG-DR funding to address capacity deficiencies and respond to the need for long-term recovery coordination at the local level. In previous disasters, supplemental funding from the EDA was used to help fill LDRM positions, however EDA did not receive any funding within the Sandy Supplemental. The Task Force and CPCB RSF teams worked with local philanthropies to fill some of these positions in New Jersey, but the lack of commitments and dedicated resources to fund them over multiple years is inhibiting the ability of local municipalities to lead and implement their own recovery.

Federal agencies can help local governments meet this need by providing guidance and technical assistance to help them understand how they can flexibly use and leverage program administration funds to partially support these positions, which have a direct tie to implementing projects under different disaster assistance program(s).

---

## PLAN EJ 2014

In the aftermath of Hurricane Sandy, environmental justice (EJ) organizations raised concerns about adverse health effects resulting from exposures (i.e. Indoor, on-site, and off-site) to environmental contaminants, particularly in industrial waterfront communities, that were caused or exacerbated by storm events. They also encouraged local and regional scale solutions that align climate adaptation and disaster planning as part of an inclusive planning process and ensure that the recovery process and cross-boundary planning answers the needs of all communities, especially those that are vulnerable to future storms.[172]

The Administration recognizes that, in addition to helping communities rebuild in ways that make them more resilient, it is important to recognize that some communities - particularly low income communities and communities of color - are disproportionately impacted by pollution and other environmental factors. EPA has laid the cornerstones for fully implementing its environmental justice (EJ) mission - that is, ensuring environmental protection for all Americans, regardless of race, color, national origin, income or education - in Plan EJ 2014. Its goals are to:

- Protect the environment and health in communities that are disproportionately impacted by pollution.
- Empower communities to take action to improve their health and environment.
- Establish partnerships with local, State, Tribal, and Federal governments and organizations to achieve healthy and sustainable communities.

Through Plan EJ 2014, the EPA developed a comprehensive suite of basic tools and guidance to integrate EJ in all its programs, policies, and activities.

In addition to Plan EJ 2014, more than one dozen federal agencies have released new or updated environmental justice strategies and annual implementation progress reports over the past four years. Further, communities across the country are integrating environmental justice and equitable development approaches to design healthy, sustainable, inclusive, and resilient neighborhoods. The Rebuilding Strategy reflects this Administration's commitment to addressing longstanding environmental and health challenges exacerbated by storm events and protecting all Americans from pollution where they live, learn, and play.

These strategies can help vulnerable and overburdened communities access and use tools and create new opportunities to address long-standing environmental and health challenges (such as indoor and outdoor air pollutants, bacteria, parasites and other contaminants) that can reduce the risk of acute and chronic illness as well as death.

Owner
**Lead:** *CPCB RSFs (FDRCs with FEMA as RSF coordinating agency)*
Status
Recommendation adopted: Funding for capacity building and coordinated local administration currently available under various Federal programs (disaster-related and non-disaster-related). The CPCB RSF is active in New Jersey and New York providing technical assistance to support States and local jurisdictions as they develop funding strategies for LDRMs.

## Build Regional Partnerships

### Challenge and Goal

Of New Jersey's 565 municipalities, 136 took the brunt of the impact of Sandy, with 37 suffering extensive damage and 99 experiencing moderate damage.[173] In New York State, Long Island, which has 15 cities and towns that are further divided into 73 incorporated villages,[174] was also particularly hard hit. With many home rule entities and independent local governments in both States, local government structures are not conducive to facilitating the cross-jurisdictional collaboration that is needed for a more efficient and effective recovery.

The Task Force worked closely with the CPCB RSF, the FDRC in each State, and a consortium of non- profit and philanthropic organizations to promote regional partnerships in the areas most impacted by Hurricane Sandy. The goal of this collaboration was to foster the development of local and regional solutions that integrate climate change adaptation and risk reduction as part of an inclusive recovery planning process. Solutions focus on coordinated planning and prioritization of long-term recovery activities as well as the coordinated implementation of those activities.

**58. RECOMMENDATION:** Support the New York Rising Community Reconstruction Program.

The New York Rising Community Reconstruction Program (NYRCR) brings communities together to facilitate a more collaborative planning process. The CPCB RSF supported the State by providing 88 community profiles (which included GIS maps, demographics, and inundation levels), conducting needs assessments, and gathering data on technical assistance requirements. The Task Force worked closely with New York Governor Andrew Cuomo to define the guidelines for the NYRCR program, identify best practices from other communities, and set aside $25 million of the State's first CDBG-DR allocation to support NYRCR planning activities.[175] The forthcoming CDBG-DR allocation to the Sandy-affected region may serve to supplement and build on these initial planning efforts as well as to help implement the proposed community recovery projects.

Within this program, each New York Rising Community (a state-determined grouping of localities) will have a planning committee drawn from the community that will assess the community's vulnerabilities to future natural disasters and needs for economic development, identify where funds should be used to repair or reconstruct critical facilities and essential public assets damaged or destroyed by the storm, and identify projects that will increase resilience while also protecting vulnerable populations and promoting sound economic development.[176] Governor Cuomo officially launched the program with Secretary Donovan on July 18, 2013.[177] The State released guidelines for NYRCR plans, including requirements for community engagement and hazard mitigation against future storms. The NYRCR program has established a cadre of consultants with a variety of capacities and expertise, which have been paired with each community. Successful completion of a NYRCR plan qualifies the community to receive access to additional recovery grants. The State estimates grants to eligible NYRCR plans will range from $3 million to $25 million, which the State anticipates using future CDBG-DR allocations to fund.[178]

As part of the NYRCR program, the State has also engaged the Long Island Regional Economic Development Council to resolve issues of regional significance and assess the collective impact of individual NYRCR plans on Long Island. The Task Force expects that this process will lead to community-driven plans that, due to regional coordination, will more effectively leverage Federal dollars. The hope is that the NYRCR program will enable the region to take advantage of planning expertise otherwise unavailable to an individual town or city and therefore push standard thinking towards truly actionable and innovative solutions that make the region more resilient. The solutions will look not only at infrastructure, but also at issues related to economic development, housing, and health and social services.

The CPCB RSF should regularly track updates on the progress of the New York planning program and work with the FDRCs, as appropriate, to ensure that resources are being provided to support recovery planning and implementation activities. Additionally, Federal agencies with local and/or regional planning resources and requirements should be directed to support and align planning activities that they fund or undertake in the impacted region. This may include NOAA, USACE, DOT, HUD, EPA, EDA, USDA, FEMA and others.

Owner
*Lead: HUD and CPCB RSF (FDRC with FEMA as RSF coordinating agency)*
Status
Recommendation adopted: Currently available for projects funded by the Sandy Supplemental.

**59. RECOMMENDATION:** Support New Jersey planning efforts, including pilots for New Jersey Local Resilience Partnerships, and encourage Federal agencies, the State of New

Jersey, non-profits, and philanthropic organizations to provide both financial and technical support for the formation and operation of the Local Resilience Partnerships.

Given its many small towns – as well as the "Home Rule" relationship between these towns, the counties, and the State of New Jersey – New Jersey has a real need for robust planning efforts in order to ensure that its communities rebuild effectively. The State has incorporated planning into its rebuilding work thus far. For example, individual towns or regional groups within Partnerships in the State's nine most impacted counties are eligible to apply for grants for consulting services on long-term planning issues through the CDBG-DR-funded and State- administered $5 million Post-Sandy Planning Assistance Grant program.[179] These grants range from $5,000 to $50,000 with a maximum of $310,000 per municipality.[180] Eligible activities include developing a strategic recovery plan, preparing community design standards specific to flood hazard areas, and analyzing local land use practices. In addition, communities are encouraged to combine their funds to pursue regional projects and solutions. New Jersey anticipates that more than 70 communities will participate in the program.

New Jersey is also coordinating a planning grant program of over $2.5 million under FEMA's Hazard Mitigation Grant Program (HMGP), which will provide eligible counties with grants to develop multi-jurisdictional hazard mitigation plans. These grants will allow municipalities or Partnerships of municipalities to collaborate with county government to develop regional resilience plans that will help New Jersey mitigate the threat of future hazards.

To provide local communities with the best available data to inform planning decisions, New Jersey has also partnered with six universities[181] to devise flood mitigation strategies for particularly flood-prone communities located near the Hudson River, Hackensack River, Arthur Kill, Barnegat Bay and Delaware Bay, in addition to collaborating with the U.S. Army Corps of Engineers on its comprehensive study. The university studies focus on repetitive flooding regions beyond what is already being addressed by current or planned U.S. Army Corps of Engineers projects.

To support these and other longer-term planning efforts, the Task Force worked together with local and Federal partners to develop a new model called the New Jersey Local Resilience Partnerships. This effort is designed to support cross-jurisdictional collaboration in several regions that have common problems and together encompass flood-prone municipalities in New Jersey. It was developed through the Task Force's engagement with a number of non- governmental partners --Sustainable Jersey (a public-private partnership that coordinates resources and policy to support local governments pursuing sustainability), New Jersey Future (a non-profit planning advocacy organization), and the New Jersey Recovery Fund (a philanthropic collaborative run by the Community Foundation of New Jersey and Geraldine R. Dodge Foundation with numerous supporting foundations).

The New Jersey Local Resilience Partnerships ("the Partnerships") are voluntary associations of small groups of adjacent communities that share common geography, flood risks, recovery challenges, and other characteristics. They serve the dual purposes of improving Sandy recovery and promoting greater cooperation among towns. The Partnerships have a bottom-up structure in which towns retain local control over land-use decisions. They will enable communities to expand their capacity to recover by bringing recovery planning and implementation capabilities to member towns on both a local and regional basis, expanding access to information and resources, and encouraging neighboring municipalities to pool resources and share services. Shared services may include joint engineering projects and cross-jurisdictional approaches to hazard mitigation. By sharing information and working together, the municipalities will be able to cooperate in securing – rather than competing with one another for – limited resources. The work of these Partnerships will foster stronger and more sustainable recovery outcomes and numerous benefits that will last far beyond recovery.

As part of their structure, the Local Resilience Partnerships will identify "Affiliate Members" that can provide technical assistance, training, and other support. Affiliate Members could include Federal, State, and county government agencies, as well as universities and non-profits with important expertise. The resources and ability of Affiliate Members to provide access to other opportunities will also enable Local Resilience Partnerships to participate in existing recovery efforts such as the development of county hazard mitigation plans. Technical assistance will help local decision-makers better participate in major recovery coordination issues such as the regional coordination of infrastructure resilience investments.

In support of these Partnerships, the New Jersey Recovery Fund is providing $1.5 million in seed funding for one year to support a Resource Center at Rutgers University as well as Disaster Recovery Managers and Resilience Coordinators to assist local governments with recovery and resilience planning. The Robert Wood Johnson Foundation is committing to fund Disaster Recovery Impact Assessments, which will help communities develop improved recovery strategies and better long-term risk adaptation measures.[182] USDA Rural Development has agreed to support Partnership efforts focused on regional rural economies as their funding and legal authorities allow. USACE will also support Partnership efforts focused on vulnerable coastal communities where funding and authority is available. FEMA, through the CPCB RSF, will support the Partnerships by working with key leadership to build capacity to convene, organize, and manage the effort. FEMA will initially assist in coordinating members, information-sharing, and Partnership activities, and facilitate relationships with other Federal, State, non-profit, and philanthropic support organizations until the effort is successfully launched. In addition, FEMA will continue to provide technical assistance, planning capabilities, and support for the implementation of recovery activities that are within the scope of the CPCB RSF.

The network of regional Resilience Coordinators and LDRMs coordinated by Sustainable Jersey and New Jersey Future respectively will also help to organize and convene the pilot Partnerships, assist in coordinating members and Partnership activities, and provide technical assistance, planning capabilities, and support for the implementation of recovery activities. Many communities have already expressed the desire to participate in such Partnerships and three pilots are ready to be operationalized. These Partnerships will create a vehicle for participating municipalities to work on matters of recovery and resilience in an efficient and cost-effective manner that fosters stronger, more sustainable outcomes.

The CPCB RSF should regularly track updates on the progress of the New Jersey planning program and work with the FDRCs, as appropriate, to ensure that resources are being provided to support recovery planning and implementation activities. Additionally, Federal agencies with local and/or regional planning resources and requirements should be directed to support and align planning activities that they fund or undertake in the impacted region. This may include NOAA, USACE, DOT, HUD, EPA, EDA, USDA, FEMA and others.

---

## LAND ACQUISITIONS

Another powerful tool for reducing risk of future losses in areas that are prone to repetitive flooding is land acquisitions. Voluntary land acquisitions by both governments and nonprofits serve a number of purposes: removing populations and structures from vulnerable areas, and providing land that can be dedicated to natural flood mitigation measures, public space or natural areas, or to building engineered flood control structures. Coordinated and targeted efforts to acquire at-risk properties from willing sellers are an important part of an effective overall risk mitigation strategy. Various mechanisms for land acquisitions include federal, state, and local open space funding, buyouts of flooded properties, deed restrictions, and easements. The Federal government should consider including the responsibility to coordinate the various Federal land acquisition mechanisms within the recovery responsibilities assigned in the NDRF. This will help avoid risk, develop resilient land use patterns, and encourage green infrastructure in vulnerable floodplains. Some examples of existing land acquisition mechanisms that could be utilized include: pre-and post-mitigation FEMA funding, CDBG-DR, NOAA's Coastal and Estuarine Land Conservation Program (CELCP), and DOI's Land and Water Conservation Fund, especially when coupled with state, county, and local open space funding. Both New Jersey and New York have implemented buy-out programs that address vulnerable flood-prone properties in certain areas, although the current levels of funding for these programs are less than the identified needs for buy-outs.

---

Owner

*Leads*: *HUD and CPCB RSF (FDRC with FEMA as RSF coordinating agency), Sustainable Jersey, and New Jersey Future*

Status

Recommendation adopted: Implementation underway for current and future Sandy recovery efforts. The CPCB RSF, New Jersey Future, and Sustainable Jersey are working with communities to help coordinate and facilitate the formation of Local Resilience Partnerships.

**60. RECOMMENDATION:** Package the variety of existing Federal resources and tools related to disaster recovery and create new ones specific to community planning and capacity building in order to establish a coordinated suite of assistance that enhances and streamlines access to the recovery expertise needed by impacted communities.

Responding to recovery needs in the aftermath of Sandy requires that local practitioners acquire new skill sets and enhanced knowledge about disaster recovery best practices and model approaches. The NDRF places great emphasis on the need for better capacity building measures for State and local governments, community-based organizations, and local actors engaged in challenging recovery operations. This includes a focus on the tools and training needed to help impacted communities improve their disaster recovery plans, processes, protocols, project management, and program administration. One of the six principles of the CPCB RSF states, "local community recovery planning and recovery capacity are essential for organizing, leading, and most importantly, sustaining long-term recovery activity."[183]

However, it is often difficult for State and local partners to find or efficiently deploy disaster recovery tools, training, case studies, best practices, funding sources, and technical assistance.

In order to meet this need, the CPCB RSF within the RSFLG will need to engage the appropriate agencies and partners to leverage their capabilities to support local recovery planning and management.

The Task Force recommends that targeted disaster recovery capacity building efforts be piloted in the New York/New Jersey/Connecticut region that would respond to urgent needs for practical expertise and that would dovetail with the planning activities in the NYRCRs and New Jersey Local Resilience Partnerships. These efforts would offer training sessions and workshops, one-on-one technical assistance, and ongoing peer learning opportunities to enhance the capabilities of LDRMs, civil servants, planners, and program administrators in the region. The Task Force also recommends that FDRCs and the CPCB RSF's in New York and New Jersey work with the States, other RSFs, academia, and non-governmental partners to develop a Sandy-specific online portal offering: tools, best practices, and links to funding opportunities; a coordinated calendar of training and technical assistance offerings in the region; blogs and discussion boards; updates on regional activities; and a forum for requesting assistance from technical experts. Efforts to establish a portal are already underway in New York and should continue to be supported.

The CPCB RSFs should be tasked with the development of this resource while the RSFLG should develop a strategy for interagency support and disseminate the results. Existing training and technical assistance funds from Federal agencies should be better coordinated to serve as a unified national disaster recovery capacity building network. In addition, future disaster appropriations should include explicit authority and funding for technical assistance.

Owner
*Lead: CPCB RSFs (FDRCs with FEMA as RSF coordinating agency)/RSFLG*
Status
Recommendation adopted: To be implemented for future projects funded by the Sandy Supplemental and will be applicable to future disaster recovery efforts nationwide.


## Facilitate Opportunities for Community and Non-Profit Engagement in Capacity Building and Actively Engage Philanthropy to Fill Capacity Gaps

### Challenge and Goal

The NDRF notes that existing highly networked individuals and organizations, both inside and outside government, are key building blocks for sustained recovery efforts. In the aftermath of a disaster, these existing networks should be tapped; resulting in a single, shared strategy for rebuilding that is facilitated by dialogue among local and regional stakeholders. While the Task Force helped to facilitate engagement between the States, foundations, and community-based organizations, much more is needed to ensure that these partnerships are successful. Ideally, where formal associations among philanthropic entities (e.g., funder collaboratives) do not exist, entities would be established and staffed by the foundations to regularly engage with State and local governments, support broad stakeholder engagement, and allow strong and capable local organizations to actively participate in long-term recovery.

Highly capable non-profit organizations and technical assistance providers in the New York and New Jersey region have the ability to meet unique needs and fill resource gaps that public-sector funding cannot address. As such, it is critical that non-profits are connected to and engaged with State and local government to maximize recovery impacts through partnership.

There is a need to enhance the working relationships between non-profits and State/local government to the benefit of the survivors they serve. As a key partner in recovery, it is important for State and local governments to dedicate resources in such a way that not only maximizes the impact they can have but that also builds the capacity of local non-profits. This investment in the capacity of non-profits yields a return on investment that is experienced by the community for years since these organizations become more capable of addressing a variety of continuing needs. Non-profits may be eligible subgrantees of States and local governments receiving CDBG-DR funds. CDBG-DR grantees are encouraged to consider this source of funding when looking to partner with non-profit organizations and leverage public and private funds.

Philanthropies generally do not consider disaster part of their normal funding priorities and, if they provide funding for these emergency events, are, historically, much more apt to fund response-oriented activities. This is because the need is clear, the media helps shine a light on areas where assistance is needed, and efforts during these periods bring in donations and produce good will. It is easy and intuitive for philanthropy and non-profits to undertake immediate relief activities, but as the response phase ebbs and recovery begins, many foundations have become interested in longer-term rebuilding processes. They want to know:

- What is the role of government and are they duplicating efforts?
- How much, if any, funding should be provided? And for what activities?
- Which local non-profits have the "know-how" to take on these tasks?
- Are there any proven models to invest in? If not, or if there are only a limited number, how can philanthropy work with government officials and non-profit leaders to identify the best ad-hoc initiatives to support?
- What is the best use of limited funds for response and/or for longer term recovery?

The Task Force recognizes the vital role of philanthropy to spur innovation in the field of disaster recovery and to support non-profits as they provide services in coordination and collaboration with government.

**61. RECOMMENDATION:** Facilitate and expand opportunities for philanthropic and non- profit engagement in recovery, including opportunities for organizations that work with vulnerable populations. The CPCB RSFs in New York and New Jersey should actively support funder collaboratives that provide grants to nonprofits working in coordination with government. This should include encouragement of sub-grants to NGOs that would assist in accomplishing the Federal outreach requirements, including those specific to vulnerable populations to ensure they are included in the recovery planning process.

The CPCB RSFs should continue to support geographically based funder collaboratives, encourage foundations to support LDRMs and the multi-jurisdictional partnerships in New York and New Jersey, and help identify specific non-profit resources that can assist government in capacity building efforts.

For future disasters, the CPCB RSFs and RSFLG should develop and disseminate guidance and sample public-private partnerships for state and local governments to leverage Federal funding and engage non-profit and community-based organizations in local capacity building and community planning efforts.

Owner
**Lead:** *CPCB RSFs (FDRCs with FEMA as RSF coordinating agency) and RSFLG*
Status
Recommendation adopted: To be implemented for future projects funded by the Sandy Supplemental and will be applicable to future disaster recovery efforts nationwide.

# IMPROVING DATA SHARING BETWEEN FEDERAL, STATE, AND LOCAL OFFICIALS

The use of data facilitates decision-making that is well-informed and leads to goals that are both clearly defined and realistically achievable. In post-disaster situations, data collection and application are especially important for on-the-ground recovery efforts, as well as for long-term policy formulation and program management.

Data and information are extremely valuable to Federal, Tribal, State, and local governments, as well as to private citizens, businesses, non-profits, and other community groups. Data and information are used to:

- Help local governments identify and design the most effective programs to meet the needs of communities.
- Help governments problem solve and streamline processes that more quickly deliver better services.
- Help governments control costs.
- Inform members of the public about the return on their investment paid through taxes.
- Inform members of the public about the availability of funding for their communities.
- Allow local planners and technology experts to design locally-focused applications.
- Allow the public to hold government accountable.

As a point of clarification for readers, the Task Force's examination of data sharing in this section is primarily confined to process-related issues at the three major recovery agencies: FEMA, HUD, and SBA. Obviously, "data sharing" is a term that can be interpreted very broadly, encompassing everything from what data Federal agencies collect to how information is passed along to victims in the immediate aftermath of a disaster. The Task Force, however, has limited its inquiry to a specific set of issues that have hindered the recovery efforts of FEMA, HUD, and SBA in response to Sandy and to other disasters in the past. The term "agencies," as used in this section, refers only to FEMA, SBA, and HUD. Nevertheless, several of the recommendations directed at these three agencies may be relevant for other agencies as well. The Task Force encourages other parts of the Federal family to consider adopting the recommendations in this section, where appropriate, and to reach out to FEMA, HUD, and SBA where coordination is necessary.

## Lack of Access to Data by Non-Governmental Third Parties

### Challenge and Goals

While shared data can be employed to facilitate and inform Federal and State responses to disasters, it can also be used to validate and provide context for decisions government officials make. Agencies and States have an interest in employing data not only to design their policies, but also to explain their policies to the public.

Non-profits working in the Sandy-affected region informed the Task Force that they would greatly benefit from having access to government data, which would help them respond more effectively and evaluate government actions. For example, community groups in New York and New Jersey told the Task Force that government data about individual needs assessments would allow them to formulate comments in response to State Action Plans by giving them a better sense of which unmet needs required attention.

In addition to using publicly available information to evaluate government programs, non-governmental entities (e.g. NGOs, academic partners, and private sector firms) can use additional data to supplement government efforts and make their efforts more effective. For example, HHS, recognizing the importance of tracking the health outcomes of individual program participants, has made grant funds available for researchers to analyze the impact of HHS programs on storm-affected communities. As they draft their proposals, grant applicants have asked for access to government data to help them determine whether their research designs are effective. Some of these applicants have pointed to existing government access portals available to potential grantees, such as http://www.healthdata.gov, as resources that provide researchers with a better understanding of the populations they intend to investigate. HHS also recently conducted an exercise in New Orleans with the local health department. Using data from HHS's Centers for Medicare and Medicaid Services (CMS), officials identified individuals who had electrically powered medical equipment and where these individuals lived. The CMS teams then visited these individuals to confirm the accuracy of the data and to learn more about their emergency preparedness plans. HHS learned that the data are accurate and hopes that this forms the basis for building nationwide capability.

Given that the Obama Administration has committed itself to making information resources accessible, discoverable, and usable by the public to promote transparency and accountability, both through its Open Government Initiative[184] and its recently announced Open Data Policy,[185] the proactive release of aggregated data in the aftermath of disasters would further an important objective of the President. Although information must be shared in a manner that complies with applicable laws and policies and protects personal privacy, it may be possible to make aggregated data available that are sufficiently scrubbed of Personally Identifiable Information (PII) but still present a useful and accurate picture of the post-disaster landscape. Having a publicly accessible portal available in the aftermath of

Sandy would have helped partners outside of government contribute more effectively to the Federal response.

**62. RECOMMENDATION:** Agencies should make aggregated, PII-scrubbed data about disaster-affected populations available to the public using a central website similar to http://www.data.gov. Specifically, FEMA, HUD, and SBA should coordinate to create a new website or adapt an existing one (such as FEMA's openFEMA site) for data posting during disasters. In addition, FEMA, HUD, and SBA should create a process for digesting raw data into an aggregated form that the public can view.

There is a growing expectation that government will make data available whenever appropriate rather than waiting for third party requests. In the Freedom of Information Act context, agencies are now posting documents proactively to promote transparency and eliminate unnecessary bureaucratic hurdles for document requestors. Similarly, groups from outside of the government that are seeking data in the wake of a disaster should not have to approach agencies to make requests when data can be posted online as a matter of course. Privacy concerns can often be addressed by masking PII through aggregation, so that data only pertain to large groups of individuals whose identities cannot be deduced.

To make publicly available data sets as accessible and user friendly as possible, they should ideally be posted on a central website that includes information from all major disaster data collecting agencies, including FEMA, HUD, and SBA.[186] As discussed above, http://www.healthdata.gov is a useful example of a publicly available data website that is comprehensive, secure, and easy to navigate. OpenFEMA could potentially serve this role since it already contains some publicly available data.

While not all data can be posted, aggregated summaries that provide context to third parties about the scope and extent of a disaster can prove invaluable, both to groups working with government (such as the HHS grant applicants described above) and to outside groups that may employ data in ways that Federal or State officials have not envisioned. In the immediate aftermath of Sandy, volunteer organizations that developed and employed information technology to direct recovery assistance to storm victims played a particularly important role in storm-affected communities. Providing these groups with access to the most current government data would have helped these groups carry out their activities even more effectively. By embracing an "open data" philosophy, the Federal Government will not only promote transparency and accountability, but also leverage non-governmental resources that can contribute to disaster recovery efforts.

Owner
*Leads: FEMA, HUD, SBA*
Status
Recommendation in process: Recommended for future disaster recovery efforts in the region and applicable to future disaster recovery efforts nationwide.

## Data Sharing between Federal Agencies and State and Local Governments

The ability of agencies and States to disseminate and receive data quickly and efficiently in the aftermath of a disaster is an essential component of a transparent and effective recovery. Whether agencies are sharing information with one another about assistance disbursed to individuals to avoid duplication of benefits or are passing information to States to help them administer their own programs, the successful exchange of data is often the difference between a productive, timely response and one that is slow and reliant on incomplete information. Failure to transmit data efficiently and effectively can lead to delays that prevent individuals and small businesses from receiving urgently needed assistance.

In the wake of Hurricane Sandy, the Task Force examined the data sharing processes of the three major Federal disaster response agencies -- FEMA, HUD, and SBA -- and identified several impediments that cause delays and inefficiencies when Federal agencies share information with one another and with State and local governments. The Task Force offers recommendations for how agencies can use data to ensure that recovery efforts are transparent and appropriately tailored to the communities that agencies are serving.

### Typical Data Sharing Arrangements

Although disasters pose unique challenges to agencies providing and requesting data, much of the work required of agencies follows a familiar pattern. FEMA is typically the first on the ground, collecting individual registrant data immediately after a disaster. Included in this registration process is an individual income screen, which establishes who in an affected area is eligible for different types of assistance. In addition to using this information for its own programs, FEMA sends these data to SBA to determine whether individuals are eligible for disaster loan assistance. In addition, HUD and FEMA exchange data about local housing needs. HUD initially identifies residents who received housing assistance before the storm so that FEMA can assess the need for its emergency housing programs. Then, once the short-term response has ended and long-term housing programs go into effect, FEMA sends HUD information about who has received emergency housing assistance and income eligibility data to inform HUD's programs and avoid duplication of benefits. Finally, as States begin to develop their CDBG-DR Action Plans, both SBA and FEMA make data available to State grantees so States can determine who qualifies for grant assistance using CDBG-DR funds. In addition, HUD will request loan data from SBA and FEMA to help formulate policy and determine allocations for CDBG-DR grants before making funds available to States.

## Identify Dedicated Points of Contact for Data Sharing Requests in Agencies and within State and Local Governments

### Challenge and Goals

Both States and agencies raised concerns that they did not have dedicated points of contact with whom to negotiate the exchange of data after Sandy. Agencies, including SBA and FEMA, wanted a central point of contact with the State governments in New York and New Jersey who would be responsible for passing data on to municipalities. Similarly, New Jersey wanted a dedicated official at FEMA who could answer questions about the State's data requests and help the State become familiar with the data available. The lack of a "go-to authority" to make and receive requests and to provide assistance meant that States and agencies lost time as they tried coordinating with one another.

**63. RECOMMENDATION:** Each agency and each State should identify a "data steward" who serves as a point of contact for data requests. This contact should not only be available after disasters, but also serve as an informational resource in advance of disasters. FEMA, HUD, and SBA should each designate an individual within their agencies that is permanently available to receive data sharing requests and related questions from States, local governments, and non-governmental entities. Each agency should then distribute the name and contact information of that individual to all 50 States. In the event of a disaster, agencies should send affected States a reminder that the data steward is available to assist them and that each State is responsible for identifying a central point of contact within the governor's office or within the primary disaster response agency to coordinate requests with Federal agencies.

One of the keys to improving the current data sharing process is to keep lines of communication open before, during, and after a disaster strikes. To that end, the Task Force recommends that FEMA, SBA, and HUD each identify a dedicated "data steward" who is available to answer questions from States and other agencies and that can provide data expertise before and during a disaster. This is in keeping with the NDRF, which states that before disaster strikes, each RSF should identify and leverage "programs that assist communities to prepare, collect and analyze relevant existing and future data necessary to plan and manage complex disaster recovery."[187]

In advance of a disaster, Federal data stewards would introduce potential State recipients to the request process and serve as reference librarians for each agency's data collection. In addition to familiarizing State officials with available data, data stewards would help States identify which data would be most helpful, the format in which the data should be delivered, and the limitations of the data (privacy requirements, aggregation, data latency, etc.). States, not knowing what information they will need, often make overly broad requests that result in an unmanageable volume of data being delivered to them by Federal agencies. This is also true for local and Tribal governments, non-profits, and community organizations that often make their own data requests. By helping to "curate" their agencies' data, the Federal data stewards would help States make better use of the information the States receive. Besides working with States on their requests, the Federal data stewards would also make sample data sharing agreements available to State officials before a disaster strikes so that recipients have an opportunity to do advanced troubleshooting, which can cut down on protracted negotiations over data sharing agreement language when disasters do occur.

The Federal data stewards should work in close coordination with agency officials, including the senior agency official for privacy and the Chief Information Officer (or an equivalent official).

Similarly, States should identify a single point of contact to make requests, and that contact should then take responsibility for passing data on to other entities within the State, including other State agencies and local governments.

Owner
*Leads: FEMA, HUD, SBA*
Status
Recommendation adopted: Currently adopted by HUD for Sandy recovery efforts and to be implemented by FEMA and SBA for future disaster recovery efforts nationwide.


## Create Data Menus to Ensure that Data Requestors Have Complete Information

### Challenge and Goals

Inexperience is a tremendous handicap to State and local governments seeking data after a disaster. Simply put, State personnel generally do not know what information to ask for and where to find it. Even States with experience responding to disasters may not be aware of all of the data potentially available from various Federal agencies.

Following Sandy, New Jersey officials, who were requesting information from FEMA for the first time, asked for a summary sheet; unfortunately, no such summary existed, which resulted in delays.

By contrast, New York City had FEMA staff embedded in the Mayor's Office of Housing Recovery Operations. Having a close point of contact familiar with both the City's goals and with FEMA's procedures and data sets made the City's process of completing a data sharing agreement much more efficient. Unfortunately, most States and localities cannot count on having someone with in-depth knowledge of an agency available to provide guidance.

**64. RECOMMENDATION:** Each agency should catalogue its disaster data in a "menu" that describes the data that it may share with States and local governments. Specifically, each agency's data steward (see recommendation 63) should create a document containing a list of all data sets that are typically requested during a disaster. Each data item description should include the fields in the data set and the units of measurement, as well as a brief description of how the data can be used by States responding to a disaster and describe the limitations of the data (privacy requirements, aggregation, data latency, etc.). This document should be distributed to disaster agencies in each State.

A data menu containing the categories of data that an agency can share with State and local governments would be an invaluable resource for States and local governments seeking sources of Federal data in the wake of a disaster. The menu should include the names and fields in each data set, the level at which data are collected (zip code, municipality, census tract, etc.), and the ways it can be employed by States and local governments during disaster recovery. SBA has developed a version of this that it began distributing in the spring of 2013 that describes the loan data it has available, how the data are broken down by field, and the unit of measurement for each field. FEMA has also started working on a similar document.

The data menu should be assembled in advance of a disaster and describe potential applications for each item listed. In addition, the data menu should include a description of how the data were originally collected so recipients understand how to interpret them. The data steward (see recommendation 63) would be charged with maintaining the data menu to ensure it is regularly updated. Ideally, each State would have access to menus from all of the major disaster response and recovery agencies so that it has a complete picture of the data available from the Federal Government.

Owner
*Leads: FEMA, HUD, SBA*
Status
Recommendation adopted: Currently adopted by SBA for Sandy recovery efforts and to be implemented by FEMA and HUD for future disaster recovery efforts nationwide.


## Create a Uniform Request Process and Uniform Data Sharing Agreement Template Common across Federal Agencies

*Challenge and Goals*

States attempting to obtain data from multiple Federal sources quickly learn that request processes vary from agency to agency. When talking with the entities that shared and received data in the aftermath of Sandy, the Task Force learned that recipients seek a dependable, uniform request process so recipients can eliminate the guesswork needed to comply with each agency's requirements. This includes the way requests are submitted, how to clarify requests, and how to draw up data sharing agreements. After Sandy, New Jersey experienced significant delays obtaining data from FEMA because State officials did not understand how to comply with the agency's specific data request submission guidelines. The State, which hoped to use information from FEMA to design its own response programs as part of its Action Plan, made several unsuccessful data requests to the agency. FEMA informed the State that its request submissions were required to provide more detail about the data sought and the proposed use of the data. Frustrated State officials reported that they struggled to find "the magic words" to unlock FEMA's data so that they could put it to use. Until they did, New Jersey could not complete its Action Plan.

Similar delays result when States have to negotiate widely varying data sharing agreements with FEMA, SBA, and HUD. Many of the agreement terms and conditions relate to safeguarding information to ensure compliance with the Privacy Act of 1974 and require some flexibility depending on the applicant and the intended use of the data. However, there are common elements in each agreement that could be standardized in advance by all three agencies, which would save States time and prevent negotiation delays due to disagreements over language. Prolonged negotiations between lawyers over agreement terms are often cited as one of the most time consuming aspects of the data sharing process.

**65. RECOMMENDATION:** FEMA, HUD, and SBA should adopt a common data sharing agreement template so that data requestors do not have to familiarize themselves with three separate forms. Attorneys and privacy officials from these agencies should meet to compare their current data sharing agreement formats and identify common boilerplate language that can serve as the basis for an interagency template. Once drafted, this template should then be distributed by each agency's data sharing steward to the States.

The adoption of a common template by the three primary disaster response agencies would make the data request process easier to understand for recipients and could eventually lay the groundwork for an interagency data hub (see recommendation 66). Agencies should distribute this template, along with guidance about how to complete it, before disasters occur, so that State points of contact are familiar with the template prior to a disaster. It should be noted, however, that although a template will streamline the process, all data agreements will have to undergo review and clearance from agency counsel and privacy officials before data containing PII can be released.

Owner
**Leads:** *FEMA, HUD, SBA*
Status
Recommendation adopted: To be implemented for future disaster recovery efforts nationwide.

**66. RECOMMENDATION:** Work towards a multi-agency integrated data repository, or "data hub," shared and operated by FEMA and HUD, that, to the extent permitted by law and Federal policy, allows those agencies to access and store one another's data and pass these data along to States in the event of a Federally declared disaster. FEMA and HUD should provide technical support and personnel resources to further this tool's development in preparation for the next disaster. In addition, agency attorneys and privacy officials should discuss what steps will be necessary to begin preparing the legal framework for a multi-agency data portal.

FEMA and HUD are already discussing how to set up an online portal that will allow both agencies to transmit information to one another instantaneously during a disaster. Each agency would have standing agreements in place to access and store one another's disaster-relevant data. Although this would require each agency to meet a number of legal requirements – including the publication of System of Records Notices (SORNs)[188] – it would eliminate the time consuming process of establishing interagency data sharing agreements each time a disaster strikes. This repository could potentially be incorporated into an existing portal/tool, such as the National Disaster Recovery Program Database, http://www.data.gov, http://www.max.gov or a new portal established by FEMA.

Owner
**Leads**: *FEMA and HUD*
**Supporting Agency:** *DOI*
Status
Recommendation in process: Recommended for implementation for future disaster recovery efforts nationwide.

## Agency Efforts to Comply with the Privacy Act

The Privacy Act, a Federal law regulating Federal agencies' collection, maintenance, use, and dissemination of certain records containing PII, places considerable restrictions on agencies' ability to share information. In general, absent consent from the person whose data are being shared, data in records covered by the Privacy Act may only be shared if the disclosure falls into one of twelve exceptions in subsection (b) of the statute. One of those exceptions is a disclosure for an official "routine use." Routine uses are defined in the Privacy Act as the use of a record for "a purpose which is compatible with the purpose for which it was collected."[189] Routine uses must be described in a SORN and should be interpreted narrowly.

**67. RECOMMENDATION:** To help make Federal data available to States, agencies should review "routine use" language in relevant SORNs to determine whether any changes are warranted that could provide greater flexibility to share information for planning purposes, to share information across State agencies and with local governments and to broaden categories of records to cover data from other sources. FEMA's Office of Chief Counsel has offered to make attorneys available to provide guidance.

The requirements of the Privacy Act are important to help the Federal Government protect privacy; however, because the routine use exception in the Privacy Act is narrow, agencies may not be able to use the exception to share Federal data with States in response to a disaster. Federal agencies should review the routine use language in relevant SORNs to determine whether changes are warranted and appropriate in disaster settings. If agencies are able to draft routine uses in a way that allows for disclosure in response to a disaster, it could help reduce the long delays that States have encountered in obtaining access to important data. Specifically, agencies can work with their privacy officers and attorneys to consider routine use language that makes it possible for State agencies to use information for program planning and design purposes.

An additional concern that the States raised was that they were unable to pass on data to subrecipients, such as local governments or other State agencies. Even in cases when States were permitted to receive data, the States were not allowed to provide the data to any other entity within the State. Instead, the States had to renegotiate agreements, which contributed to additional delays.

Owner
*Lead*: FEMA and HUD
Status
Recommendation adopted: To be implemented for future disaster recovery efforts nationwide.

## DATA SHARING AND ACCOUNTABILITY: THE PMO

The Program Management Office (PMO) provides a concrete example of the ways in which open and transparent data sharing practices between agencies can encourage smarter and more effective decision making in recovery and rebuilding efforts. The size, complexity, and urgency of the funding for Hurricane Sandy recovery made it clear -- even before the Sandy Supplemental was enacted – that the Task Force needed a central coordinating office that would work closely with agencies, OMB, and the oversight community, such as the agency Inspectors General and the Recovery Accountability and Transparency Board (RATB). PMO was also established to leverage lessons learned from Hurricane Katrina as well as best practices from ARRA.

## Challenge and Goals

The Sandy Supplemental provided about $50 billion in relief funding for communities affected by Hurricane Sandy and other disasters in 2011, 2012, and 2013.[190] The funds were appropriated to 19 different federal agencies to be administered through more than 60 different programs. To meet the challenge of monitoring these many programs, the Task Force established PMO to serve as a central source for information about the progress and performance of Sandy Supplemental funding. PMO centrally collects and shares data across agencies.

**68. RECOMMENDATION:** Continue functions of PMO to track the progress of the Sandy Supplemental funding and performance.

The Task Force created PMO in January 2013 to serve as the data-driven cross-agency management organization within the Task Force, coordinating with OMB and the oversight community.

PMO's mission was to support the Task Force and partner agencies by promoting efficiencies and information sharing across agencies in order to speed assistance to and maximize the impact of relief funds for Sandy-affected communities, families, and individuals, while also promoting the transparent and responsible use of federal resources. Since its inception, PMO has worked to fulfill this mission by focusing its efforts on four primary areas:

1) Transparency: PMO worked to develop public facing financial and performance updates, as well as machine-readable data sets for public consumption in order to keep taxpayers informed about the progress of recovery. These are expected to be published by October 1, 2013.

2) Cross Agency Coordination: PMO served as the Task Force's office responsible for coordinating matters related to budget execution and performance management across the 19 federal agencies funded by the Sandy Supplemental.

3) Data: In recognition of the lessons learned from both Hurricane Katrina and ARRA about the importance of accountability, PMO focused on data. PMO collected and analyzed agency financial and performance data to understand the progress of recovery on the ground.

4) Oversight Support: PMO played a support role to RATB and, by extension, to agency Inspectors General (IGs), by providing data and information, as well as by convening agency stakeholders, in support of the oversight community. These functions are also particularly important in light of the lessons from Katrina that demonstrate that accountability and transparency are critical elements of a successful recovery.

While each of these functions is routinely addressed within every agency—as well as within state entities, which are, in some cases, charged with program implementation—PMO has worked to bring together agency experts in these areas to ensure that Task Force and agency efforts are aligned. Especially given the breadth of the funding and affected agencies—each with their own set of governing statutes, regulations, and data systems—the PMO roles described above served to ensure regular and open communication across agencies and oversight organizations, as well as allowed the development of a single, consistent, source of information about the progress of spending and performance across the agencies. Activities and stakeholders supporting each of these functions are described in the sections below.

## Promoting Transparency

The tracking and coordination provided through PMO has primarily served the needs of government leadership and staff within agencies, the oversight community, the Executive Office of the President (EOP), and the Task Force. These organizations are charged with overseeing and managing program implementation, and keeping track of progress to date is an important component of their roles. The data that PMO collects serve many purposes: the data are critical to internal management and can also be useful to the public, helping demonstrate the nature of taxpayers' investment (e.g., what programs were funded, and at what levels) and the return in terms of long-term recovery for Sandy-impacted families and communities.

One key lesson from ARRA is that there is a tremendous amount of public interest in understanding where the funds are going and what they are buying. To expand on those lessons, after building the underlying reporting mechanisms and establishing day-to-day operations, PMO turned its attention to developing a way in which non-sensitive data and information could be shared with the public. In coordination with Task Force agencies, as well as with OMB and the White House, PMO began to design both narrative and graphic updates on progress for the public, which will be published to a public website. Following the lead of the http://www.data.gov efforts, PMO also worked to develop granular information, such as funds and performance by state, in machine-readable formats that the public can download and analyze.[191] PMO expects these data to be published by October 1, 2013.

## Cross Agency Coordination

PMO worked with a broad range of stakeholders and established a PMO working group which provided critically important feedback and information. This working group met on a weekly basis and consisted of representatives from each of the 19 agencies that the Sandy Supplemental funded. The weekly conversations were the principal drivers of PMO's work and allowed PMO to move quickly to develop reporting processes with maximal agency input and also provided a constructive forum for interagency problem solving and information sharing.

Each week, PMO presented proposals for data collection and analysis and facilitated a discussion around the implications of these proposals. In this way, PMO was able to quickly meet its data collection goals while fully leveraging the wisdom and experience of the group. By taking a consensus-based approach, PMO was able to collect the necessary data while also ensuring that PMO's processes were relevant and workable for the affected agencies. PMO staff also provided extensive technical assistance to help partner agencies navigate PMO's reporting processes. This assistance has been a critical component for ensuring consistency across agencies, and the need for this kind of agency-specific technical assistance will continue into the future.

Through PMO, agencies were able to work together to identify and address common program implementation and budget execution concerns. A good example of this was the development of a waiver policy proposal to provide much-needed flexibility for the permissible duration of rebuilding projects. Finally, agencies productively used PMO to share information about their agency's activities or funding opportunities that could have an impact on another agency. For example, EPA shared its revised Title VI term and condition, as well as its updated guidance regarding SRF and Superfund grants, so other members of the PMO working group could see possible ways of highlighting the need to comply with non-discrimination laws while also providing guidance to recipients about limited English proficiency issues and public participation. The very existence of this Sandy Supplemental-focused forum enabled simple and efficient cross-agency information sharing which might otherwise have taken longer or not have occurred at all.

## Focusing on the Data

Another primary PMO strategy for advancing its mission was to focus on the data. In particular, lessons learned from Katrina illustrated the importance of accountability in the disaster context, and in keeping with the administration's focus on data-driven policy formulation, a focus on the data was perhaps the most critical component of the PMO strategy, as it supported and enhanced each of the others.[192] Again, while each agency has their own internal process for monitoring and reporting relevant data, by providing a comprehensive view of the data across the broad range of programs funded in the Sandy Supplemental, PMO became the primary source of information about interagency progress to date. This centralized effort obviated the need for ad hoc inquiries of more than 60 programs.

The primary datasets the Task Force focused on were the financial metrics that detailed the progress of spending and preliminary performance metrics to illustrate what the significant federal investment has and will produce.[193] Since the process of providing Federal aid to communities begins with shifting money from federal agencies to State and local recipients, PMO began by tracking financial metrics. Typically, once Federal dollars reach the State and local level, funds are distributed by recipients and the work on the ground commences.[194] This work was captured though PMO's performance reporting process, which measured progress in terms of three main metrics: the people, businesses, and projects served by these funds. Through a monthly report, PMO provides aggregated agency data on the numbers of people served, businesses assisted, and projects planned, started, and completed.

By providing ongoing technical assistance to agencies, and by leveraging very simple technology, PMO was able to effectively compile and manage dynamic agency data while designing and deploying standardized products. These products present a great deal of information to a broad audience. In line with the principles of data-driven policies that the government is increasingly implementing, these simple datasets were provided to a range of stakeholders with varying needs and are intended to enhance the recovery effort. Furthermore, by regularly informing agency staff, leadership, and the oversight community about the status, recipients, and results of the supplemental funding, the Task Force is enabling more informed, consistent policy– making, which should lead to better outcomes on the ground.[195]

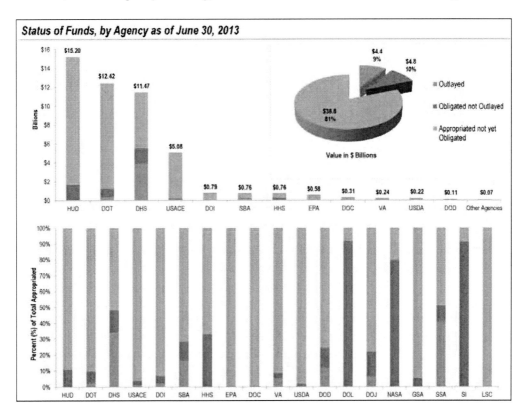

Status of Funds, by Agency as of June 30, 2013

## Supporting the Oversight Community

Lessons learned from Katrina underscore the importance of the oversight function. Nearly eight years after the storm, multiple agency IGs found that funds moved too slowly and were not adequately managed.[196] In a more extreme example, a 2007 GAO report assessing the Hurricane Katrina recovery process noted that there was a lack of proper oversight on contracts in several housing programs. GAO concluded that this lack of oversight may have resulted in millions of dollars in fraudulent charges to FEMA, illustrating the need for appropriate levels of oversight in post-disaster scenarios.[197] In the Sandy Supplemental, Congress responded to this inherent difficulty in meeting the dual objectives of getting money out quickly while maintaining appropriate controls, and as such gave RATB the authority to take on an extended oversight role over Sandy projects. Established by ARRA, RATB had broad transparency and accountability missions over the stimulus funding, and the Sandy Supplemental extended RATB's accountability mission to also apply to Sandy Supplemental funding. The vigilant oversight that RATB applied proved to be extraordinarily effective for ARRA funding: only 987 potential cases of fraud were identified (0.04% of the total awards) and DOJ filed charges for less than $3 million (or .0001%) in ARRA funding not related to taxes.[198] As the primary convener of agencies funded in the Supplemental, PMO was well suited to support this work by facilitating conversation, communicating agency concerns, and, most importantly, by compiling and providing agency data to OMB, RATB, and relevant agency IGs.

Another mechanism the Sandy Supplemental included to help ensure this significant investment was adequately managed and documented was the requirement that agencies develop enhanced Internal Control Plans (ICPs) to identify incremental risks associated with Sandy recovery programs.[199] PMO worked to ensure that agencies understood this requirement and assisted with the development and delivery of the plans to OMB. In these plans, agencies identified risks associated with Sandy Supplemental funding, as well as the specific hazard mitigation strategies they would use to address each risk. For example, HUD's ICP laid out a series of additional steps taken to oversee the funds, including increased grantee monitoring and additional reporting requirements, while EPA's ICP detailed proactive IG engagement before the funds were awarded and how specific additional information would be used by both EPA and the States. The plans are a foundational source of information for oversight and provide important information about steps agencies are taking internally to prevent waste, fraud, and abuse.

In addition to working closely with the agencies and OMB, PMO also worked with RATB to define roles, data needs, and to share information. In a series of conversations since the passage of the Sandy Supplemental, PMO, OMB, and RATB have worked to identify their respective responsibilities and how to support them. PMO shared data and information with RATB to support their work towards preventing and identifying waste, fraud, and abuse. This proactive approach to oversight—enabled by sharing data and information about recipients of federal funds, the progress of spending, and program performance—serves government's collective objectives: to see disaster funds spent responsibly so storm-affected families, businesses, and communities recover and rebuild quickly and without waste.

Owner
*Lead: Sandy Recovery Tracking Team*
Status
Recommendation adopted: Currently available for the Sandy Supplemental and replicable for future supplemental appropriations.

**69. RECOMMENDATION:** Document the functions and processes used by the Task Force recovery in a "PMO toolkit," which could be quickly deployed in the event of future supplemental funding.

For any large supplemental appropriation in the future, whether in response to a disaster or otherwise, good government requires that a comprehensive view of the funding be available. Quickly establishing PMO was critical to creating that picture during the Sandy recovery. Given this experience, the Task Force will, over the course of the wind-down period, create a toolkit that identifies the processes, stakeholders, and considerations required to quickly establish a similar interagency tracking function for large-scale and complex funding situations.

Owner
**Lead:** *Task Force*
Status
Recommendation adopted: In development, for use in future supplemental appropriations

# BEYOND THE TASK FORCE: DRIVING IMPLEMENTATION AND MONITORING PROGRESS

The President established the Task Force to ensure that the highest levels of government were engaged on the rebuilding and recovery efforts. As part of their work on the Task Force, the constituent Federal agencies have made important and detailed commitments to the region's recovery. Though the Task Force will wind down its operations over the sixty days following the submission of this Rebuilding Strategy to the President, the recovery will continue for years. In order to build on the extraordinary partnership forged among agencies over the last nine months, there must be a plan for implementing the recommendations and monitoring the progress of the recovery. To that end, the Task Force has developed a framework to maintain a similar degree of Cabinet-level engagement over the long-term. This includes both the implementation and monitoring of: the progress of the Task Force policy recommendations; the Sandy Supplemental funding; and performance metrics as contemplated in EO 13632.

## Implementation

While many of the recommendations that the Task Force suggests have already been adopted and implemented, there are a significant number that will require additional work by the agencies well into the future. To ensure that these efforts continue to be driven to completion, the Task Force has developed a framework for implementation that the agencies will use moving forward, including implementation plans with major milestones for each recommendation and regular checkpoints for interagency coordination.

Furthermore, on a quarterly basis, the agency principals will convene in a forum, co-chaired by the Secretaries of DHS and HUD, and attended by the relevant agency regional administrators (or other agency leadership as appropriate), to provide the cabinet-level engagement required to see that these recommendations are fully implemented. These regular meetings will be used to highlight successes and escalate challenges across all of the recommendations and policy areas relevant to the recovery and to rebuilding the region. All relevant Sandy stakeholders at the EOP and agencies will also be engaged in these meetings.

## Monitoring Progress

The complementary function to implementation is accountability, which occurs through monitoring. To this point, the Executive Order requires that the Task Force's Rebuilding Strategy include a "plan for monitoring progress." Thus, this Rebuilding Strategy identifies a plan that calls for two components of monitoring, to be owned by a Sandy Recovery tracking team. The Sandy Recovery tracking team will continue the work of the PMO, monitoring Sandy Supplemental funding and the cumulative outputs and outcomes in the storm-impacted communities, and will also set up a process to monitor the progress of the recommendations.

## Continued Coordination

The two components of the Task Force's succession plan -- implementation and monitoring -- are intended to ensure agency accountability for the commitments that have been made to improve the outcomes for Sandy-affected communities and to ensure that the administration is working to mitigate against future risk as effectively as possible. This model of active and engaged senior leadership -- combined with consistent data collection, analysis, and dissemination -- will serve these goals well. The model also serves to facilitate the Executive Order's charge to identify "specific outcomes, goals, and actions . . . that could support the affected region's rebuilding."

These coordinated efforts, led through the interagency forums described above, and supported by regular data and analysis, will serve to both effectively implement and rigorously monitor the recovery effort, thus ensuring that the Sandy Supplemental funds are put to work quickly, responsibly, and transparently, and that the recommendations identified by the Task Force, agency partners, and local stakeholders are expediently implemented. This will guarantee a full recovery and a more secure future for the region.

## APPENDICES

## I. Executive Order -- Establishing the Hurricane Sandy Rebuilding Task Force

*Executive Order 13632, December 7, 2012*
ESTABLISHING THE HURRICANE SANDY REBUILDING TASK FORCE
By the authority vested in me as President by the Constitution and the laws of the United States of America, it is hereby ordered as follows:

**Section 1. Purpose.** Hurricane Sandy made landfall on October 29, 2012, resulting in major flooding, extensive structural damage, and significant loss of life. A dangerous nor'easter followed 9 days later causing additional damage and undermining the recovery effort. As a result of these events, thousands of individuals were displaced and millions lost power, some for an extended period of time. Over 1,600 stores were closed, and fuel distribution was severely disrupted, further complicating the recovery effort. New York and New Jersey -- two of the Nation's most populous States -- were especially hard hit by these storms.

The Federal Emergency Management Agency (FEMA) in the Department of Homeland Security is leading the recovery efforts to assist the affected region. A disaster of Hurricane Sandy's magnitude merits a comprehensive and collaborative approach to the long-term rebuilding plans for this critical region and its infrastructure. Rebuilding efforts must address economic conditions and the region's aged infrastructure -- including its public housing, transportation systems, and utilities -- and identify the requirements and resources necessary to bring these systems to a more resilient condition given both current and future risks.

This order establishes the Hurricane Sandy Rebuilding Task Force (Task Force) to provide the coordination that is necessary to support these rebuilding objectives. In collaboration with the leadership provided through the National Disaster Recovery Framework (NDRF), the Task Force will identify opportunities for achieving rebuilding success, consistent with the NDRF's commitment to support economic vitality, enhance public health and safety, protect and enhance natural and manmade infrastructure, and ensure appropriate accountability. The Task Force will work to ensure that the Federal Government continues to provide appropriate resources to support affected State, local, and tribal communities to improve the region's resilience, health, and prosperity by building for the future

**Sec. 2.** Establishment of the Hurricane Sandy Rebuilding Task Force. There is established the Hurricane Sandy Rebuilding Task Force, which shall be chaired by the Secretary of Housing and Urban Development (Chair).

a.  In addition to the Chair, the Task Force shall consist of the head of each of the following executive departments, agencies, and offices, or their designated representatives
    i.    the Department of the Treasury;
    ii.   the Department of the Interior;
    iii.  the Department of Agriculture;
    iv.   the Department of Commerce;
    v.    the Department of Labor;
    vi.   the Department of Health and Human Services;
    vii.  the Department of Transportation;
    viii. the Department of Energy;
    ix.   the Department of Education;
    x.    the Department of Veterans Affairs;
    xi.   the Department of Homeland Security;
    xii.  the Environmental Protection Agency;
    xiii. the Small Business Administration;
    xiv.  the Army Corps of Engineers;
    xv.   the Office of Management and Budget;
    xvi.  the National Security Staff;
    xvii. the Domestic Policy Council;
    xviii. the National Economic Council;
    xix.  the Council on Environmental Quality;
    xx.   the Office of Science and Technology Policy;
    xxi.  the Council of Economic Advisers;
    xxii. the White House Office of Public Engagement and Intergovernmental Affairs;
    xxiii. the White House Office of Cabinet Affairs; and
    xxiv. such other agencies and offices as the President may designate.

b. The Chair shall regularly convene and preside at meetings of the Task Force and determine its agenda as the Task Force exercises the functions set forth in section 3 of this order. The Chair's duties shall also include:

    i. communicating and engaging with States, tribes, local governments, Members of Congress, other stakeholders and interested parties, and the public on matters pertaining to rebuilding in the affected region;

    ii. coordinating the efforts of executive departments, agencies, and offices related to the functions of the Task Force; and

    iii. specifying the form and subject matter of regular reports to be submitted concurrently to the Domestic Policy Council, the National Security Staff, and the Chair.

**Sec. 3. Functions of the Task Force.** Consistent with the principles of the NDRF, including individual and family empowerment, leadership and local primacy, partnership and inclusiveness, public information, unity of effort, timeliness and flexibility, resilience and sustainability, and psychological and emotional recovery, the Task Force shall:

a. work closely with FEMA in the coordination of rebuilding efforts with the various intergovernmental activities taken in conjunction with the NDRF;

b. (b) describe the potentially relevant authorities and resources of each member of the Task Force;

c. identify and work to remove obstacles to resilient rebuilding in a manner that addresses existing and future risks and vulnerabilities and promotes the long-term sustainability of communities and ecosystems;

d. coordinate with entities in the affected region in efforts to:

    i. ensure the prompt and orderly transition of affected individuals and families into safe and sanitary long-term housing;

    ii. plan for the rebuilding of critical infrastructure damaged by Hurricane Sandy in a manner that accounts for current vulnerabilities to extreme weather events and increases community and regional resilience in responding to future impacts;

    iii. support the strengthening of the economy; and

    iv. understand current vulnerabilities and future risks from extreme weather events, and identify resources and authorities that can contribute to strengthening community and regional resilience as critical infrastructure is rebuilt and ecosystem functions are restored;

e. prior to the termination of the Task Force, present to the President a Hurricane Sandy Rebuilding Strategy (Strategy) as provided in section 5 of this order;

f. engage local stakeholders, communities, the public, Members of Congress, and other officials throughout the areas affected by Hurricane Sandy to ensure that all parties have an opportunity to share their needs and viewpoints to inform the work of the Task Force, including the development of the Strategy; and

g. communicate with affected tribes in a manner consistent with Executive Order 13175 of November 6, 2000, regarding the consultation and coordination with Indian tribal governments.

**Sec. 4. Task Force Advisory Group.** The Chair shall, at his discretion, establish an Advisory Group to advise the Task Force and invite individuals to participate in it. Participants shall be elected State, local, and tribal officials and may include Governors, Mayors, County Executives, tribal elected officials, and other elected officials from the affected region as the Chair deems appropriate. Members of the Advisory Group, acting in their official capacity, may designate employees with authority to act on their behalf. The Advisory Group shall generally advise the Task Force as requested by the Chair, and shall provide input on each element of the Strategy described in section 5 of this order.

**Sec. 5. Hurricane Sandy Rebuilding Strategy.**

a. Within 180 days of the first convening of its members, the Task Force shall prepare a Strategy that includes:
   i. a summary of Task Force activities;
   ii. a long-term rebuilding plan that includes input from State, local, and tribal officials and is supported by Federal agencies, which is informed by an assessment of current vulnerabilities to extreme weather events and seeks to mitigate future risks;
   iii. specific outcomes, goals, and actions by Federal, State, local, and tribal governments and the private sector, such as the establishment of permanent entities, as well as any proposed legislative, regulatory, or other actions that could support the affected region's rebuilding; and
   iv. a plan for monitoring progress.
b. The executive departments, agencies, and offices listed in section 2(a) of this order shall, as appropriate and to the extent permitted by law, align their relevant programs and authorities with the Strategy.

**Sec. 6. Administration.**

a. The Task Force shall have a staff, headed by an Executive Director, which shall provide support for the functions of the Task Force.
b. The Executive Director shall be selected by the Chair and shall supervise, direct, and be accountable for the administration and support of the Task Force.
c. At the request of the Chair, other executive departments and agencies shall serve in an advisory role to the Task Force on issues within their expertise.
d. The Task Force may establish technical working groups of Task Force members, their representatives, and invited Advisory Group members and elected officials, or their designated employees, as necessary to provide advice in support of their function.
e. The Task Force shall terminate 60 days after the completion of the Strategy described in section 5 of this order, after which FEMA and the lead agencies for the Recovery Support Functions, as described in the NDRF, shall continue the Federal rebuilding coordinating roles described in section 3 of this order to the extent consistent with the NDRF.

**Sec. 7. General Provisions.**

a. For purposes of this order, "affected tribe" means any Indian tribe, band, nation, pueblo, village, or community that the Secretary of the Interior acknowledges to exist as an Indian tribe pursuant to the Federally Recognized Indian Tribe List Act of 1994 (25 U.S.C. 479a), located or with interests in the affected area.

b. To the extent permitted by law, and subject to the availability of appropriations, the Department of Housing and Urban Development shall provide the Task Force with such administrative services, facilities, staff, equipment, mobile communications, and other support services as may be necessary for the Task Force to carry out its functions, using funds provided from the Disaster Relief Fund by agreement with FEMA and any other available and appropriate funding.

c. Members of the Task Force, Advisory Group, and any technical working groups shall serve without any additional compensation for their work on the Task Force, Advisory Group, or technical working group.

d. Nothing in this order shall be construed to impair or otherwise affect:
   i. the authority granted by law to an executive department, agency, or the head thereof, or the status of that department or agency within the Federal Government; or
   ii. the functions of the Director of the Office of Management and Budget relating to budgetary, administrative, or legislative proposals.

e. This order shall be implemented consistent with applicable law, and subject to the availability of appropriations.

f. This order is not intended to, and does not, create any right or benefit, substantive or procedural, enforceable at law or in equity by any party against the United States, its departments, agencies, or entities, its officers, employees, or agents, or any other person.

BARACK OBAMA
THE WHITE HOUSE,
December 7, 2012.


# II. Definitions

### *Sustainability*

Sustainability is the creation and maintenance of conditions under which humans and nature can exist in productive harmony and fulfill the social, economic and other requirements of present and future generations. Sustainability involves providing for the long-term viability of the people and economy of the region and its natural ecosystems, which requires consideration of the risks posed by a changing climate, the practicality of maintaining a long-term presence in the most vulnerable areas, and the need to protect and restore the natural ecosystems. The specific definition of sustainability will vary when shifting the scale of a sustainability assessment between individuals, neighborhoods, communities, cities, and regions. Individuals, communities, or regions will need to state what they want to sustain, why they value that, how long they intend to sustain it, and what costs (social, ecological, and economic) they are willing to accept in order to sustain what they value. As individuals and societies evolve, their specific definition of sustainability, based on how they answer these four questions, will evolve as well.

The Task Force also recognizes elements and challenges of implementing sustainability. To maintain resilience in the face of a constantly shifting set of needs and values, sustainability efforts will need to utilize an integrated approach to problem-solving that optimizes the desired social, economic, and environmental effects of an action while minimizing known negative effects, as well as adapting to unknown and unintended effects as they surface.[200]

### Resilience

For individuals and communities, resilience means the ability to anticipate, prepare for, and adapt to changing conditions and withstand, respond to, and recover rapidly from disruptions. Disruptions can include deliberate attacks, accidents, potential threats, and naturally occurring incidents. Discussions of resilience will vary depending on the focus of the effort and stakeholders involved (e.g., individuals, communities, regions), the scale and time frame of planning and rebuilding efforts, and the expected return frequency and severity of the event or stressor.

A resilient recovery to Hurricane Sandy will foster the development of systems that build physical, economic, environmental, and social capacity to reduce vulnerabilities and manage known risks. These increased capacities should be designed to allow future incident responders to maintain acceptable levels of functioning across all systems and quickly adapt system structures to changing risk and vulnerability scenarios. Furthermore, a resilient rebuilding strategy will consider interdependent system elements interacting across multiple scales.[201]

### Risk Assessment and Risk Management

Making informed decisions at community and regional scales to mitigate risks posed by potential hazards is a core element of the Task Force strategy. Risk assessment is a process for determining what hazards exist, characterizing the effect a hazard might have on valued elements in a community or region, and calculating the risk of a hazard occurring and affecting a valued element. Hazard identification characterizes the timing of occurrence (and re-occurrence), what effects may occur from the hazard, and the magnitude of a hazard. Vulnerability assessment describes effects to a specific receptor when exposed to a hazard, the social or ecological value of the receptor, and how resilient the receptor and its supporting systems are to effects from the hazard. Exposure assessment collects information about the human and ecological systems that the identified hazards could affect.

Risk management is a response strategy, advancing a set of actions that emphasize risk reduction across a range of possible futures (hazard mitigation strategies) and revising response strategies periodically in light of new knowledge. Risk management strategies must be resilient enough to promote long-term investments, yet sufficiently flexible so as to sustain social and economic progress by taking advantage of improvements in risk knowledge, tools, and technologies.[202] Incorporating risk assessment and risk management into broader rebuilding and response planning efforts provides an objective and logical framework for assessing risks and vulnerabilities as new information is collected and made available to decision makers. Risk-informed decisions must consider a whole-systems perspective. Risk managers should understand how multiple human and ecological systems may interact during extreme events and consider the potential for concurrent extreme events as well as the spatial and temporal nature of these hazards.[203]

### Hazard Mitigation

Hazard mitigation refers to efforts using non-structural measures to reduce loss of life, property, and resources by lessening the impact of disasters. Hazard mitigation measures broadly aim to avoid, reduce, rectify, or eliminate impacts and risks to affected communities. Hazard mitigation measures include but are not limited to investments in measures such as zoning, rehabilitation of coastal ecosystems that buffer floods, relocating homes and businesses away from the most vulnerable areas, non-structural efforts to improve the resilience of public infrastructure and key resource lifelines as well as reduce the risk of specific vulnerabilities from natural hazards, and management and social programs to reduce future risks.

It is important that approaches to hazard mitigation and risk reduction are not only physical interventions (i.e., the development and enhancement of community-based social networks) but are also invaluable components to community resilience. Members of the whole community—including individuals with disabilities, others with access and functional needs and limited English proficiency, as well as racially and ethnically diverse communities—benefit from hazard mitigation actions as the entire community can expect fewer disruptive disaster impacts and a decreased need for supplemental resource support.[204]

### Vulnerable Populations

The Task Force understands that the affected areas include a diversity of businesses, neighborhoods, residents, and workers that may have been disproportionately vulnerable to the impacts of Hurricane Sandy due to their location, limited financial or other resources, less access to emergency services and support, or other disadvantages. Accordingly, the Task Force's Rebuilding Strategy seeks to address the needs of such "vulnerable populations," which is meant to include: low-income communities, overburdened populations,[205] children and youth, elderly individuals, certain communities of color, households and people with limited English proficiency, immigrants, individuals with chronic medical conditions, people who are homeless or at risk of homelessness, and individuals with disabilities.

## III. Acronyms and Abbreviations

| ABFE | Advisory Base Flood Elevation |
|------|-------------------------------|
| ACF | Administration for Children and Families (HHS) |
| ACHP | Advisory Council on Historic Preservation |
| ACL | Administration for Community Living (HHS) |
| AFL-CIO | American Federation of Labor and Congress of Industrial Organizations |
| ARRA | American Recovery and Reinvestment Act of 2009 |
| BW-12 | Biggert-Waters Flood Insurance Reform Act of 2012 |
| CDBG-DR | Community Development Block Grant – Disaster Recovery |
| CDC | Centers for Disease Control and Prevention (HHS) |

| CDFI | Community Development Financial Institution |
|---|---|
| CEQ | White House Council on Environmental Quality |
| CHP | Combined Heat and Power |
| CMS | Centers for Medicare and Medicaid Services (HHS) |
| CNCS | Corporation for National and Community Service |
| CPCB RSF | Community Planning and Capacity Building Recovery Support Function |
| DHS | U.S. Department of Homeland Security |
| DOC | U.S. Department of Commerce |
| DOD | U.S. Department of Defense |
| DOE | U.S. Department of Energy |
| DOI | U.S. Department of the Interior |
| DOJ | U.S. Department of Justice |
| DOL | U.S. Department of Labor |
| DOT | U.S. Department of Transportation |
| ED | U.S. Department of Education |
| EDA | Economic Development Administration (DOC) |
| EJ | Environmental Justice |
| EOP | Executive Office of the President |
| EPA | U.S. Environmental Protection Agency |
| ETA | Employment and Training Administration (DOL) |
| FAA | Federal Aviation Administration (DOT) |
| Fannie Mae | Federal National Mortgage Association |
| FCC | Federal Communications Commission |
| FDRC | Federal Disaster Recovery Coordinator |
| FEMA | Federal Emergency Management Agency (DHS) |
| FHA | Federal Housing Administration (HUD) |
| FHFA | Federal Housing Finance Agency |
| FHWA | Federal Highway Administration (DOT) |
| FIO | Federal Insurance Office (Treasury) |
| FIRM | Flood Insurance Rate Map |
| FRA | Federal Railroad Administration (DOT) |
| Freddie Mac | Federal Home Loan Mortgage Corporation |
| FTA | Federal Transit Administration (DOT) |
| FY | Fiscal Year |
| GAO | Government Accountability Office |
| GDP | Gross Domestic Product |
| GIS | Geographical Information System |
| GSA | General Services Administration |
| GSE | Government Sponsored Enterprise |
| GSP | Gross State Product |
| HHS | U.S. Department of Health and Human Services |
| HMGP | Hazard Mitigation Grant Program |
| HRSA | Health Resources and Services Administration (HHS) |

**(Continued)**

| | |
|---|---|
| HUBZone | Historically Underutilized Business Zone |
| HUD | U.S. Department of Housing and Urban Development |
| IBC | International Building Code |
| IBHS | Insurance Institute for Business and Home Safety |
| ICC | International Code Council |
| ICP | Internal Control Plan |
| IG | Inspector General |
| IPCC | Intergovernmental Panel on Climate Change |
| IRC | International Residential Code |
| IRS | Internal Revenue Service (Treasury) |
| ISO | Independent Service Operator |
| ITAC | Industrial and Technical Assistance Corporation |
| JFO | Joint Field Office |
| LDRM | Local Disaster Recovery Manager |
| LEED | U.S. Green Building Council's Leadership in Energy and Environmental Design |
| LMI | Low and Moderate Income |
| LSC | Legal Services Corporation |
| LWD | New Jersey Department of Labor and Workforce Development |
| MitFLG | Mitigation Framework Leadership Group |
| NAS | National Academy of Sciences |
| NASA | National Aeronautics and Space Administration |
| NDRF | National Disaster Recovery Framework |
| NFIP | National Flood Insurance Program |
| NGO | Non-Governmental Organization |
| NIEHS | National Institute of Environmental Health (HHS) |
| NIH | National Institutes of Health (HHS) |
| NIST | National Institute of Standards and Technology (DOC) |
| NOAA | National Oceanic and Atmospheric Administration (DOC) |
| NPCC | New York City Panel on Climate Change |
| NSS | White House National Security Staff |
| NPS | National Park Service (DOI) |
| NTIA | National Telecommunications Information Administration (DOC) |
| NYCHA | New York City Housing Authority |
| NYRCR | New York Rising Community Reconstruction Program |
| OFN | Opportunity Finance Network |
| OHHLHC | Office of Healthy Homes and Lead Hazard Control (HUD) |
| OIPI | Office of International and Philanthropic Innovation (HUD) |
| OMB | White House Office of Management and Budget |
| OSHA | Occupational Safety and Health Administration (DOL) |
| OSTP | White House Office of Science and Technology Policy |

| PHA | Public Housing Authority |
|---|---|
| PII | Personally Identifiable Information |
| PLA | Project Labor Agreement |
| PMO | Program Management Office (Task Force) |
| PPD-21 | Presidential Policy Directive 21: Critical Infrastructure Security and Resilience |
| PPD-8 | Presidential Policy Directive 8: National Preparedness |
| RATB | Recovery Accountability and Transparency Board |
| Risk MAP | Risk Mapping, Assessment, and Planning |
| RSF | Recovery Support Function |
| RSFLG | Recovery Support Framework Leadership Group |
| Sandy | Disaster Relief Appropriations Act, 2013 |
| SBDC | Small Business Development Center |
| SFHA | Special Flood Hazard Areas |
| SHPO | State Historic Preservation Officer |
| SI | Smithsonian Institution |
| SORN | System of Records Notices |
| SRF | State Revolving Fund |
| SRIA | Sandy Recovery Improvement Act |
| SSA | Social Security Administration |
| SSBCI | State Small Business Credit Initiative |
| STEP | Sheltering and Temporary Essential Power Program (FEMA) |
| Task Force | Hurricane Sandy Rebuilding Task Force |
| TIFIA | Infrastructure Finance Innovation Act (FHWA/DOT) |
| TIGER | Transportation Investment Generating Economic Recovery (DOT) |
| Treasury | U.S. Department of the Treasury |
| USACE | U.S. Army Corps of Engineers (DOD) |
| USDA | U.S. Department of Agriculture |
| USGCRP | U.S. Global Change Research Program |
| USGS | U.S. Geological Survey (DOI) |
| VA | U.S. Department of Veterans Affairs |
| WBC | Women's Business Center |
| WETP | Worker Education and Training Program (NIH/HHS) |

## IV. Agency Accomplishments

### Corporation for National and Community Service

The Corporation for National and Community Service (CNCS), through its AmeriCorps programs, has deployed more than 3,600 national service participants in the six states that Hurricane Sandy affected. Additionally, CNCS has established and is implementing a long-term recovery strategy in New Jersey and New York. AmeriCorps members have mucked and gutted more than 3,700 homes, including 1,443 in New Jersey and 1,958 in New York. National service members have leveraged the help of 30,000 volunteers, collaborated with the

American Red Cross in operating 45 shelters, and coordinated with more than 200 non-profits and community-based organizations. The AmeriCorps National Civilian Community Corps program will deploy up to 20 members every six weeks to both New York and New Jersey to continue to assist communities as they rebuild impacted communities.

### *Department of Agriculture*

As of July 1, 2013, USDA obligated $2.8 million to 20 projects for emergency food assistance, infrastructure, and economic programs that will help rehabilitate farmland, watersheds, and flood plains, as well as provide erosion control and infrastructure at National historic sites, forests, and non-industrial private forest lands. USDA has steadily utilized state programs and leveraged funding for housing, utility, and business recovery, and USDA is providing economic, technical, and scientific investments in data and studies to support recovery in the region. USDA's efforts immediately following the storm included providing emergency food assistance for low income households, coordinating with state and local governments to identify available USDA programs, and processing applications for emergency loans, the Emergency Conservation Program, the Emergency Forest Restoration Program, and municipal debris removal. Other efforts have included working with states and municipalities on planning and restoration for flood plain easements, soil and water conservation, fisheries and hatcheries, and National Forests. USDA is currently accelerating its efforts to review and approve projects as quickly as possible, while ensuring that each project is a sound investment in the restoration and rehabilitation of impacted areas.

### *Department of Commerce*

### Economic Development Administration

EDA has aided Sandy recovery primarily through enhancing information sharing capabilities and providing targeted technical assistance. A key facet of implementing the NDRF is to establish a common framework for sharing information about agency programs, community impacts, and troubleshooting gaps in recovery assistance. Advancements in this area included the convening of "Economic Recovery Practitioner All Hands" conference calls, establishing recovery topic-focused working groups with key stakeholders from Federal, State, academic, and private sector organizations, and facilitating regular Federal and State partner coordination meetings to share recovery information and collaborate on common recovery objectives. Through enhanced communication, these advancements provided opportunities to share recovery and resilience best practices. In the area of targeted technical assistance, EDA implemented peer-to-peer forums to assist the New Jersey tourism industry, held "Access to Capital Meetings" to inform business resources of traditional and non-traditional financing mechanisms, and provided risk management resource information to small businesses in the impacted region.

### National Oceanic and Atmospheric Administration

In the immediate aftermath of Hurricane Sandy, NOAA vessels began surveying obstructions of waterways that lead to critical petroleum facilities within the Port of New York and New Jersey, which helped to restore the flow of emergency fuel supplies by the following morning. Furthermore, NOAA embedded five senior staff members in FEMA's New York and New Jersey JFOs for rotating details from December 2012 through June 2013 and developed a set of joint principles on Infrastructure Rebuilding Systems alongside USACE. NOAA is actively informing recovery and resilience efforts by working with impacted communities to provide technical assistance, strengthen long-term coastal observations and monitoring, and advance charting and mapping. As highlighted in the President's Climate Action Plan, NOAA, USACE, and FEMA released a new sea level rise planning tool that includes interactive maps and a sea level rise calculator to improve community understanding of future flood risks and planning. Additionally, NOAA is working to advance integration of natural and built systems in disaster response, recovery, and mitigation through fostering partnerships and contributing technical expertise to efforts, such as the USACE's Comprehensive Study.

### Department of Education

Following Hurricane Sandy, the U.S. Department of Education (ED) provided Project School Emergency Response to Violence (SERV) awards for New York, New Jersey, and Connecticut totaling $3 million. Project SERV provides for restoration of the learning environment after a disrupting event and– although the program began as a response to violent incidents—, has been expanded to include major events that disrupt the learning environment. Examples of allowable funds usage include financing mental health services, overtime for teachers and counselors, security, and substitute staff.

### Department of Energy

DOE has been providing technical assistance to the affected States to help them develop pilot projects, financial mechanisms, and policy and market development tools and promote cost-effective investments in resilient energy generation and storage using Sandy recovery funds. DOE is collaborating with the Task Force, DOE National Laboratories, and State and local governments to advance emerging programs that address key energy resilience initiatives using public-private partnerships launched by the States later this year. These projects include: developing a Hoboken Microgrid Plot, enhancing New York and New Jersey fuel coordination, holding a regional roundtable to monetize microgrid investments in New York, New Jersey, and Connecticut, and providing direct assistance to states on leveraging Sandy Supplemental funding to finance emerging energy opportunities.

### Department of Health and Human Services

As the Coordinating Agency for the Health and Social Services Recovery Support Function (HSS RSF) under the NDRF, HHS deployed Field Coordinators to New York and New Jersey in the days following Hurricane Sandy to guide RSF efforts, and deployed subject matter experts from the Administration for Children and Families (ACF) and the National Institutes of Health (NIH) to conduct program and impact assessments as well as to provide technical assistance. HHS convened and supported multi-sector and interagency Task Forces on the needs of children, youth, and families, on environmental health, and on other issues related to Sandy recovery. ACF also led the Immediate Federal Disaster Case Management Program in New Jersey. At the time of the transition to the State Grant Program, ACF had provided disaster case management services to support 4,186 New Jersey Sandy survivor households. ACF is also awarding Sandy Supplemental funding for new construction or significant rebuilding of Head Start centers in New York and New Jersey that suffered catastrophic damage, $475 million through the Social Services Block Grant, and approximately $2 million to support family violence prevention and services in affected communities. The Substance Abuse and Mental Health Services Administration is using Sandy Supplemental funding to support behavioral health treatment to impacted populations upon referral by FEMA crisis counselors, restore the capability of medication assisted substance abuse treatment services in the impacted areas, ensure the disaster distress helpline connects individuals to services and supports the crisis center network in the affected regions, and provide resilience training to educators on caring for their pupils in disaster areas. The Administration for Community Living (ACL) awarded the Connecticut and New Jersey State Units on Aging funding to reimburse the States for home delivered meals to homebound seniors after Sandy struck. ACL staff also worked with specific Area Agencies on Aging to coordinate relocation and recovery efforts by FEMA and displaced seniors. NIH has announced several funding opportunities, funded by the Sandy supplemental, to recover losses resulting from Sandy to NIH-supported research, including to help restore their research and facilities. NIH's National Institute of Environmental Health Sciences (NIEHS) carried out a process to update Federal and State guidance on mold remediation for protection of volunteers, homeowners, and cleanup workers during March 2013. Also, NIEHS's Worker Education and Training Program (WETP) released a supplemental funding request to provide safety and health training to support recovery, rebuilding, and resilience in preparing for current and potential future disasters within Sandy-affected areas. As of June 2013, WETP had trained over 929 workers in New York and New Jersey. Hurricane health and safety booklets ordered included 35,945 copies in English, 15,781 copies in Spanish, and 290 copies in Vietnamese. The Health Resources and Services Administration (HRSA) prepared, in collaboration with federal partners, the FEMA Guidance For HRSA Community-Based Service Delivery Grantees and the HRSA Disaster Response and Recovery-Flexibilities and Capabilities guidance, which serve as tools that support HRSA's operations, strategic information, and coordination. Additionally, CDC and the Office of the Assistant Secretary for Preparedness and Response are funding research activities in several areas.

### Department of Homeland Security: FEMA

FEMA has provided funding to the impacted region through the traditional Stafford Act programs of Individual Assistance, Public Assistance, and HMGP. As prescribed in the NDRF, FDRCs were appointed, and the six RSFs were activated and deployed. The Sandy Recovery Improvement Act of 2013 (SRIA) authorized several significant changes to the way FEMA may deliver disaster assistance under a variety of programs. Forms of aid provided by FEMA include: Individuals and Households Program distributions to 180,000 survivors, totaling $1.4 billion; Transitional Shelter Assistance Program assistance for 6,000 survivors in New York and 5,500 in New Jersey; direct housing refurbishing for 115 housing units in Fort Monmouth, NJ; and $2.4 billion obligated in Public Assistance funds. The Hurricane Sandy disaster response comprised a full implementation of the six RSFs, which were deployed in regional JFOs. A federal Recovery Support Strategy was also developed for each state to outline the interagency federal approach to support the recovery efforts.

### Department of Housing and Urban Development

In the aftermath of Hurricane Sandy, HUD worked closely with impacted states and other Federal agencies to provide for the needs of affected individuals and communities. Working alongside FEMA, New York City, New York State, and New Jersey, HUD aimed to ensure housing for displaced residents over the short-, medium-, and long-term. HUD also worked in conjunction with FHA and FHFA to protect homeowners from potential foreclosures caused by the storm. Due to swift action after the passage of the appropriations bill, HUD was able to begin allocating $5.4 billion in CDBG-DR funding within eight days of the storm, which communities are using to help rebuild houses, businesses, and critical infrastructure. HUD, together with the Task Force, has identified innovative ways to encourage and incentivize resilient rebuilding in the Sandy-affected region to ensure communities will be better able to withstand future storms. HUD has instituted a uniform flood risk reduction standard that applies to all reconstruction projects that the Sandy Supplemental funds, thereby ensuring a basic level of protection for those projects that take into account the future risks of climate change.

### *Department of the Interior*

DOI owns and manages land along the coast that is important to coastal resilience and tourism. DOI aids recovery through the delivery of actionable scientific information, providing storm surge data that identified the extent and elevation above land surface of the storm surge, served storm-related geospatial information on a daily basis, and documented storm impacts to coastal barriers, all of which informed response and recovery as well as provided a new baseline to assess vulnerability of the reconfigured coast. Actions taken by DOI on those parks and refuges can assist in both coastal resilience and economic restoration, as well as enable sites to be the subject of long-term research and monitoring of effectiveness. Since Hurricane Sandy, DOI has allocated $445 million to 234 projects that will help repair facilities, reopen roads, and restore services in national parks, wildlife refuges, beaches, and public lands so that they may be reopened to the public. This funding will also provide for investments in scientific data and studies to support recovery, as well as assessments of risk and resilience, in the region. As part of this initiative, DOI repaired damage to heat, utilities, walkways, and docks in order to reopen the Statue of Liberty National Monument in time for the Fourth of July and restored Fire Island National Seashore and Gateway National Recreation Area in time for peak tourist weekends and holidays. DOI has also worked with USACE to restore Jamaica Bay Salt Marsh Islands at Gateway National Recreation Area. Looking forward, an additional $342 million will be allocated to support projects for coastal restoration and resilience at DOI assets, including national parks, refuges, and tribal lands across the region.

### *Department of Labor*

DOL's worker protections agencies have worked closely with Federal, State, and local partners to ensure the safety and health of workers who were involved in Sandy response efforts, as well as in current and future recovery projects. ETA provided $70.3 million in National Emergency Grants (NEGs) to New York, New Jersey, Connecticut, West Virginia, and Rhode Island for continuing cleanup and recovery efforts. This included $20.5 million provided by the Disaster Relief Recovery Act of 2013 and $49.8 million provided by ETA's WIA Dislocated Worker National Reserve, which funds NEGs. DOL's Occupational Safety and Health Administration (OSHA) deployed Safety & Health professionals throughout the impacted areas immediately after Sandy's landfall to protect workers engaged in storm response and recovery work, conducting over 4,900 outreach briefings and intervention activities and reaching over 63,000 workers, which resulted in the removal of 7,900 workers from workplace hazards. OSHA also engaged with State and local communities in the impacted region by providing Susan Harwood grants to community organizations in New York and New Jersey for recovery-specific training and education, holding two Sandy-specific wage conferences for hundreds of stakeholders involved in rebuilding projects, and implementing a compliance assistance plan for contractors and subcontractors that were awarded storm recovery contracts by FEMA, SBA, HUD, EPA, or USACE. Furthermore, DOL's Wage and Hour Division (WHD) has engaged in outreach for the Hurricane Sandy initiative on a continuing basis, such as on May 14 when WHD staff provided Davis-Bacon Act compliance assistance training to the agency representatives of the Sandy PMO. In addition, to ensure labor standards protections for workers engaged in cleanup and rebuilding activities under the Hurricane Sandy initiative, WHD has, to- date, initiated 139 investigations of contractors and employers for compliance with the requirements of the Fair Labor Standards Act, Service Contract Act, and/or Davis-Bacon Act.

### *Department of the Treasury*

While Treasury did not receive Sandy Supplemental funding, a variety of accomplishments were achieved through standard emergency operations. Treasury provided effective governmental assistance to the Financial Service sector through Federal interagency coordination, which Treasury chaired and was established to resolve issues, ensure adequate communication among affected parties, and identify heightened requirements for resilience. Treasury's CDFI Fund contacted all certified CDFIs in the affected region to survey need and assess impact. Treasury and IRS also lifted income eligibility restrictions for Low Income Housing Tax Credit-financed projects, so displaced residents could rent units in these buildings. Additionally, IRS announced that 401(k)s and similar employer-sponsored retirement plans could make loans and hardship distributions to victims of Hurricane Sandy and members of their families prior to February 1, 2013. In June 2013, Treasury used the conference of SSBCI state program managers to promote flexible capital provisions for small businesses still recovering from Hurricane Sandy.

### *Department of Transportation*

Letters to proceed on recovery work currently total $6.8 billion, more than 50% of the $12.4 billion authorized to repair and protect the nation's largest transportation system. These funds have been used to repair and rebuild transit assets and facilities, reopen roads and bridges, and restore services at impacted airports. As part of these efforts, the Secretary of Transportation directed $185 million in Hurricane Sandy Relief funding be dedicated to the Hudson Yards Right-of-Way Preservation project. This "game changing" project will help pave the way for two desperately-needed, flood-resistant tunnels under the Hudson River, running between New York and New Jersey. Additionally, DOT played an instrumental role positioning assets leading up to the storm's impact and for recovering immediately after. FTA, for example, worked expediently to develop a new emergency relief program to facilitate recovery grants. Working with other agencies and the White House, DOT administered a host of waivers, special permits, and other regulatory flexibilities to expedite operations in the aftermath of the storm. By working around the clock to repair damage, FAA restored normal air traffic operations quickly, and the Maritime Administration was able to dispatch vessels for emergency relief. In addition to dispatching staff to the region to begin damage assessments, FTA worked closely with FEMA and GSA to procure 250 buses to replace lost commuter rail and transit service in New Jersey, which allowed commuters to take buses to ferry terminals for the trip into Manhattan.

### Department of Veterans Affairs

The VA Manhattan Medical Center was severely damaged during Hurricane Sandy, as were multiple VA cemeteries. VA was authorized $234 million from Hurricane Sandy supplemental, $232 million of which has been allocated to repair, reoutfit, and resupply the Manhattan facility. The National Cemetery Administration has completed all of the work at the affected cemeteries, and VA expects to fully obligate the funds for the repair of the Manhattan Medical Center in FY 2016. As of June 30, 2013, VA had obligated $15.9 million in supplemental funds.

### Environmental Protection Agency

Hurricane Sandy's flooding and wind damage impacted more than 200 waste water treatment plants and over 80 drinking water plants, resulting in the release of potentially millions of gallons of raw sewage and impacting the clean drinking water of dozens of communities. EPA deployed over 200 people to help with the initial response and is now working to manage the funds appropriated to the Agency, with the long-term goals of strengthening sewage and drinking water systems to better withstand disasters and supporting other agencies' effort to better protect human health and the environment. Following Hurricane Sandy, EPA assessed 40 drinking water facilities and 23 wastewater treatment plants in New Jersey as well as 40 drinking water and 23 wastewater plants in New York. Since that time, EPA has been appropriated funds for water treatment, monitoring, and storage and has worked both to manage its programs and provide expertise to states and other agencies.

### Small Business Administration

SBA has played an integral role in the response and recovery efforts in the Sandy-affected region and is committed to providing small businesses with the access to capital, resources, and opportunities to rebuild their businesses. As of July 2013, SBA approved $2.4 billion in loans to 36,137 businesses and homeowners needing assistance to repair, rebuild, and restart the local economy. As of July 3013, SBA has provided 32,194 home loans for $1.9 billion and 3,943 business loans for $448.3 million. Additionally, SBA has deployed disaster response teams to the area, worked closely with its resource partners to provide technical assistance and counseling to small businesses, and ensured small businesses get increased opportunities to Federal and local contracting opportunities. SBA has awarded $19 million, received earlier this year through ad-hoc authority, to provide targeted small business management and technical assistance. The first award was made to individual resource partners in the amount of $5,811,000, and the second was made to resource partner collaborative proposals in the amount of $13,189,000. Between April 9, 2013 and June 30, 2013, 4,297 clients were served using these funds. As of July 2013, 27.1 percent of Sandy-related prime contract dollars obligated in the Federal Procurement Database System went to small businesses, exhibiting a strong Federal commitment to small business contracting. Within these Sandy related prime contracts, almost half went to local businesses.

*United States Army Corps of Engineers*

USACE partnered with NOAA to develop Infrastructure Systems Rebuilding principles to promote a unified strategy for each agency's approach to activities associated with rebuilding and restoration efforts in the wake of Hurricane Sandy. Working under mission assignments from FEMA at the New York and New Jersey Disaster Recovery JFOs, USACE coordinated development of Mission Scoping Assessments and Recovery Support Strategies for Infrastructure Systems pursuant to the NDRF. As of August 2013, roughly 3.6 million cubic yards of sand has been placed on beaches in support of repairs to projects damaged by Hurricane Sandy. Of the 33 coastal storm damage reduction projects in the process of being repaired due to Hurricane Sandy, 18 contracts have been awarded, 11 contractors have received notices to proceed, and 4 projects have been restored to their authorized design profile. Of the 135 navigation projects affected by Hurricane Sandy in the Corps North Atlantic Division, Lakes and Rivers Division, and South Atlantic Division, 24 contracts have been awarded, 23 contractors have received notices to proceed, and 9 activities have been completed. An evaluation of the performance of storm damage reduction projects in areas affected by Hurricane Sandy is forthcoming. USACE, in collaboration with other agencies (as described on page 43) also contributed to the development and fielding of the Sea Level Rise Tool for Sandy Recovery. USACE is working on the Comprehensive Study, which will inform the effort to promote more resilient communities that are sustainable and support the coastal ecosystem. This study will also identify activities warranting further analysis and institutional barriers to implementation.


# V. Addressing Future Risks

"But for the sake of our children and our future, we must do more to combat climate change. Now, it's true that no single event makes a trend. But the fact is the 12 hottest years on record have all come in the last 15. Heat waves, droughts, wildfires, floods -- all are now more frequent and more intense. We can choose to believe that Superstorm Sandy, and the most severe drought in decades, and the worst wildfires some states have ever seen were all just a freak coincidence. Or we can choose to believe in the overwhelming judgment of science -- and act before it's too late."[206] President Barack Obama

It is clear that we are vulnerable to a wide spectrum of natural disasters that will continue to strike the United States. This is why the mission of the Task Force is vital to ensuring that we learn how to rebuild smarter so we are better prepared for the next storm nature throws our way.

*Extreme Rainfall*

Extreme rainfall events have increased in intensity and number in many regions of the U.S., especially over the last three decades. The largest increases have been in the Midwest and Northeast regions,[207] and, in parts of the Northeast, there has also been an increase in flooding events.[208] This may be associated with the increase in both mean and extreme precipitation, although other factors (e.g., antecedent soil moisture) also have important influences on flooding. Warmer air can contain more water vapor than cooler air. Global analyses show the amount of water vapor in the atmosphere has, in fact, increased over both land and oceans. Climate change also alters dynamical characteristics of the atmosphere that, in turn, affect weather patterns and storms. In the mid-latitudes, where most of the continental U.S. is located, there is an upward trend in extreme precipitation in the vicinity of fronts associated with mid-latitude storms.

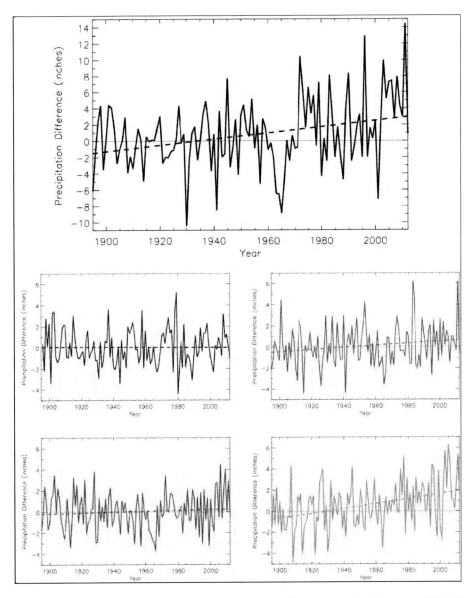

Figure 1. Precipitation anomaly (deviations from the 1901-1960 average, inches) for annual (black), winter (blue), spring (green), summer (red), and fall (orange) for the northeastern U.S during 1901-2012. Dashed lines indicate the best fit by minimizing the chi-square error statistic. Based on a new gridded version of COOP data from the National Climatic Data Center, the CDDv2 data set (R. Vose, personal communication, July 27, 2012). Note that the annual time series is on a unique scale. Trends are upward and statistically significant annually and for the fall season. From Kunkel et al. (2013).

Figure 1 shows an annual and seasonal time series of precipitation anomalies for the period of 1895-2011. Annual precipitation has varied over time, showing a clear shift towards greater variability and higher totals since 1970. The wettest year since 1895 was 2011, while the 2nd driest year occurred in 1996. The 1960s were characterized by a very severe, long-term drought that was particularly intense in the New England region, where it spanned almost the entire decade. The Northeast's three driest years were 1930, 1941, and 1965. Summer precipitation does not exhibit an overall trend but, over the past 10 years, there have been a few very wet summers, including 2006 (wettest on record) and 2009 (second wettest on record). Precipitation trends are not statistically significant for winter, spring, or summer; the upward annual and fall trends (as seen in Figure 1) are statistically significant, with magnitudes of +0.39 and +0.24 inches/decade, respectively.[209]

Figure 2 shows a time series of an index for the number of extreme daily precipitation events for the northeastern U.S. An extreme event is defined here as one with a 2-day precipitation total exceeding the threshold for a 5-yr recurrence interval. There is substantial decadal-scale variability in the number of extreme precipitation events since the 1930s. The most dominant feature is the high values in the 1990s and 2000s. The highest index value occurred in 1996. The index was quite low in the 1960s, coinciding well with the drought that affected the Northeast during that period.

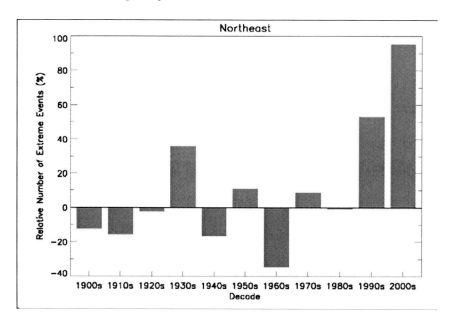

Figure 2. Decadal time series of extreme precipitation index for the occurrence of 2-day, 1 in 5-year extreme precipitation, for the Northeastern region, during 1901-2012. Based on daily COOP data from long-term stations in the National Climatic Data Center's Global Historical Climate Network data set. Values are expressed as anomalies with respect to a reference period of 1901-1960. Only stations with less than 10% missing daily precipitation data for the period 1895-2011 are used in this analysis. Events are first identified for each individual station by ranking all 2-day precipitation values and choosing the top N/5 events, where N is the number of years of data for that particular station. Then, event numbers for each year are averaged for all stations in each 1x1° grid box. Finally, a regional average is determined by averaging the values for the individual grid boxes. This regional average is the extreme precipitation index. The bar for the 2000s includes the 12-yr period of 2001-2012.

The recent elevated level in extreme precipitation also manifests itself in estimates of shorter rainfall recurrence intervals. These values are used extensively in engineering design and governmental regulations (e.g., building codes). Commonly these rainfall extremes are known as the 50- or 100-year storm and represent the amount of rainfall that can be expected to occur on average once in 50 or 100 years, respectively. In terms of these design specifications, an increase in extreme rainfall lowers the expected recurrence interval of a specific precipitation amount. DeGaetano (2009) shows that what would be expected to be a 100-year event based on 1950-1979 data occurs with an average return interval of 60 years when data from the 1978-2007 period are considered.[210] Similarly, the amount of rain that constituted a 50-year event during 1950-1979 is expected to occur on average once every 30 years based on the more recent data.

The latest projections of future climate over the U.S. suggest that mean annual precipitation will increase in the Northeast. This is part of a large continental pattern of precipitation increase in northern latitudes. The contiguous U.S. straddles the transition zone between drier conditions in the sub-tropics (south) and wetter conditions at higher latitudes (north). Because the precise location of this transition zone varies somewhat among models, projected changes in precipitation in central areas of the U.S. range from small increases to small decreases. However, the Northeast is within the belt of northern latitude increases, these increases being concentrated seasonally in winter and spring. In addition, model projections indicate that the recent trend towards a greater percentage of precipitation falling in heavy rain events will continue. Heavy-precipitation events that are presently rare will become more common in the future.

There is a high degree of certainty that the heaviest precipitation events will increase everywhere, and by large amounts. This consistent model projection is well understood and is a direct outcome of the increase in atmospheric moisture caused by warming. There is also more certainty regarding dry spells, as the annual maximum number of consecutive dry days increases in future model projections. Thus, both extreme wetness and extreme dryness increase.

### Hurricanes

There has been a substantial increase in virtually every measure of hurricane activity in the Atlantic since the 1980s (Figure 3) relative to the 1970s and 1980s. However, values were also high in the 1960s.[211]

The increases illustrated in Figure 3 are linked, in part, to higher sea surface temperatures in the region which Atlantic hurricanes form in and move through. Numerous factors influence these local sea surface temperatures, including human-induced emissions of heat-trapping gases and particulate pollution and natural variability. However, hurricanes respond to more than just sea surface temperature. How hurricanes respond also depends on how the local atmosphere responds to changes in local sea surface temperatures, and this atmospheric response depends critically on the cause of the change. For example, the atmosphere responds differently when local sea surface temperatures increase due to a local decrease of particulate pollution that allows more sunlight through to warm the ocean, versus when sea surface temperatures increase more uniformly around the world due to increased amounts of heat-trapping gases. Thus, the link between hurricanes and ocean temperatures is complex and this is an active area of research. The high values in the 1960s indicate that natural decadal-scale variability is quite high and is likely a component of the recent changes.

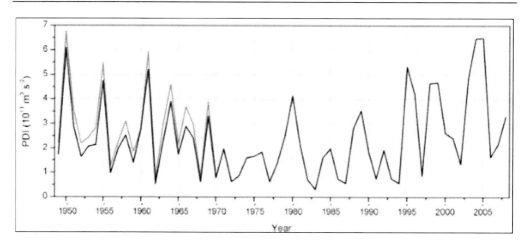

Figure 3. Recent variations of the Power Dissipation Index (PDI), a measure of overall hurricane intensity in a hurricane season, in the north Atlantic (from Villarini and Vecchi, 2012).

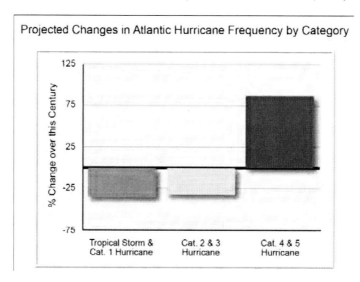

Figure 4. Model projections of percentage changes in Atlantic hurricane and tropical storm frequencies for different storm categories, by the late this century. Projected changes are for the period 2081-2100 compared with the period 2001-2020. (Figure source: NOAA Geophysical Fluid Dynamics Laboratory).

Climate models that incorporate the best understanding of all these factors project further increases in the frequency and intensity of the strongest Atlantic hurricanes (Figure 4), as well as increased rainfall rates in response to continued warming of the tropical oceans by heat-trapping gases. Although the current generation of climate models tends to underestimate the frequency of the strongest hurricanes for the current climate, the distribution of hurricane intensities in the latest models is believed to be realistic enough to use the relative changes in the projections.[212]

### Winter Storms

Over the U.S., historical changes in winter storm frequency and intensity are small and not significant with the exception that there is limited evidence of an overall increase in winter storm activity near the northeast and northwest U.S. coastlines during the second half of the 1950-2010 period. However, for the Northern Hemisphere as a whole, there is evidence of an increase in both winter storm frequency and intensity during the cold season since 1950, with storm tracks having shifted slightly towards the poles.

The characteristics that constitute a severe winter storm vary regionally. Snowfall greater than 10 inches is common in many parts of the Northeast, and thus often only a short-term inconvenience. However, the same snowfall across the Southeast might cripple the region for a week or longer. A Regional Snowfall Index[213] has been formulated that takes into account the typical frequency and magnitude of snowstorms in each region of the eastern two-thirds of the U.S., providing perspectives on decadal changes in extreme snowstorms since 1900. An analysis based on the area receiving snowfall of various amounts shows there were more than twice the number of extreme regional snowstorms from 1961-2010 (21) as there were in the previous 60 years (9) (Figure 5). The greater number of extreme storms in recent decades is consistent with other findings of recent increases in heavier and more widespread snowstorms.[214]

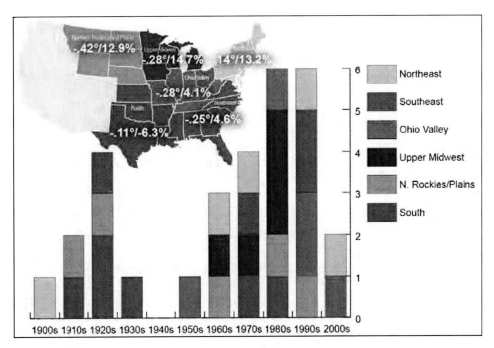

Figure 5. Number of extreme snowstorms (upper 10 percentile) occurring each decade within the six U.S. climate regions in the eastern two-thirds of the contiguous U.S. (Based on an analysis of the 50 strongest storms for each of the six climate regions from October 1900-April 2010). The inset map shows the boundaries of each climate region. These regions were selected for consistency with NOAA's monthly to annual operational climate monitoring activities. The map includes standardized temperature anomalies and precipitation departures from the 20th century mean calculated across all snow seasons in which each storm occurred. The snow season is defined as December-March for the South and Southeast regions and November-April for the other four regions.[215]

These extreme storms occurred more frequently in snow seasons that were colder and wetter than average (Figure 5), but not exclusively. Approximately 35% of the snow seasons in which these events occurred were warmer than average and 30% drier than average. The implications are that even if temperatures continue to warm as they have over the past several decades, for the next few decades, at least, such record storms are possible as they have been observed during otherwise warmer- and drier-than-average seasons. However, future changes in winter storm frequency and intensity are uncertain.

## *Sea Level Rise*

### Introduction
Coastal planning, management, and risk assessment require analysis of future conditions, particularly future sea levels, for the purpose of identifying and evaluating decision options that are resilient to environmental change. The impacts of Hurricane Sandy are evidence that coastal plans currently underestimate extreme flooding because they do not adequately account for sea level rise and the possibility of low probability, high impact storm surge events.

Any amount of sea level rise will increase the flooding caused by coastal storm events, and recent work on the U.S. Atlantic coast demonstrates that the probability of coastal erosion increases with higher rates of sea level rise. Flood risk is also related to decision factors such as time horizon (i.e., life of the investment), the spatial extent of a planning area, and risk tolerance (i.e., willingness to accept a higher or lower probability of impacts). Risk perception, tolerance, and ability to address risks vary considerably among and within coastal communities. Considering the limits of tolerable risk is an active area of research and public debate, but is important for more resilient recovery and planning.

The sections that follow summarize the current scientific understanding of projected sea level rise globally and in the Sandy-affected region, the implications of sea level rise in assessing communities' coastal flood risks, and considerations for incorporating this information in determining risk tolerances and in evaluating potential hazard mitigation options.

### Sea Level Rise and Risk Management in the U.S. Northeast
Global sea level has been rising at varying rates since the end of the last Ice Age (21,000 years ago) and is expected to continue beyond the end of this century. Over eight million people live in 100-year oceanic coastal flood hazard areas as mapped by FEMA. Further, more than 100 million people (33% of the U.S. population) live in counties that border the ocean and/or contain 100-year coastal flood hazard areas (excluding Great Lakes counties).[216] Many of the nation's assets related to military readiness and security, energy, commerce, transportation, and ecosystems are already located at or near the tidal coastal lines. Any increase in relative sea level[217] increases the frequency and severity of coastal flooding in manmade and natural systems, even if storm patterns remain the same. Hurricane Sandy is a vivid reminder that we must find ways to contain costs resulting from exposure and increasing risk.

FEMA is providing information about current risk based on historic conditions, including new ABFE maps for parts of coastal New York and New Jersey. Using the best available scientific information to address flood risk, including ABFEs, has immediate, short-term benefits to communities, but does not account for increasing flood risk resulting from future sea level rise. In order to reduce vulnerability and increase resilience further into the future, long-term decisions such as where to locate new developments or critical infrastructure should incorporate information on future risk, such as sea level rise projections.[218]

FEMA and CEQ have been working with federal agencies and with the New York City Panel on Climate Change (NPCC) to provide the best available information on future sea level rise in a planning tool developed for decision makers in the Northeast.[219] This section provides a synthesis of the scientific information on sea level rise incorporated in the planning tool and on risk management considerations in using sea level rise information.

## Methods for Determining Future Sea Level Rise

There are two major approaches to looking ahead: one extrapolates past trends and the other relies on models of processes expected to drive future trends. The recent report, Global Sea-Level Rise Scenarios for the US National Climate Assessment (Parris et al 2012 – hereafter referred to as the Interagency Global SLR Scenarios), builds upon efforts by USACE and the National Climate Assessment to provide guidance on sea level rise estimates for these purposes.[220]

Coastal management decisions based solely on a most probable or likely outcome can lead to vulnerable assets resulting from inaction or maladaptation.[221] The Interagency Global SLR Scenarios provides four plausible global sea level rise scenarios derived from current, peer-reviewed research. The scenarios do not precisely predict future changes, but describe potential future conditions in a manner that supports decision-making under conditions of uncertainty.[222] This provides decision makers with alternative scenarios that can be employed based on risk tolerance.[223]

Sea level rise is highly variable over time and along different parts of the US coast. Changes in vertical land movement and ocean dynamics may be applied with different degrees of confidence based on available regional or local data. The Interagency Global SLR Scenarios can be used in the absence of more locally or regionally relevant sea level rise estimates, as is the case in New York City. Modeled on the Intergovernmental Panel on Climate Change (IPCC), NPCC was convened by Mayor Michael Bloomberg in August 2008 as part of PlaNYC, the City's long-term sustainability plan.[224] The NPCC consists of scientists who study climate change and its impact, as well as legal, insurance, and risk management experts. In the wake of Hurricane Sandy, Mayor Bloomberg's office is re-convening NPCC to provide updated climate risk information, including sea level rise projections. NPCC has developed next generation sea level rise projections for the immediate metropolitan area.[225] The approach relies on latest global climate models outputs and emerging research to project changes in six sea level components (three global and three local).

## Global Mean Sea Level Rise

Global Sea Level Rise Scenarios for the US National Climate Assessment (Parris et al 2012) states very high confidence (>90% ) that global mean sea level will rise at least 0.2 meters (8 inches) and no more than 2.0 meters (6.6 feet) by 2100. At this stage, the greatest uncertainty surrounding estimates of future global sea level rise is the rate and magnitude of ice sheet loss, primarily from Greenland and West Antarctica. The Highest Scenario of global sea level rise by 2100 is derived from a combination of estimated ocean warming from the

IPCC AR4 global sea level rise projections and a calculation of the maximum possible glacier and ice sheet loss by the end of the century. The Intermediate-High Scenario assumes recent rates of ice sheet loss, but not the possibility of faster rates as temperature rises. The Intermediate-Low Scenario is based primarily on ocean warming and does not assume significant contributions increase in ice sheet loss. The Lowest Scenario is based on a linear extrapolation of the historical sea level rise rate derived from tide gauge records beginning in 1900 (1.7 mm/yr). The rate of global mean sea level rise derived from satellite altimetry (1992 to 2010) has been substantially higher (3.2 mm/yr), approaching twice the rate of the longer historical record from tide gauges. Thus, the Lowest Scenario should be considered only where there is a great tolerance for risk.

A highly significant correlation is present between increasing global mean temperature and global mean sea level rise.[226] The IPCC and more recent studies anticipate that oceanic circulation and thermal expansion due to heat transfer will continue to drive global mean sea level rise even if warming ceases.[227] The Intermediate-Low and Lowest Scenarios are optimistic scenarios of future environmental change that assume rates of ice sheet loss and ocean warming slightly higher or similar to recent observations.

**U.S. Northeast Sea Level Rise**

Sea level rise has been rising along the entire US Atlantic coast, and it has been rising faster in the Mid- Atlantic region (Virginia, Maryland, and Delaware, including the Chesapeake Bay) and the Carolinas primarily due to subsidence.[228] In the Mid-Atlantic region, possible causes of subsidence include sediment consolidation, glacio-isostatic adjustment (GIA), groundwater extraction, and tectonics.[229] Sallenger et al. (2012) detect a "hotspot" of accelerated sea level rise along the 1,000 km of coast from Cape Hatteras, North Carolina to near Boston, Massachusetts and suggest it may be related to circulation changes in the North Atlantic Ocean.[230] Dynamical sea level rise resulting from ocean circulation patterns could be additive to the global mean sea level rise trend, creating even higher sea levels and potential coastal impacts in Boston, New York, and Washington, DC when compared to the southeastern U.S.[231] The causal mechanisms and persistence of this regional sea level rise acceleration remain an area of scientific debate.[232] However, the observed rates of sea level rise and the evidence presented by Yin et al. (2010), Sallenger et al. (2012), and more recently by Boon (2012) are sufficient to suggest that experts and decision makers should consider accelerated rates along the northeast coast in their risk-averse, worst-case scenarios.[233]

The NPCC projects that, by the 2020s, sea level at the Battery at the southern tip of Manhattan will rise by between 2 and 11 inches.[234] By the 2050s, the range expands to 6 to 32 inches. The broad range in the 2050s is primarily due to uncertainty about how much ice loss from ice sheets, mountain glaciers, and land-based ice caps will contribute to sea level rise, although thermal expansion of the ocean and dynamical changes in ocean height are important as well. After the 2050s, uncertainties associated with the melting of ice sheets, mountain glaciers, and land-based ice caps are projected to increasingly dominate.

**Physical Science Limitations on Current Flood Risk Information**

In many cases, FIRMs provided by FEMA are based on analyses and data that are 20 years old or more. The coastal storm flood data depicted in these maps often do not consider future sea level rise, the combination of coastal flooding factors, and/or shoreline change.

Sea levels continue to influence extreme weather events, including hurricanes and northeasters, which have been and continue to be the primary driver of the highest water levels affecting coastal communities.[235] The general consensus is that it is likely the average maximum wind speed of hurricanes will increase throughout the coming century, although possibly not in every ocean basin, and the frequency of heavy precipitation will increase over the 21st Century.[236] Sea level rise amplifies factors that contribute to coastal flooding: high tides, storm surge, high waves, and high runoff from rivers and creeks.[237] For example, coastal damage from Hurricane Sandy in much of the New York Metropolitan Region is a result of high waves and storm surge occur during an astronomically high tide.

Shoreline change is a dynamic process that is driven by both climate (e.g., storminess, sea level rise) and non-climate (e.g., sediment availability, tectonic uplift, or subsidence) factors. Historical trends of coastal erosion in the northeastern U.S. are well-documented.[238] Predicting future trends of coastal change in response to storms and sea level rise is an active area of research that is critical to a comprehensive view of future risk. Recent work on the U.S. Atlantic coast demonstrates that the probability of coastal erosion increases with higher rates of sea level rise, and that explicit consideration of both climate and non-climate factors increases confidence in predictions.[239]

Efforts remain underway to develop updated coastal storm flood data for portions of the New York and New Jersey coast most severely affected by Sandy. The Task Force previously advised use of FEMA's ABFEs plus 1 foot for rebuilding in the region. In the July-October timeframe, FEMA will release most of the Preliminary Digital Flood Insurance Rate Maps for coastal areas in both states, which will replace the ABFEs and refine the 1%-annual-chance (100-year) coastal flood elevations based on improved modeling. Thus, considering the impact of different weather events combined with scenarios of sea level rise and shoreline change is crucial in developing hazard profiles for emergency planning and vulnerability, impact, and adaptation assessments.[240]

## Coastal Flood Risk Management Constraints

In addition to the factors described above, coastal flood risk is also related to planning choices that often include these common considerations: location or planning area, time horizon or planned life of use/investment, and risk tolerance.[241] Risk tolerance refers to a community's or decision maker's willingness to accept a higher or lower probability of impacts.

Risk perception, tolerance, and ability to address risks vary considerably among and within coastal communities. For example, power stations or airports at specific locations along the coast may be critically important to the regional or national economy and thus may be protected with a large flood control structure based on projected long-term, regional, and/or global scale risks. However, such flood control structures may have adverse effects on adjacent parts of the coast or create a false sense of reduced risk as sea level rises and coastal flooding increases.[242] Over time, the ability to incrementally increase the height of flood control structures may be limited. Some communities are already facing limits to their ability to adapt to risk, presenting challenging questions for policy makers about managing consequences.[243]

Factors considered in determining risk tolerance should include, among other things:

- Potential for catastrophic loss of human lives, critical infrastructure, livelihoods, and ecosystem function.
- Perceived fairness and voluntary nature of risks.
- Adaptive capacity or the ability or potential of a system to respond successfully to a coastal flooding event, including adjustments in both behavior and in resources and technologies.

Incorporating sea level rise into coastal plans can improve risk profiles. However, understanding the limits of tolerable risk is an active area of research and public debate.

## VI. The Importance of Outreach and Community Engagement

After Sandy struck the eastern seaboard, mayors up and down the coast worked to identify necessary steps to protect their community; philanthropists scrambled to determine where their support could make the biggest impact; officials at local, State, and Federal agencies worked long hours to implement programs to assist residents in rehabilitating their homes. Amid the chaos and destruction caused by Hurricane Sandy, it was immediately clear to the Task Force that an effective plan for recovery and rebuilding would be the result of addressing needs on the ground, not the product of just one voice. The Task Force's approach reflects this reality, and throughout the process of aiding the rebuilding and recovery efforts following Hurricane Sandy, we have taken steps to ensure that a wide range of viewpoints are heard and incorporated into our work.

Community engagement was key to each and every step of the Task Force's work and the development of this Rebuilding Strategy. The Task Force designed its community engagement strategy to maintain a thorough public presence that would assist in rebuilding, keep stakeholders informed of Task Force efforts, and obtain feedback on Task Force proposals. The Task Force worked closely with State RSFs to align with the work of the NDRF. The Task Force established a formal Advisory Group composed of State, local, and Tribal elected leaders from the most severely impacted cities and towns in the region. Additional outreach extended to State and local officials from other affected areas, subject matter experts and think tanks, advocacy organizations, community-based organizations, philanthropic organizations and foundations, and private partners.

The extensive efforts of the Task Force to engage a wide variety of perspectives and incorporate a diverse set of opinions in the development of our policy recommendations reflect a commitment to the principles that guided our work. Whether identifying areas in which communities could bolster resilience, providing data in a clear and transparent way, working to ensure that funds were spent efficiently and equitably, or working to ensure that systems were put in place to boost the capacity of communities to respond to disasters, engagement of key stakeholders in the region was vital to the Task Force's success. Likewise, nowhere was an active engagement strategy more important than in our efforts to expand regional coordination and maintain local primacy so as to enable smaller communities to access the knowledge and resources that would otherwise be out of reach.

### Engagement Model

In order to ensure we addressed the needs and ideas of a wide variety of stakeholders, the Task Force pursued a policy-driven community engagement plan to maintain a public presence with those directly involved in recovery and rebuilding efforts and to obtain feedback on our policy proposals throughout the development process. The Task Force followed an engagement framework based upon the International Association for Public Participation (IAP2) Spectrum,[244] to define our goals and commitment to the stakeholders. This approach was applied to the work conducted on each of the Task Force policy priority issues, including: resilience, infrastructure, housing, small business, insurance, capacity building, and data sharing.

The Task Force engaged Members of Congress, state officials, and local stakeholders such as advocacy groups, community-based organizations, philanthropies, think tanks, and private partners to ensure all stakeholders had an opportunity to share their needs and viewpoints. Through policy focused roundtables, local workshops, policy calls, and several hundred meetings with individuals, small groups, and regional meetings, the Task Force engaged a wide variety of viewpoints which helped inform its information gathering and policy work and remove obstacles to rebuilding.

The Task Force identified four key approaches that were vital to effective outreach and communication. Each outlined a clear, deliverable, goal for the Task Force to pursue when working with stakeholders:

- **Inform:** To provide the stakeholder with balanced and objective information to assist them in understanding the problems, alternatives, opportunities, and/or solutions.
- **Consult:** To obtain stakeholder feedback on analysis and/or decisions.
- **Involve:** To work directly with the stakeholder throughout the process to ensure that public concerns and aspirations are consistently understood and considered.
- **Collaborate:** To partner with the stakeholder in each aspect of the decision including the development of alternatives and the identification of the preferred solution.

To ensure that the Task Force was engaging stakeholders throughout the development of its policy recommendations, we employed a five-phase timeline to guide our community outreach and engagement process:

In **Phase I**, Task Force staff identified key stakeholders, creating a comprehensive list of experts, organizations, and community members that could provide key input. To do so, Task Force staff held briefings and one-on-one meetings with Federal and local partners to collaborate regarding whom to bring into the process.

**Phase II** consisted of outreach to nearly 450 stakeholders in the region and in Washington, D.C. The Chair hosted meetings with Advisory Group members and advocacy groups. Various cabinet members including DHS Secretary Janet Napolitano and Former DOT Secretary Ray LaHood participated in site visits to see the devastation first hand and announce investment in the region. Task Force staff worked to inform relevant parties of the Task Force's objectives through briefings, conference calls, and one-on- one meetings.

In **Phase III**, members of the Task Force consulted and collaborated with members of the affected communities and key stakeholders to validate specific policy proposals. Through workshops, roundtables, and stakeholder meetings, the Task Force sought to include an abundance of voices in order to maximize the variety of opinions and ensure it was identifying key needs.

In **Phase IV**, the Task Force engaged with stakeholders to finalize policy priorities and recommendations while maintaining strong communication within the affected communities.

Finally, In **Phase V**, the Task Force will provide briefings, fact sheets, and background calls to interested stakeholders with details and context on the final policy recommendations included in this report.

### *Advisory Group*

The Task Force's outreach strategy is reflective of the reality that it is the governors, mayors, and local elected officials in the affected regions who are on the ground dealing with much of the day-to-day aftermath of the storm. In order to ensure the officials on the front lines of recovery efforts had both the resources they needed and had a voice, the Chair, in accordance with the Executive Order governing the Task Force, established an Advisory Group composed of elected officials that represented the worst-hit regions. With a focus on flood risk, housing, small business, capacity building, resilient infrastructure and energy, and flood and other hazard insurance, the Advisory Group has served as a direct line of communication between communities affected by the storm and those developing plans for rebuilding and recovery. Through participation in regional meetings, regular conference calls on policy priorities, and informal one-on-one meetings and consultations, Advisory Group members provided direct input into the development of the Rebuilding Strategy, ensured that the Task Force's activities and recommendations reflect the input of those directly affected, as well as addressed the challenges those directly affected face as they continue to rebuild their communities.

The Advisory Group consisted of 37 members, including the CDBG-DR grantees: Governors of New York, New Jersey, Rhode Island, Maryland, and Connecticut, and the Mayor of New York City; the Chairman of the Shinnecock Tribe; 12 additional local New York officials; and 18 additional local officials from New Jersey. The Task Force held three in-person meetings of the Advisory Group, one in New York, New Jersey, and Washington, and six in-depth policy calls discussing proposed sections of the Rebuilding Strategy. One-on-one meetings with Advisory Group members in their regions were also held.

### *Members of Congress*

The Task Force facilitated communication between Members of Congress and State and local elected officials to further ensure that the needs in the region were being met. By working closely with Senators and Representatives of the affected regions, the Task Force ensured that they remained informed of the work of the Task Force and the progress of recovery efforts. Task Force staff briefed Members of Congress and over 30 staffers from the Connecticut, Maryland, New Jersey, New York, and Rhode Island delegations on the initial Sandy Supplemental CDBG-DR allocation and eligible uses for these funds. The Chair and Executive Director met with members of the New York and New Jersey delegation to update them on the recovery progress. Congressional delegation trips were made to Connecticut and Rhode Island to discuss the recovery effort and tour areas impacted by Sandy. Congressional conference calls and individual briefings were held for Capitol Hill staffers on various issues such as mold remediation, impending risk standards announcements, and forbearance modifications to extend foreclosure relief to homeowners adversely impacted by Hurricane Sandy.

## VII. Hurricane Sandy Rebuilding Task Force Staff and Agency Designees

### *Task Force Staff and Agency Detailees*

Laurel Blatchford – Executive Director
Marion McFadden – Chief Operating Officer
Rachel Haltom-Irwin – Chief of Staff
Michael Passante – New Jersey State Director
Jamie S. Rubin – New York State Director

| | | |
|---|---|---|
| Adriana Akers | Sarah Gillespie | Laura Olson |
| Christopher Armstrong | Jose Gil Montanez | Roger Mouafo |
| Robin A. Barnes | Janet Golrick | Rima Oueid |
| Donna Battistoni | Alicia Gould | Henk Ovink |
| Peter Bondi | Katherine Greig | Olivia Papp |
| Alex Boota | James Hairston | Darshini Patel |
| Nat Bottigheimer | Tianhao He | Jacob Press |
| Kevin Bush | Andrew Heimowitz | Liza Purcell |
| Irene Chang-Cimino | Charles Imohiosen | Micah Ragland |
| Adria Crutchfield | Aaron Jacobs | Zachary Richner |
| Scott Davis | Naveen Jawaid | Stewart Sarkozy-Banoczy |
| Fernanda da Rocha | Fae Jencks | Josh Sawislak |
| David Dietz | Omar Khan | Justin Scheid |
| Jennifer DiLorenzo | Diane Kinnane | R. Tom Sizemore III, M.D. |
| Mark Dowd | Karen Lake | Benjamin Spinelli |
| Hannah Edwards | Gina Lee | Lily Sugrue |
| Sandra Edwards | Jacob Leibenluft | Sarah Tippens |
| Sarah Ellis-Peed | Aracely Macias | Jason Washington |
| Warren Flood | Betsy Mallow | Matthew Weinberg |
| Felipe Floresca | Sara Meyers | Kevin Werner |
| DeShaunta Franklin | Rafaela Monchek | Samuel Winningham |
| Stephanie Gidigbi | Hannah Mullen | Kirsten Wolfington |
| Brendan Gilfillan | | |

Program Management Office Working Group
Task Force Congressional and Intergovernmental Affairs Working Group
Task Force Communications Working Group

*Task Force Member Agency Lead Designees and Additional Federal Contributors*

| | |
|---|---|
| **U.S. Department of the Treasury:** | John Fassl |
| **U.S. Department of the Interior:** | Jon Jarvis |
| **U.S. Department of Agriculture:** | Max Finberg |
| **U.S. Department of Commerce:** | Matt Erskine & Renee Stone |
| **U.S. Department of Labor:** | Robert Asaro-Angelo |
| **U.S. Department of Health and Human Services:** | Nicole Lurie, M.D. |
| **U.S. Department of Transportation:** | Vinn White |
| **U.S. Department of Energy:** | Pat Hoffman |
| **U.S. Department of Education:** | David Esquith |
| **U.S. Department of Veterans Affairs:** | Jose Riojas |
| **U.S. Department of Homeland Security:** | Rafaela Monchek |
| **U.S. Department of Housing and Urban Development:** | Janet Golrick |
| **U.S. Environmental Protection Agency:** | Lisa Feldt |
| **Small Business Administration:** | Megan K. Smith |
| **U.S. Army Corps of Engineers:** | Mark Mazzanti |
| **White House Office of Management and Budget:** | Jim Holm |
| **White House National Security Staff:** | Ahsha Tribble |
| **White House Domestic Policy Council:** | Carlos Monje |
| **National Economic Council:** | Ronald Minsk |
| **White House Council on Environmental Quality:** | Lowry Crook and Susan Ruffo |
| **White House Office of Science and Technology Policy:** | Tammy Dickinson |
| **White House Council of Economic Advisors:** | Cynthia Nickerson |
| **White House Office of Public Engagement and Intergovernmental Affairs:** | David Agnew |
| **White House Office of Cabinet Affairs:** | Ali Zaidi |
| **Corporation for National and Community Service:** | Kelly L. DeGraff |
| **Federal Communications Commission:** | Gene Fullano |
| **National Endowment for the Arts:** | Dan Lurie |

# End Notes

[1] After striking the Caribbean as a Category 3 Hurricane, Sandy weakened over the Atlantic Ocean. Though the storm weakened in power, it grew massively in size. Sandy sustained Hurricane-force wind in the Atlantic as a Category 1 hurricane before making landfall in Brigantine, N.J. as a post-tropical cyclone. For the purpose of clarity, this Strategy will refer to the storm as "Hurricane Sandy" or simply "Sandy." For more information, see: National Hurricane Center, "Tropical Cyclone Report: Hurricane Sandy," 02/12/2013, http://www.nhc.noaa.gov/data/tcr/AL182012_Sandy.pdf.

[2] National Hurricane Center, "Tropical Cyclone Report: Hurricane Sandy," 02/12/2013, http://www.nhc.noaa.gov/data/tcr/ AL182012_Sandy.pdf.

[3] Ibid.

[4] FEMA, "Hurricane Sandy: Timeline," accessed 7/22/2013, http://www.fema.gov/hurricane-sandy-timeline.

[5] FEMA, "Superstorm Sandy Update – Nov. 10, 2012," 10/11/2012, http://www.fema.gov/employee-news-and-announcements/superstorm-sandy-update-nov-10-2012.

[6] FEMA, "Hurricane Sandy: Timeline," 12/07/2012, http://www.fema.gov/hurricane-sandy-timeline.

[7] NOAA, "Service Assessment, Hurricane/Post-Tropical Cyclone Sandy," 05/2013, http://www.nws.noaa.gov/os/assessments/pdfs/Sandy13.pdf.

[8] FEMA, "Disaster Declarations for 2012," accessed 07/22/2013, http://www.fema.gov/disasters/grid/year/2012; FEMA, "Disaster Declarations for 2013," accessed 07/22/2013, http://www.fema.gov/disasters/grid/year/2013.

[9] NOAA, "Service Assessment, Hurricane/Post-Tropical Cyclone Sandy," 05/2013, http://www.nws.noaa.gov/os/assessments/pdfs/Sandy13.pdf.

[10] U.S. Climate Change Science Program and the Subcommittee on Global Change Research, "Coastal Sensitivity to Sea-Level Rise: A Focus on the Mid-Atlantic Region," Table 2: Shoreline Length by Major Water Body and Likelihood of Shore Protection (miles), 01/2009, http://risingsea.net/ERL/New_Jersey_shoreline_length.pdf.

[11] New Jersey Division of Travel and Tourism, "2012 Tourism Economic Impact Study," 2012, http://www.visitnj.org/new-jersey-tourism-research-and-information

[12] U.S. Census Bureau, "Population and Housing Occupancy Status: 2010 - United States -- Metropolitan Statistical Area; and for Puerto Rico: 2010 Census National Summary File of Redistricting Data," http://www.factfinder2.census.gov/faces/tableservices/jsf/pages/productview.xhtml?pid=DEC_10_NSRD_GCTPL2.US24PR&prodType=table

[13] Bureau of Economic Analysis, "Economic Growth Continues Across Metropolitan Areas In 2011," 02/22/2013, http://www.bea.gov/newsreleases/regional/gdp_metro/gdp_metro_newsrelease.htm.

[14] New York City Special Initiative for Resilient Rebuilding, "PlaNYC: A Stronger, More Resilient New York," 06/11/2013, http://www.nyc.gov/html/sirr/html/report/report.shtml.

[15] About Long Island, 2013, http://www.longisland.com/long-island.html.

[16] U.S. Census Bureau, 2012, http://www.quickfacts.census.gov/qfd/states/36/36059.html; U.S. Census Bureau, 2012, http://www.quickfacts.census.gov/qfd/states/36/36103.html.

[17] U.S. Census Bureau Statistical Abstract: State Rankings, 2012, http://www.census.gov/compendia/statab/rankings.html.

[18] U.S. Census Bureau, County Business Patterns, accessed 07/22/2013, http://www.census.gov/econ/cbp/.

[19] Task Force analysis of data from U.S. Census Bureau Patterns, Moody's (2012), U.S. Bureau of Economic Analysis, FEMA, ESRI, 05/22/2013.

[20] American Society of Civil Engineers, "Report Card on America's Infrastructure," 2013, http://www.infrastructurereportcard.org/states/.

[21] Ibid.

[22] According to FEMA, flood hazard areas identified on the Flood Insurance Rate Map are identified as a Special Flood Hazard Area (SFHAs). SFHA are defined as the area that will be inundated by the flood event having a 1-percent chance of being equaled or exceeded in any given year. National Flood Insurance Program, "Flood Zones," 05/15/2012, http://www.fema.gov/national-flood-insurance-program-2/flood-zones.

[23] Congressional Research Service, "The National Flood Insurance Program: Status and Remaining Issues for Congress," 02/06/2013, http://www.fas.org/sgp/crs/misc/R42850.pdf.

[24] New York City Special Initiative for Resilient Rebuilding, "PlaNYC: A Stronger, More Resilient New York", 06/11/2013 http://www.nyc.gov/html/sirr/downloads/pdf/final_report/Ch4_Buildings_FINAL_singles.pdf.

[25] Federal Reserve Bank of New York, "Small Business Credit Survey, 2013," 05/2013, http://www.newyorkfed.org/smallbusiness/2013/pdf/full-report.pdf.

[26] National Hurricane Center, "Tropical Cyclone Report: Hurricane Sandy," 02/12/2013, http://www.nhc.noaa.gov/data/tcr/AL182012_Sandy.pdf.

[27] NOAA, "Service Assessment, Hurricane/Post-Tropical Cyclone Sandy," 05/2013, http://www.nws.noaa.gov/os/assessments/pdfs/Sandy13.pdf.

[28] Ibid.

[29] According to NOAA, the 2013 Consumer Price Index (CPI) cost adjusted value of Hurricane Sandy was $65.7 billion. The costliest storm was Hurricane Katrina, with a 2013 CPI cost adjusted value of $148.8 billion, and the third costliest Hurricane was Hurricane Andrew, with a 2013 CPI cost adjusted value of $44.8 billion. Source: NOAA, "Billion-Dollar Weather/Climate Disasters," accessed 08/06/2013, http://www.ncdc.noaa.gov/billions/events.

[30] NOAA, "Service Assessment, Hurricane/Post-Tropical Cyclone Sandy," 05/2013, http://www.nws.noaa.gov/os/assessments/pdfs/Sandy13.pdf.

[31] NOAA, "Billion-Dollar U.S. Weather/Climate Disasters 1980-2012," accessed 07/11/2013, http://www.ncdc.noaa.gov/billions/events.pdf.

[32] EQECAT, "Post-Landfall Loss Estimates - Hurricane Sandy," 11/01/2012, http://www.eqecat.com/catwatch/post-landfall-loss-estimates-superstorm-sandy-released-2012-11-01/.

[33] Department of Energy "Comparing the Impacts of Northeast Hurricanes on Energy Infrastructure," 04/2013, http://www.energy.gov/sites/prod/files/2013/04/f0/Northeast%20Storm%20Comparison_FINAL_041513c.pdf.

[34] National Hurricane Center, "Tropical Cyclone Report: Hurricane Sandy," 02/12/2013, http://www.nhc.noaa.gov/data/tcr/AL182012_Sandy.pdf.

[35] National Hurricane Center, "Tropical Cyclone Report: Hurricane Sandy," 02/12/2013, http://www.nhc.noaa.gov/data/tcr/AL182012_Sandy.pdf.

[36] David Turetsky, Chief, Public Safety & Homeland Security Bureau, Federal Communications Commission, Remarks NENA 2013 Conference & Expo Charlotte, NC 06/18/2013, http://www. transition.fcc.gov/Daily_Releases/Daily_Business/2013/db0621/DOC-321744A1.pdf.

[37] Peter M. Rogoff, FTA Administrator, Testimony before the Senate Banking, Housing, and Urban Affairs Committee, Subcommittee on Housing, Transportation, and Community Development, 12/20/2012, http://www.fta.dot.gov/newsroom/12908_14967.html.

[38] MTA, 10/28/2012, http://www.mta.info/Alert_hurricaneSandy.htm.

[39] Rudin Center for Transportation NYU Wagner Graduate School of Public Service, "Transportation During and After Hurricane Sandy," 11/2012, http://wagner.nyu.edu/files/faculty/publications/sandytransportation.pdf.

[40] Federal Transit Administration, "Superstorm Sandy Public Transit Projects – Review of Cost Estimates," 01/31/2013.

[41] Rudin Center for Transportation NYU Wagner Graduate School of Public Service, "Transportation During and After Hurricane Sandy," 11/2012, http://wagner.nyu.edu/files/faculty/publications/sandytransportation.pdf.

[42] Amtrak, "Hurricane Sandy," 11/29/2012, http://www.commerce.senate.gov/public/?a=Files.Serve&File_id=c449a06d-c1d6-41be-8326-8e625faeb211.

[43] Ibid.

[44] Climate Central, "Sewage Overflows From Hurricane Sandy," 04/2013, http://www.climatecentral.org/pdfs/Sewage.pdf.

[45] Ibid.

[46] State of New Jersey Department of Environmental Protection, "Christie Administration Advises Residents To Be Alert For Local Boil Water Advisories," 10/31/2012, http://www.state.nj.us/dep/newsrel/2012/12_0132.htm; New York State Department of Health, "Drinking Water Advisories Following Hurricane Sandy," 12/2012, http://www.health.ny.gov/environmental/water/drinking/boilwater/sandy/.

[47] New York City Special Initiative for Resilient Rebuilding, "PlaNYC: A Stronger, More Resilient New York," 06/11/2013, http://www.nyc.gov/html/sirr/html/report/report.shtml.

[48] Information provided by FEMA.

[49] NJ Spotlight, "NJ Hospital Officials Begin Planning, Building for the Next Sandy," 02/21/2013, http://www.njspotlight.com/stories/13/02/20/hospital-officials-begin-planning-building-for-the-next-sandy/.

[50] The Star-Ledger, "Hurricane Sandy aftermath: Some NJ schools reopen with no heat, no lunch," 11/06/2012, http://www.nj.com/news/index.ssf/2012/11/hurricane_sandy_aftermath_some.html.

[51] Information provided by FEMA.

[52] Office of the Governor of New York, "New York State Hurricane Sandy recovery needs summary," 11/26/2012, http://www.governor.ny.gov/assets/documents/sandyimpactsummary.pdf.

[53] NJMEP Ongoing Post Sandy Outreach, Data on Calls Made November 2-16, 2012.

[54] U.S. Department of Commerce, Office of the Chief Economist, draft report "Economic Impact of Super Storm Sandy", 08/2013

[55] NOAA Fisheries, "Regional Impact Evaluation: An Initial Assessment of the Economic Impacts of Sandy on New Jersey and New York Commercial and Recreational Fishing Sectors," 03/2013, http://www.st.nmfs.noaa.gov/Assets/economics/documents/sandy/Final_Report_Sandy_Regional_Impact_Evaluation_MSA.pdf.

[56] Insurance Information Institute, "Over 90 Percent of the New Jersey and New York Sandy Insurance Claims Have Been Settled; Likely to Be Third Largest Storm Ever for U.S. Insurers," 4/19/2013, http://www.iii.org/press_releases/over-90-percent-of-the-new-jersey-and-new-york-sandy-insurance-claims-have-been-settled-likely-to-be-third-largest-hurricane-ever-for-us-insurers.html.

[57] Figures expressed in 2012 dollars. Source: FEMA, "Significant Flood Events as of April 30, 2013," updated 06/24/2013, http://www.fema.gov/policy-claim-statistics-flood-insurance/policy-claim-statistics-flood-insurance/policy-claim-13-9.

[58] New York Department of Financial Services, as of 06/14/2013; New Jersey Department of Banking and Insurance, as of 6/18/2013; FEMA, as of 06/25/2013.

[59] FEMA, "Hurricane Sandy: Timeline," 12/07/2012, http://www.fema.gov/hurricane-sandy-timeline.

[60] FEMA, "Superstorm Sandy Update – Nov. 10, 2012," 10/11/2012, http://www.fema.gov/employee-news-and-announcements/superstorm-sandy-update-nov-10-2012.

[61] FEMA, "Hurricane Sandy: Timeline," 12/07/2012, http://www.fema.gov/hurricane-sandy-timeline.

[62] FEMA, "Sandy Update – Nov. 21, 2012", 11/21/2012, https://www.fema.gov/employee-news-and-announcements/sandy-update-nov-21-2012.

[63] These values are based on agencies classifying programs into one primary category that describes the intended use of funds. These are not direct line items from the Sandy Supplemental, but rather show the different types of program themes that have been funded explicitly and implicitly.

[64] This data is not based on 100 percent of all obligated and outlayed funds and includes data that was submitted to the PMO by agencies. This data does account for approximately 90 per cent of obligated and outlayed funds.

[65] Presidential Policy Directive 8, http://www.dhs.gov/presidential-policy-directive-8-national-preparedness.

[66] National Disaster Recovery Framework, 09/2011, http://www.fema.gov/pdf/recoveryframework/ndrf.pdf.

[67] FEMA, "Recovery Support Functions," accessed 07/19/2013, http://www.fema.gov/recovery-support-functions.

[68] Values represent the 2013 Consumer Price Index (CPI) cost adjusted value. NOAA, "Billion-Dollar U.S. Weather/ Climate Disasters 1980-2012," accessed 07/11/2013, http://www.ncdc.noaa.gov/billions/events.pdf.

[69] IPCC, 2012: Summary for Policymakers. In: Managing the Risks of Extreme Events and Disasters to Advance Climate Change Adaptation [Field, C.B., V. Barros, T.F. Stocker, D. Qin, D.J. Dokken, K.L. Ebi, M.D. Mastrandrea, K.J. Mach, G.-K. Plattner, S.K. Allen, M. Tignor, and P.M. Midgley (eds.)]. A Special Report of Working Groups I and II of the Intergovernmental Panel on Climate Change. Cambridge University Press, Cambridge, UK, and New York, NY, USA, pp. 1-19.

[70] Buro Happold, "Sandy Success Stories," 06/2013, http://www.sandysuccessstories.org.

[71] Multihazard Mitigation Council, "Natural Hazard Mitigation Saves: An Independent Study to Assess the Future Savings from Mitigation Activities," 2005, http://c.ymcdn.com/sites/www.nibs.org/resource/resmgr/MMC/hms_vol1.pdf.

[72] FEMA, "Changes in the Flood Insurance Program: Preliminary Considerations for Rebuilding," http://www.dec.ny.gov/docs/water_pdf/fpmfemacfip.pdf.

[73] U.S. Global Change Research Program, "Sea Level Rise Tool for Sandy Recovery," http://www.globalchange.gov/what-we-do/assessment/coastal-resilience-resources.

[74] The National Science and Technology Council (NSTC) within the Office of Science and Technology Policy was established by Executive Order on November 23, 1993. This Cabinet-level Council within the executive branch coordinates science and technology policy across the diverse entities that make up the Federal research and development enterprise. The work of the NSTC is organized under five primary committees: Environment, Natural Resources and Sustainability (CENRS); Homeland and National Security; Science, Technology, Engineering, and Math (STEM) Education; Science; and Technology. Each of these committees oversees subcommittees and working groups focused on different aspects of science and technology and working to coordinate across the Federal government.

[75] Matthew J.P. Cooper, Michael D. Beevers, and Michael Oppenheimer, "Future Sea Level Rise and the New Jersey Coast: Assessing Potential Impacts and Opportunities," 11/2005, http://www.princeton.edu/step/people/faculty/michael-oppenheimer/recent-publications/Future-Sea-Level-Rise-and-the-New-Jersey-Coast-Assessing-Potential-Impacts-and-Opportunities.pdf.

[76] U.S. Global Change Research Program, "Sea Level Rise Tool For Sandy Recovery," http://www.globalchange.gov/what-we-do/assessment/coastal-resilience-resources.

[77] OSTP, "Implementation of Federal Prize Authority: Progress Report,"03/2012, http://www.whitehouse.gov/sites/default/files/microsites/ostp/competes_report_on_prizes_final.pdf.

[78] McKinsey & Company, "And the Winner Is..." Capturing the promise of philanthropic prizes, 2009

[79] Executive Order 13632, 12/07/2012, http://www.gpo.gov/fdsys/pkg/DCPD-201200936/pdf/DCPD-201200936.pdf.

[80] Bureau of Economic Analysis, "Gross Domestic Product by Metropolitan Area: Advance Statistics for 2011 and Revised Statistics for 2001–2010, 03/2013, http://www.bea.gov/scb/pdf/2013/03%20March/0313_gdp-by-metro_area.pdf.

[81] Rural Policy Research Institute – Rural Futures Lab & the University of Missouri, "Regional Resilience Research and Policy Brief," 02/2012; Community and Regional Resilience Institute, "How Geographic Scale Matters in Seeking Community Resilience," 2009; Cutter, S. L. (ed.), "American Hazardscapes: The Regionalization of Hazards and Disasters," 2001.

[82] The Civil Rights Act of1964, 42 U.S.C. § 2000d et seq., available at http://www.gpo.gov/fdsys/pkg/ USCODE-2010-title42/pdf/USCODE-2010-title42-chap21-subchapV-sec2000d.pdf

[83] Such efforts are undertaken in conformance with Executive Order 12898 and the Federal Interagency Working Group on Environmental Justice Memorandum of Understanding (2011). Source: EPA, "Memorandum Of Understanding On Environmental Justice And Executive Order 12898," http://www.epa.gov/environmentaljustice/resources/publications/interagency/ej-mou-2011-08.pdf.

[84] Executive Order 13604, 03/22/2012, http://www.gpo.gov/fdsys/pkg/DCPD-201200202/pdf/DCPD-201200202.pdf.

[85] The White House, "Report To The President: Rebuilding America's Infrastructure: Cutting Timelines and Improving Outcomes for Federal Permitting and Review of Infrastructure Projects," 05/2013, http://www.whitehouse.gov/sites/default/files/omb/reports/report-to-the-president-rebuilding-americas-infrastructure.pdf.

[86] The White House, "Report To The President: Rebuilding America's Infrastructure: Cutting Timelines and Improving Outcomes for Federal Permitting and Review of Infrastructure Projects," 05/2013, http://www.whitehouse.gov/sites/default/files/omb/reports/report-to-the-president-rebuilding-americas-infrastructure.pdf.

[87] Estimates based on data reported by agencies funded in the supplemental appropriation, Hurricane Sandy Rebuilding Task Force analysis.

[88] Based on an analysis compiled by the Infrastructure Steering Committee

[89] The White House, "Report To The President: Rebuilding America's Infrastructure: Cutting Timelines and Improving Outcomes for Federal Permitting and Review of Infrastructure Projects," 05/2013, http://www.whitehouse. gov/sites/default/files/omb/reports/report-to-the-president-rebuilding-americas-infrastructure.pdf.

[90] GAO, "Hurricane Katrina: GAO's Preliminary Observations Regarding Preparedness, Response, and Recovery," 03/08/2006, http://www.gao.gov/products/GAO-06-442T; Executive Office of the President, "The Federal Response to Hurricane Katrina: Lessons Learned," 02/23/2006, http://www.library.stmarytx.edu/acadlib/edocs/katrinawh.pdf.

[91] Specifically, sections 402, 403, 404, 406, 407, or 502 of the Stafford Act. The Sandy Supplemental stated, "Provided further, That, notwithstanding the preceding proviso, recipients of funds provided under this heading that use such funds to supplement Federal assistance provided under section 402,403, 404,406, 407, or 502 of the Robert T. Stafford Disaster Relief and Emergency Assistance Act (42 U.S.C. 5121 et seq.) may adopt, without review or public comment, any environmental review, approval, or permit performed by a Federal agency, and such adoption shall satisfy the responsibilities of the recipient with respect to such environmental review, approval or permit." Disaster Relief Appropriations Act, 2013, http://www.gpo.gov/fdsys/pkg/PLAW-113publ2/html/PLAW-113publ2.htm.

[92] Executive Order 13604, 03/22/2012, http://www.gpo.gov/fdsys/pkg/DCPD-201200202/pdf/DCPD-201200202.pdf.

[93] ACHP, "Program Alternatives – 36 CFR § 800.14," last updated 05/09/2013, http://www.achp.gov/progalt/.

[94] These data reflect $18 billion in funds appropriated specifically for infrastructure and over $2 billion in CDBG-DR and Public Assistance funds allocated to infrastructure projects as of June 28, 2013.

[95] EPA's Environmental Finance Advisory Board has examined SRF programs across the country, and concluded that "state programs that have leveraged their SRF funds have provided greater assistance as a percentage of their capitalization grants than those that have not leveraged." Source: EPA Environmental Finance Advisory Board, "Report on the Relative Benefits of Direct and Leveraged Loans in State Revolving Loan Fund (SRF) Programs," 08/2008.

[96] New York State Environmental Facilities Corporation, http://www.nysefc.org/Default.aspx?tabid=114; New Jersey Environmental Infrastructure Fund, "Frequently Asked Questions," updated 07/07/2010, http://www.njeit.org/faqs.htm#general1.

[97] Federal Highway Administration, "MAP-21 – Moving Ahead for Progress in the 21st Century," 09/25/2012, http:// www.fhwa.dot.gov/map21/qandas/qap3.cfm; EPA, "Drinking Water State Revolving Fund Program Operations Manual," 10/2006, http://www.epa.gov/ogwdw/dwsrf/pdfs/manual_dwsrf_programoperationalmanual.pdf.

[98] The White House, "Fiscal Year 2014 Budget Overview," accessed 07/24/2013, http://www.whitehouse.gov/omb/overview.

[99] The White House, Fiscal Year 2014 Budget, http://www.whitehouse.gov/sites/default/files/omb/budget/fy2014/assets/budget.pdf; The President's Budgets for Fiscal Years 2010-2014; S. 652: "Building and Upgrading Infrastructure for Long-Term", 112th Congress.

[100] National Hurricane Center, "Tropical Cyclone Report: Hurricane Sandy," 02/12/2013, http://www.nhc.noaa.gov/data/tcr/AL182012_Sandy.pdf.

[101] Ibid.

[102] Stony Brook University, "In the Aftermath of Superstorm Sandy: A Message from President Stanley," http://www.stonybrook.edu/sb/sandy/index.shtml; ICF International, "Combined Heat and Power: Enabling Resilient Energy Infrastructure for Critical Facilities," 03/2013,

[103] DOE Office of Energy Efficiency and Renewable Energy, "CHP: Enabling Resilient Energy Infrastructure," 04/03/2013, http://www1.eere.energy.gov/manufacturing/distributedenergy/pdfs/chp_enabling_resilient_energy_infrastructure.pdf.

[104] American Council for an Energy-Efficient Economy, "How CHP Stepped Up When the Power Went Out During Hurricane Sandy," 12/06/2012, http://www.aceee.org/blog/2012/12/how-chp-stepped-when-power-went-out-d.

[105] ICF International, "Combined Heat and Power: Enabling Resilient Energy Infrastructure for Critical Facilities," 03/2013, http://www1.eere.energy.gov/manufacturing/distributedenergy/pdfs/chp_critical_facilities.pdf.

[106] 2008 New York City Mechanical Code, with January 1-December 31, 2011 Supplement, Section MC 1305.11.1.3.

[107] DOE, "U.S. Energy Sector Vulnerabilities to Climate Change and Extreme Weather," 07/2013, http://energy.gov/sites/prod/files/2013/07/f2/20130716-Energy%20Sector%20Vulnerabilities%20Report.pdf.

[108] Moving Ahead for Progress in the 21st Century Act (MAP-21), P.L. 112-141.

[109] Federal Transit Administration and FEMA, "Memorandum of Agreement between the U.S. Department of Transportation Federal Transit Administration and the U.S. Department of Homeland Security Federal Emergency Management Agency," 03/03/2013, http://www.fta.dot.gov/documents/FTA_FEMA_MOA.pdf.

[110] Some agencies and organizations have used the term "green infrastructure" more narrowly to define natural systems for stormwater management; however, the Task Force's Strategy Report is using the more expansive definition provided here.

[111] ESA PWA, Analysis Of The Costs And Benefits Of Using Tidal Marsh Restoration As A Sea Level Rise Adaptation Strategy In San Francisco Bay," 02/22/2013, http://www.bay.org/assets/FINAL%20D211228_00%20Cost%20and%20Benefits%20of%20Marshes%20022213.pdf; Shepard CC, Crain CM, Beck MW, "The Protective Role of Coastal Marshes: A Systematic Review and Meta-analysis," 11/23/2011, http://www.plosone.org/article/info%3Adoi%2F10.1371%2Fjournal.pone.0027374.

[112] Environmental Sensitivity Index (ESI) Atlases are a collection of maps that provide a concise summary of coastal resources that are at risk in the event of an oil or chemical spill. There are three distinct components to the maps and data: biological resources (such as birds and shellfish beds), sensitive shorelines (such as marshes and tidal flats), and human-use resources (such as public beaches and parks). Source: NOAA, ESI Maps, http://www.response.restoration.noaa.gov/esi.

[113] Leatherman, S.P., "Migration of Assateague Island, Maryland, by inlet and overwash processes," 1979; Donnelly, J.P., J. Butler, S. Roll, M. Wengren, and T. Webb III., "A backbarrier overwash record of intense storms from Brigantine, New Jersey," 2004; Roman, C.T., J.A. Peck, J.R. Allen, J.W. King, and P.G. Appleby, "Accretion of a New England (USA) salt marsh in response to inlet migration, storms, and sea-level rise," 1997; Fisher, J.J., and E.J. Simpson., "Washover and tidal sedimentation rates s environmental factors in development of a transgressive barrier shoreline" In: Leatherman, S.P. (ed.), "Barrier Islands: From the Gulf of St. Lawrence to the Gulf of Mexico," 1979.

[114] Costanza, Robert, Octavio Perez-Maqueo, M. Luisa Martinez, Paul Sutton, Sharolyn J. Anderson, and Kenneth Mulder, "The Value of Coastal Wetlands for Hurricane Protection," Ambio, 2008; USGS, "Meeting the science needs of the Nation in the wake of Hurricane Sandy—A U.S. Geological Survey science plan for support of restoration and recovery," http://www.pubs.usgs.gov/circ/1390/.

[115] Arkema, K.K., et. al., "Coastal habitats shield people and property from sea-level rise and storms," 07/14/2013, http://www.nature.com/nclimate/journal/vaop/ncurrent/full/nclimate1944.html.

[116] Disaster Relief Appropriations Act, 2013, http://www.gpo.gov/fdsys/pkg/PLAW-113publ2/html/PLAW-113publ2.htm.

[117] Federal agencies do not formally "adopt" the I-Codes, but do use them as guides for design and construction of Federal facilities. In general, Federal facilities are designed to conform with or exceed local building codes.

[118] The Rapid Repair program restored service to 11,744 buildings containing 20,257 residential units and 54,000 individuals. Source: City of New York, "Mayor Bloomberg Announces First-Of-Its-Kind NYC Rapid Repairs Program Completes Work On More Than 20,000 Homes Damaged By Hurricane Sandy," 03/22/2013, http://www.nyc.gov/portal/site/nycgov/menuitem.c0935b9a57bb4ef3daf2f1c701c789a0/index.jsp?pageID=mayor_press_release&catID=1194&doc_name=http%3A%2F%2Fwww.nyc.gov%2Fhtml%2Fom%2Fhtml%2F2013a%2Fpr109-13.html&cc=unused1978&rc=1194&ndi=1.

[119] DHS Office of Inspector General, "FEMA's Sheltering and Temporary Essential Power Pilot Program," 12/2012, http://www.oig.dhs.gov/assets/Mgmt/2013/OIG_13-15_Dec12.pdf.

[120] Red Bank Green, 03/2013, http://www.redbankgreen.com/2013/03/sea-bright-drops-unworkable-fema-fix.html.

[121] New York City Mayors office, http://www.nyc.gov/html/om/html/2013a/pr109-13.html.

[122] New York State Homes and Community Renewal, Office of Community Renewal, "State Of New York Action Plan For Community Development Block Grant Program Disaster Recovery," 04/2013, http://www.nyshcr.org/Publications/CDBGActionPlan.pdf.

[123] New Jersey Department of Community Affairs, "Community Development Block Grant Disaster Recovery Action Plan," approved 04/29/2013, http://www.state.nj.us/dca/announcements/pdf/CDBG-DisasterRecovery ActionPlan.pdf.

[124] City of New York, "Community Development Block Grant – Disaster Recovery Partial Action Plan A," http://www.nyc.gov/html/cdbg/downloads/pdf/cdbg-dr_full.pdf.

[125] A significant number of low-income households were impacted by the storm. Reports released in March 2013 by New York University's Furman Center for Real Estate and Urban Policy and by Enterprise Community Partners, Inc. indicate that 43% of those who registered for FEMA assistance were renters. Of all renter registrants, 64% in New York City and 67% in New Jersey are low income and less likely to have insurance. Sources: The Furman Center and the Moelis Institute for Affordable Housing Policy, "Sandy's Effects on Housing in New York City," 03/2013, http://www.furmancenter.org/files/publications/SandysEffectsOn HousingInNYC.pdf; Enterprise, "Measuring the Response to Hurricane Sandy," http://www.practitionerresources.org/showdoc.html?id=67899.

[126] New Jersey Department of Community Affairs, "Community Development Block Grant Disaster Recovery Action Plan," approved 04/29/2013, http://www.state.nj.us/dca/announcements/pdf/CDBG-DisasterRecoveryActionPlan.pdf.

[127] In October 2012 before Hurricane Sandy, single-family homeowner foreclosure filings in New York, New Jersey, and Connecticut were on the rise. Realty Trac Inc. reported an increase in default, auction, and repossession filings of 140% in New Jersey, 123% in New York and 41% in Connecticut from a year before.

In a February 2013 National Foreclosure Report, CoreLogic reports that in January 2013, New Jersey (at 7.2%) ranked second and New York (at 5.1%) third in the country behind Florida with the highest foreclosure inventory as a percentage of all mortgaged homes. The national average in January 2013 was 2.9%. In the March 2013 CoreLogic report, New Jersey (at 7.3%) and New York (at 5.0%) continue to rank second and third in the nation behind Florida. Sources: RealtyTrac, 11/13/2013, http://www.realtytrac.com/content/foreclosure-market-report/october-2012-us-foreclosure-market-report-7474; CoreLogic, 02/28/2013, http://www.corelogic.com/about-us/news/corelogic-reports-61,000-completed-foreclosures-in-january.aspx; CoreLogic, 04/30/2013, http://www.corelogic.com/about-us/news/corelogic-reports-55,000-completed-foreclosures-in-march.aspx.

[128] Munich Re estimates that applying the standard adds a few thousand dollars in construction costs per home but this cost is likely to be exceeded by expected savings on insurance premiums and deductibles, which in the Alabama pilot ranged between 25-50% Sources: Munich Re, "Interview: Carl Hedde Head of Risk Accumulation," http://www.munichreamerica.com/ind_cat_ mngmnt_hedde_ibhs.shtml; Insurance Institute for Business & Home Safety, "Disaster Safety Review: 20 Years After Hurricane Andrew Are We building Stronger?" 2012, http://www.disastersafety.org/wp-content/uploads/DSR-andrew-08-20121.pdf.

[129] FEMA, "Protecting Your Businesses," updated 03/01/2013, http://www.fema.gov/protecting-your-businesses.

[130] SBA Office of Advocacy, 2013, http://www.sba.gov/sites/default/files/files/WEB_11_Advo_Brochure.pdf.

[131] SBA Office of Advocacy, "Frequently Asked Questions," 09/2012, http://www.sba.gov/sites/default/files/FAQ_Sept_2012.pdf.

[132] 61.6% of workers with a disability are employed by a firm with fewer than 500 employees, and 62.7% of workers with a high school education or less are employed by a firm with fewer than 500 employees. Source: SBA Research and Statistics, "The Small Business Economy 2012," Appendix A, http://www.sba.gov/sites/default/files/files/Appendix_A_2012.xls.

[133] SBA, "Small Business Development Centers (SBDCs)," accessed 07/24/2013, http://www.sba.gov/content/small-business-development-centers-sbdcs.

[134] SBA, "Women's Business Centers," accessed 07/22/2013, http://www.sba.gov/local-assistance/wbc.

[135] SCORE, "About SCORE," accessed 07/22/2013, http://www.score.org/about-score.

[136] Business USA, accessed 07/22/2013, http://www.business.usa.gov/about-us.

[137] SBA Disaster Loan Application data, 2011-2012.

[138] SBA Disaster Loan Approval data, 2013.

[139] Ibid.

[140] Ibid.

[141] Ibid.

[142] SBA Disaster Loan Terms.

[143] SBA Microloan Program Data

[144] Treasury, "State Small Business Credit Initiative," updated 3/19/2013, http://www. treasury.gov/resource-center/sb-programs/Pages/ssbci.aspx.

[145] Ibid.

[146] A prime contract is a contract that is awarded directly by the Federal government to a business. It is distinct from a subcontract, which is a contract in which a business performs part or all of the obligations of another's contract.

[147] Task Force analysis of Federal Procurement Data System data, 08/01/2013, https://www.fpds.gov/.

[148] Ibid.

[149] SBA, "Goaling Program," accessed 07/24/2013, http://www.sba.gov/about-sba-services/2636.

[150] U.S. Department of Commerce, Office of the Chief Economist, draft report "Economic Impact of Super Storm Sandy

[151] According to the Bureau of Labor Statistics, unemployment rates in New Jersey, New York State, and New York City decreased by 0.9, 1.0, and 0.7 percentage points between September 2012 and June 2013, respectively. In comparison, national unemployment fell 0.2 percentage points in the same period. Source: Bureau of Labor Statistics, "Unemployment Rates for States," 06/2013, http://www.bls.gov/web/laus/laumstrk.htm; New York State Department of Labor, "Labor Statistics for the New York City Region," 06/2013, http://www.labor.ny.gov/stats/nyc/.

[152] Congressional Research Service, "The National Flood Insurance Program: Status and Remaining Issues for Congress", 02/06/2013 http://www.fas.org/sgp/crs/misc/R42850.pdf

[153] New York numbers from DFS as of June 14, 2013; New Jersey numbers from DBI and Insurance as of June 18, 2013; NFIP numbers from FEMA as of June 25, 2013.

[154] Office of the Governor of New York, "Governor Cuomo Announces DFS Investigation Identifies Banks with Worst Sandy Aid Statistics", 03/19/2013, https://www.governor.ny.gov/press/03192013cuomo_dfs_worst_sandy_aid

[155] Congressional Research Service, "The National Flood Insurance Program: Status and Remaining Issues for Congress", 02/06/2013, http://www.fas.org/sgp/crs/misc/R42850.pdf

[156] Federal Reserve Bank of New York, "2013 Small Business Borrowers Poll: Superstorm Sandy Insurance", 05/2013, http://www.newyorkfed.org/smallbusiness/2013

[157] Vrem, M.J. "Communicating Risk - Ten Key Learnings from the FloodSmart Campaign," Gilbert F. White National Flood Policy Forum 2010 Assembly, 2010 http://www.asfpmfoundation.org/pdf_ppt/2010_GFW_Forum_Background_Reading.pdf

[158] Society for Risk Analysis, "Policy Tenure Under the U.S. National Flood Insurance Program (NFIP)", 2011, http://cedm.epp.cmu.edu/files/pdfs/Erwann%20et%20al%20on%20flood%20insurance.pdf

[159] Lynda F. Williams, ICPD, Campaign Manager, America's PrepareAthon!

[160] FEMA

[161] "Buildings constructed after December 31, 1974, or after the publication of a flood insurance rate map (FIRM), are charged an actuarial premium that reflects the property's risk of flooding. Subsidized rates, on the other hand, are determined by a statutory mandate that requires rates to be affordable so individuals are encouraged to participate. Owners of properties built prior to the issuance of a community's flood hazard map or January 1, 1974 (Pre-Firm structures), usually pay subsidized rates and are exempted from the NFIP's floodplain management standards. Even properties that are remapped into higher-risk areas pay the subsidized rates — a situation that exacerbates the financial challenges facing the NFIP." Congressional Research Service, "The National Flood Insurance Program: Status and Remaining Issues for Congress," 02/06/2013, http://www.fas.org/sgp/crs/misc/R42850.pdf.

[162] Federal Emergency Management Agency, "National Flood Insurance Program – Frequently Asked Questions" 25/01/2013http://www.fema.gov/region-vi/national-flood-insurance-program-reform-frequently-asked-questions.

[163] U.S. Government Accountability Office, "National Flood Insurance Program Report", 2013, http://www.gao.gov/highrisk/national_flood_insurance/why_did_study.

[164] Special Initiative for Resilient Rebuilding, "PlaNYC: A Stronger, More Resilient New York", 06/11/2013 http://www.nyc.gov/html/sirr/downloads/pdf/final_report/Ch_2_ClimateAnalysis_FINAL_singles.pdf.

[165] V-zones are coastal areas with a 1percent or greater chance of flooding and an additional hazard associated with storm waves. These areas have a 26 percent chance of flooding over the life of a 30-year mortgage. https://msc.fema.gov/webapp/wcs/stores/servlet/info?storeId=10001&catalogId=10001&langId=-1&content=floodZones&title=FEMA%2520Flood%2520Zone%2520Designations.

[166] For this analysis, PD&R defines "LMI" is determined as people in households that are 80% or less of the HUD determined Area Median Income (AMI)

[167] New Jersey Department of Community Affairs Community Development Block Grant Disaster Recovery Action Plan. 01/29/2013. http://www.nj.gov/dca/announcements/pdf/CDBG-DisasterRecoveryActionPlan.pdf.

[168] Multihazard Mitigation Council, "Natural Hazard Mitigation Saves", 2005, http://c.ymcdn.com/sites/www.nibs.org/resource/resmgr/MMC/hms_vol1.pdf

[169] FEMA, "Mitigation Ideas: A Resource for Reducing Risk to Natural Hazards", 02/2013, http://www.fema.gov/library/viewRecord.do?id=6938.

[170] Special Initiative for Resilient Rebuilding, "PlaNYC: A Stronger, More Resilient New York", 06/11/2013 http://www.nyc.gov/html/sirr/downloads/pdf/final_report/Ch_2_ClimateAnalysis_FINAL_singles.pdf.

[171] The White House, "Statement of Administration Policy: S. 1940–Flood Insurance Reform and Modernization Act of 2011," 06/25/2012, http://www.whitehouse.gov/sites/default/files/omb/legislative/sap/112/saps1940s_20120625.pdf.

[172] Sandy Regional Assembly, "Sandy Regional Assembly Recovery Agenda," 04/2013, http://dl.dropboxusercontent.com/u/4969505/NYC-EJA/SandyRegionalAssemblyRecoveryAgenda_WEB_033013.pdf.

[173] New Jersey State Office of Emergency Management and FEMA, Comprehensive Damage Assessment, 5/8/2013.

[174] New York State Local Government, "Local Government in Long Island" http://www.nyslocalgov.org/pdf/Long_Island_Local_Govt.pdf.

[175] The New York State CDBG-DR Action Plan provides that "New York State will establish the Community Reconstruction Zone (NYRCR) planning grants. The State anticipates allocating approximately $25 million from this first allocation to provide planning grants to targeted communities selected by a NYRCR planning committee. Later allocations will be used to implement successful NYRCR plans." Source: New York State Office of Community Renewal, "State Of New York Action Plan For Community Development Block Grant Program Disaster Recovery," 04/2013, http://www.nyshcr.org/Publications/CDBGActionPlan.pdf.

[176] New York State Guidance for Community Reconstruction Zone Plans, accessed 07/23/2013, http://www.nysandyhelp.ny.gov/community-reconstruction-program.

[177] State of New York, "Governor Cuomo Designates 102 New York Rising Communities Eligible to Receive More Than $750 Million for Storm Reconstruction," 07/18/2013, http://www.governor.ny.gov/press/07182013-ny-rising-communities%20.

[178] Ibid.

[179] "Christie Administration Announces Post-Sandy Planning Assistance Grant Program," http://www.nj.gov/governor/news/news/552013/approved/20130618e.html.

[180] For more information, please see http://www.nj.gov/dca/services/lps/pdf/Post%20Sandy%20Planning%20Assistance%20Grant%20Program%20Guidelines.pdf.

[181] Rutgers University, Stevens Institute of Technology, New Jersey Institute of Technology, Stockton College, Monmouth University and Montclair State University.

[182] These assessments will draw on a framework for Health Impact Assessments (HIAs) created by the National Research Council and supported by The Health Impact Project, a collaboration of the Robert Wood Johnson Foundation and the Pew Charitable Trusts.

[183] FEMA, "Community Planning and Capacity Building Recovery Support Function," 09/2011, http://www.fema.gov/pdf/recoveryframework/community_planning_cpacity_building_rsf.pdf.

[184] "Executive departments and agencies should harness new technologies to put information about their operations and decisions online and readily available to the public." Source: The White House, "Memorandum for the Heads of Executive Departments and Agencies – Transparency and Open Government," 01/21/2009, http://www.whitehouse.gov/sites/default/files/omb/assets/memoranda_fy2009/m09-12.pdf.

[185] The White House, "Memorandum for the Heads of Executive Departments and Agencies: Open Data Policy – Managing Information as an Asset," 05/09/2013, http://www.whitehouse.gov/sites/ default/files/omb/memoranda/2013/m-13-13.pdf.

[186] As with all information releases, agencies should abide by applicable Fair Information Practice Principles.

[187] National Disaster Recovery Framework, 09/2011, http://www.fema.gov/pdf/recoveryframework/ndrf.pdf.

[188] Generally speaking, System of Record Notices (SORNs) are a Federal Register notice required by the Privacy Act that documents containing the rules for collection, maintenance, use, and dissemination of data sets containing PII. Please see the Privacy Act and OMB guidance for a more detailed description of SORNs.

[189] Privacy Act 5 U.S.C. 552a (a)(7), effective 01/07/2011, http://www.gpo.gov/fdsys/granule/USCODE- 2010-title5/USCODE-2010-title5-partI-chap5-subchapII-sec552a/content-detail.html.

[190] Disaster Relief Appropriations Act, 2013, http://www.gpo.gov/fdsys/pkg/PLAW-113publ2/html/PLAW-113publ2.htm.

[191] Machine readable data are that which is structured to allow for automated processes; this enables data that are readily retrieved, downloaded, organized, and searchable.

[192] This updated the 1993 Government Performance and Results Act (GPRA), revising the existing performance framework to increase the use of performance information driving program decision-making. This includes agencies producing more relevant and frequent data to inform agency decisions and operations. Source: GPRA Modernization Act of 2010, http://www.gpo.gov/fdsys/pkg/PLAW-111publ352/pdf/PLAW-111publ352.pdf.

[193] Note that PMO has focused on program administrative and financial data, and not on issues surrounding duplication of benefits. These issues are included in the Data Sharing Policy section of this document beginning on page 116

[194] Each agency has its own processes and funding sequence, but this is a typical sequence for grants and contracts which are not funded on a reimbursable basis.

[195] Center for American Progress, "The CitiStat Model: How Data-Driven Government Can Increase Efficiency & Effectiveness," 04/2007, http://www.americanprogress.org/wp-content/uploads/issues/2007/04/pdf/citistat_report.pdf.

[196] HUD Office of Inspector General, Audit Report 2013-FW-0001, 03/28/2013, http://www.hudoig.gov/Audit_Reports/2013-FW-0001. pdf; HUD Office of Inspector General, Memorandum 2013-IE-0803, 03/29/2013, http://www.hudoig.gov/Audit_Reports/2013-IE-0803.pdf; EPA Office of Inspector General, "Lessons Learned: EPA's Response to Hurricane Katrina," 9/14/2006, http://www.epa.gov/oig/reports/2006/20060914-2006-P-00033.pdf; DHS Office of Inspector General, "A Performance Review of FEMA's Disaster management Activities in Response to Hurricane Katrina," 03/2006, http://www.oig.dhs.gov/assets/Mgmt/OIG_06-32_Mar06.pdf; DHS Office of Inspector General, "Management Advisory Report: Recoupment of Improper Disaster Assistance Payments," 12/2010, http://www.oig.dhs.gov/assets/Mgmt/OIG_11-21_Dec10.pdf; GAO, "Hurricanes Katrina and Rita Disaster Relief Continued Findings of Fraud, Waste, and Abuse," 03/2007, http://www.gao.gov/new.items/d07300.pdf; GAO, "Disaster Recovery: Experiences from Past Disasters Offer Insights for Effective Collaboration after Catastrophic Events, 07/2009, http://www.gao.gov/assets/300/293529.pdf.

[197] GAO, "Hurricane Katrina: Ineffective FEMA Oversight of Housing Maintenance Contracts in Mississippi Resulted in Millions of Dollars of Waste and Potential Fraud," 11/2007, http://www.gao.gov/assets/270/269550.pdf.

[198] The White House, "A New Way of Doing Business: How The Recovery Act Is Leading The Way To 21st Century Government," 02/2011, http://www.whitehouse.gov/sites/default/files/new_way_of_doing_business.pdf.

[199] OMB Circular A-123, Management's Responsibility for Internal Control, establishes the requirement for all agencies to establish ICPs "to prevent waste, fraud, and abuse of Federal program funds." The Disaster Relief Act required agencies to expand existing internal controls to address specific risks associated with Sandy-

recovery related funding. Source: The White House, "Memorandum for the heads of Executive Departments and Agencies -- Accountability for Funds Provided by the Disaster Relief Appropriations Act, 03/12/2013, http://www.whitehouse.gov/sites/default/files/omb/memoranda/2013/m-13-07.pdf.

[200] Executive Order No. 13514, Federal Leadership in Environmental, Energy, and Economic Performance, October 5, 2009; National Environmental Policy Act section 101, 42 U.S.C. 4331United Nations General Assembly, 2005 World Summit Outcome, 60th Session, September 15, 2005.

[201] Presidential Policy Directive 8, National Preparedness, March 30, 2011; Presidential Policy Directive 21, Critical Infrastructure Security and Resilience, February 12, 2013. HHS, National Health Security Strategy of the United States of America, December 2009; NOAA and USACE, Infrastructure Systems Rebuilding Principles, February 28, 2013; CEQ, Progress Report of the Interagency Climate Change Adaptation Task Force: Recommended Actions in Support of a National Climate Change Adaptation Strategy, 2010.

[202] National Research Council, Science and Decisions: Advancing Risk Assessment, 2009.

[203] EPA, "Risk Assessment Principles and Practices,", 2004, http://www.epa.gov/osa/pdfs/ratf-final.pdf; FEMA, "Risk Assessment: A How-to Guide to Mitigate Terrorist Attacks,"01/2005, http://www.fema.gov/library/viewRecord.do?id=1559; Sayers, Paul., Y. Li, G. Galloway, E. Penning-Rowsell, F. Shen, K. Wen, Y. Chen, and T. Le Quesne, Flood Risk Management: A Strategic Approach, UNESCO, 2013.

[204] FEMA, National Mitigation Framework, May 2013; National Environmental Policy Act section 1508.2042 U.S.C. 4331; Presidential Policy Directive 8, National Preparedness, March 30, 2011.

[205] Plan EJ 2014: EPA's Plan EJ 2014 defines "overburdened populations" as minority, low-income, tribal, and indigenous populations or communities in the ES that potentially experience disproportionate environmental harms and risks as a result of greater vulnerability to environmental hazards. This increased vulnerability may be attributable to an accumulation of negative and a lack of positive environmental, health, economic, or social conditions within these populations.

[206] Remarks by the President in the State of the Union Address, 2/12/13, http://www.whitehouse.gov/state-of-the-union-2013

[207] Kunkel, K.E, L.E. Stevens, S.E. Stevens, L. Sun, E. Janssen, D. Wuebbles, and J.G. Dobson, "Regional Climate Trends and Scenarios for the U.S. National Climate Assessment. Part 9. Climate of the Contiguous United States," 2013, NOAA Technical Report NESDIS.

[208] Peterson, T.C., R.J. Heim, Jr., R. Hirsch, D.P. Kaiser, H. Brooks, N.S. Diffenbaugh, R.M. Dole, J.P. Giovannettone, K. Guiguis, T.R. Karl, R.W. Katz, K.E. Kunkel, D. Lettenmaier, G.J. McCabe, C.J. Paciorek, K. Ryberg, S. Schubert, V.B.S. Silva, B.C. Stewart, A.V. Vecchia, G. Villarini, R.S. Vose, J. Walsh, D. Wolock, K. Wolter, C.A. Woodhouse, M. Wehner, and D. Wuebbles, "Monitoring and understanding changes in heat waves, cold waves, floods and droughts in the United States: State of knowledge," 2013, Bull. Amer. Meteor. Soc.

[209] Kunkel, K.E, L.E. Stevens, S.E. Stevens, L. Sun, E. Janssen, D. Wuebbles, J. Rennells, A. DeGaetano, and J.G. Dobson, "Regional Climate Trends and Scenarios for the U.S. National Climate Assessment. Part 1. Climate of the Northeast U.S.," 2013, NOAA Technical Report NESDIS.

[210] DeGaetano, A. T., "Time-Dependent Changes in Extreme-Precipitation Return-Period Amounts in the Continental United States," 2009, J. Appl. Meteorol. Climatol.

[211] Villarini, G. and Vecchi, G.A., "21st Century Projections of North Atlantic Tropical Storms from CMIP5 Models," 2012, http://www.gfdl.noaa.gov/news-app/story.58.

[212] Knutson, T., J. Sirutis, G. Vecchi, S. Garner, M. Zhao, H. Kim, M. Bender, R. Tuleya, I. Held, and G. Villarini, "Dynamical Downscaling Projections of Twenty-First-Century Atlantic Hurricane Activity: CMIP3 and CMIP5 Model-Based Scenarios," 2013, J. Climate. doi:10.1175/JCLI-D-12-00539.1, in press.

[213] Squires, M.F., J.H. Lawrimore, R.R. Heim, D.A. Robinson, M. Gerbush, T. Estilow, C. Tabor, and A. Wilson, "Development of new snowstorm indices and databases at the National Climatic Data Center," 2009, Eos, Transactions of the AGU, 90(52), Fall Meeting Supplement, Abstract IN13A-1076 Poster.

[214] Kocin, P.J., L.W. Uccellini, "A snowfall impact scale derived from northeast storm snowfall distributions," 2004, Bull. Amer. Meteor. Soc., 85, 177–194. doi: 10.1175/BAMS-85-2-177

[215] Kunkel, K.E., T.R. Karl, H. Brooks, J. Kossin, J. Lawrimore, D. Arndt, L. Bosart, D. Changnon, S.L. Cutter, N. Doesken, K. Emanuel, P.Ya. Groisman, R.W. Katz, T. Knutson, J. O'Brien, C. J. Paciorek, T. Peterson, K. Redmond, D. Robinson, J. Trapp, R. Vose, S. Weaver, M. Wehner, K. Wolter, D. Wuebbles, "Monitoring and understanding changes in extreme storms: state of knowledge," Bull. Amer. Meteor. Soc., 94, doi: http://dx.doi.org/10.1175/BAMS-D-12-00066.1.

[216] Crowell, M, Westcott, J, Phelps, S, Mahoney, T, Coulton, K, and Bellomo, D, "Estimating the United States Population at Risk from Coastal Flood-Related Hazards," 2013, In: Coastal Hazards, C.W. Finkl (ed.), Springer: 151-183.

[217] Relative sea level – The height of the sea with respect to a specific point on land.

[218] Intergovernmental Panel on Climate Change (IPCC), "Summary for Policymakers. In: Managing the Risks of Extreme Events and Disasters to Advance Climate Change Adaptation," 2012, A Special Report of Working Groups I and II of the Intergovernmental Panel on Climate Change. Cambridge University Press, Cambridge, UK, and New York, NY, USA; Parris, A., P. Bromirski, V. Burkett, D. Cayan, M. Culver, J. Hall, R. Horton,

K. Knuuti, R. Moss, J. Obeysekera, A. Sallenger, and J. Weiss, "Global Sea Level Rise Scenarios for the US National Climate Assessment, 2012, NOAA Tech Memo OAR CPO-1.

[219] State and local officials, community planners, and infrastructure managers

[220] Parris, A., P. Bromirski, V. Burkett, D. Cayan, M. Culver, J. Hall, R. Horton, K. Knuuti, R. Moss, J. Obeysekera, A. Sallenger, and J. Weiss, "Global Sea Level Rise Scenarios for the US National Climate Assessment, 2012, NOAA Tech Memo OAR CPO-1.

[221] Weeks, D., Malone, P., and L. Welling, "Climate change scenario planning: A tool for managing parks into uncertain futures," 2011, Park Science, Volume 28, Number 1; Gray, S., "From Uncertainty to Action: Climate Change Projections and the Management of Large Natural Areas," 2011, BioScience 61(7); Intergovernmental Panel on Climate Change (IPCC), "Summary for Policymakers. In: Managing the Risks of Extreme Events and Disasters to Advance Climate Change Adaptation," 2012, A Special Report of Working Groups I and II of the Intergovernmental Panel on Climate Change. Cambridge University Press, Cambridge, UK, and New York, NY, USA.

[222] Moss, R., Edmonds, J. A., Hibbard, K.A., Manning, M.R., Rose, S.K., van Vuuren, D. P., Carter, T., Emori, S., Kainuma, M., Kram, T., Meehl, G. A., Mitchell, G. F. B., Nakicenovic, N., Riahi, K., Smith, S.J., Stouffer, R.J., Thomson, A.M., Weyant, J.P., and T.J. Wilbanks, "The next generation of scenarios for climate change research and assessment," 2010, Nature 463, 747-756 (11 February 2010) | doi:10.1038/nature08823; Weeks, D., Malone, P, and L. Welling, "Climate change scenario planning: A tool for managing parks into uncertain futures," 2011, Park Science, Volume 28, Number 1; Gray, S., "From Uncertainty to Action: Climate Change Projections and the Management of Large Natural Areas," 2011, BioScience 61(7).

[223] Parris, A., P. Bromirski, V. Burkett, D. Cayan, M. Culver, J. Hall, R. Horton, K. Knuuti, R. Moss, J. Obeysekera, A. Sallenger, and J. Weiss, "Global Sea Level Rise Scenarios for the US National Climate Assessment," 2012, NOAA Tech Memo OAR CPO-1.

[224] New York City Panel on Climate Change (NPCC), "Climate Change Adaptation in New York City: Building a Risk Management Response," 2010, prepared for use by the New York City Climate Change Adaptation Task Force, Annals of the New York Academy of Sciences, New York, NY.

[225] NPCC, "Climate Risk Information 2013: Observations, Climate Change Projections, and Maps," 2013, NPCC2, Prepared for use by the City of New York Special Initiative on Rebuilding and Resiliency, New York, New York.

[226] Rahmstorf, S., "A semi-empirical approach to projecting future sea-level rise," 2007, Science; Vermeer, M., Rahmstorf, S., "Global sea level linked to global temperature," 2009, Proceedings of the National Academy of Sciences, DOI: 10.1073/pnas.0907765106; Grinsted, A., Moore, J., Jevrejeva, S., "Reconstructing sea level from paleo and projected temperatures 200 to 2100 AD," 2010, Climate Dynamics.

[227] Meehl, G.A., Hu, A., Tebaldi, C., Arblaster, J.M., Washington, W.M., Teng, H., Sanderson, B.M., Ault, T., Strand, W.G., White, J.B., "Relative outcomes of climate change mitigation related to global temperature versus sea-level rise," 2012, Nature Clim. Change 2.

[228] CCSP, "Coastal Sensitivity to Sea-Level Rise: A Focus on the Mid-Atlantic Region. A report by the US Climate Change Science Program and the Subcommittee on Global Change Research," U.S. Environmental Protection Agency, Washington D.C., USA.

[229] Poag, C.W., Koeberl, Christian, Reimold, W.U., "The Chesapeake Bay Crater," 2004, New York; Hayden, T., Kominz, M., Powars, D., Edwards, L., Miller, K., Browning, J., and Kulpecz, A., "Impact effects and regional tectonic insights: Backstripping the Chesapeake Bay impact structure," 2008, Geology, v. 36.

[230] Sallenger, A., Doran, K, and Howd, P., "Hotspot of accelerated sea-level rise on the Atlantic coast of North America," Nature Climate Change, DOI: 10.1038/NCLIMATE1597.

[231] Yin J, Griffies SM, Stouffer RJ, "Spatial variability of SLR in twenty-first century projections," 2010, J Climate 23:4585–4607.

[232] Chambers, D.P., Merrifield, M.A., Nerem, R.S., "Is there a 60-year oscillation in global mean sea level?" 2012, Geophysical Research Letters 39, L18607.

[233] Boon, John D., "Evidence of Sea Level Acceleration at U.S. and Canadian Tide Stations, Atlantic Coast, North America," Journal of Coastal Research, 28(6); Yin J, Griffies SM, Stouffer RJ, "Spatial variability of SLR in twenty-first century projections," 2010, J Climate 23:4585–4607; Sallenger, A., Doran, K, and Howd, P., "Hotspot of accelerated sea-level rise on the Atlantic coast of North America," Nature Climate Change, DOI: 10.1038/NCLIMATE1597.

[234] Relative to a 2002 baseline.

[235] Zhang K., Douglas B. C., Leatherman S. P., "Twentieth-Century Storm Activity along the U.S. East Coast," 2000, J. Climate, 13; Grinsted, A., Moore, J.C., Jevrejeva, S., "Projected Atlantic hurricane surge threat from rising temperatures," 2013, Proceedings of the National Academy of Sciences. DOI: 10.1073/pnas.1209980110.

[236] Intergovernmental Panel on Climate Change (IPCC), "Summary for Policymakers. In: Managing the Risks of Extreme Events and Disasters to Advance Climate Change Adaptation," 2012, A Special Report of Working Groups I and II of the Intergovernmental Panel on Climate Change. Cambridge University Press, Cambridge, UK, and New York, NY, USA.

[237] Cayan, D.R., P.D. Bromirski, K. Hayhoe, M. Tyree, M.D. Dettinger and R.E. Flick, "Climate change projections of sea level extremes along the California coast," 2008, Climatic Change, 87, (Suppl 1), doi:10.1007/s10584-007-9376-7.

[238] Hapke, C.J., Himmelstoss, E.A., Kratzmann, M., List, J.H., and Thieler, E.R., 2011, National assessment of shoreline change; historical shoreline change along the New England and Mid-Atlantic coasts: U.S. Geological Survey Open-File Report 2010-1118, 57 p.

[239] Gutierrez, B.T., Plant, N.G., Thieler, E.R., "A Bayesian network to predict coastal vulnerability to sea level rise," 2011, J. Geophys. Res. 116, F02009.

[240] Horton, R. M., V. Gornitz, D. A. Bader, A. C. Ruane, R. Goldberg, and C. Rosenzweig, "Climate Hazard Assessment for Stakeholder Adaptation Planning in New York City," 2011, J Appl Meteorol Clim, 50, 2247-2266. doi:10.1175/2011JAMC2521.1.

[241] Mote, P., Petersen, A., Reeder, S., Shipman, H. and Binder, L., "Sea Level Rise in the Coastal Waters of Washington State," 2008, A report by the University of Washington – Climate Impacts Group and the Washington Department of Ecology.

[242] Smits, A.J.M., Nienhuis, P.H., and Saeijs, H.L.F., "Changing Estuaries, Changing Views," 2006, Hydrobiologia 565; Parris, A. and L. Lacko, "Climate change adaptation in the San Francisco Bay: A case for managed realignment," 2009, Shore and Beach, vol. 77.

[243] Dow, K, Berhout, F, Preston, B, Klein, R.J.T, Midgley, G, Shaw, R.B., "Limits to adaptation," 2013 Nature Climate Change 3, doi:10.1038/nclimate1847.

[244] International Association for Public Participation, http://www.iap2.org/.

In: Hurricane Sandy Rebuilding Strategy and Progress Update     ISBN: 978-1-63321-826-0
Editor: Lorayne Tucker                                  © 2014 Nova Science Publishers, Inc.

*Chapter 2*

# HURRICANE SANDY REBUILDING STRATEGY: PROGRESS UPDATE - SPRING 2014[*]

## *Hurricane Sandy Rebuilding Task Force*

## BACKGROUND

On August 19, 2013, the Hurricane Sandy Rebuilding Task Force released its Rebuilding Strategy for the Sandy impacted region. The Rebuilding Strategy included a long-term plan for rebuilding that guides Sandy Supplemental spending to drive regional coordination and make communities more resilient to future disasters. The Rebuilding Strategy also aligns federal, state and local policies to achieve seven goals that are important to the long-term rebuilding of the region in the most economically efficient, ecologically robust and innovative ways possible. These goals are:

- Promoting Resilient Rebuilding through Innovative Ideas and a Thorough Understanding of Current and Future Risk
- Ensuring a Regionally Coordinated, Resilient Approach to Infrastructure Investment
- Restoring and Strengthening Homes and Providing Families with Safe, Affordable Housing Options
- Supporting Small Businesses and Revitalizing Local Economies
- Addressing Insurance Challenges, Understanding, and Affordability
- Building State and Local Capacity to Plan for and Implement Long-Term Recovery and Rebuilding
- Improving Data Sharing Between Federal, State, and Local Officials

The Rebuilding Strategy identified 69 specific recommendations across these broad goals as well as specific member agencies[1] to lead the implementation of each of them. Since the publication of the Rebuilding Strategy, these agencies have continued to work closely

---

[*] This is an edited, reformatted and augmented version of document issued June 2014.

together to move the recommendations forward and deliver on their commitments to the region and the President.

This report includes an update on the implementation of the Rebuilding Strategy goals and an additional section on the internal efforts to improve data sharing and accountability through the Sandy Program Management Office (PMO). This report is organized by each of the seven Rebuilding Strategy goals and the PMO; recommendations are grouped according to these goals. Each section of this report includes background information from the original Rebuilding Strategy, identifies the relevant leading agencies[1], and includes brief updates on highlighted areas of progress made since the publication of the Rebuilding Strategy through the spring of 2014. A full list of the Rebuilding Strategy recommendations is included as an appendix to this document. To learn more about the Task Force or the Sandy Supplemental, or to see the status of the Sandy Supplemental funding, please visit the following websites:

- Executive Order 13632, establishing the Hurricane Sandy Rebuilding Task Force: http://www.gpo.gov/fdsys/ pkg/DCPD-201200936/pdf/DCPD-201200936.pdf
- Disaster Relief Appropriations Act, 2013, or "Sandy Supplemental," which provided $50 billion in disaster relief funding to Federal agencies: http://www.gpo.gov/fdsys /pkg/PLAW-113publ2/pdf/PLAW-113publ2. pdf
- Recovery.gov Hurricane Sandy maps, for the latest status of Sandy Supplemental funds by state: http:// www.recovery.gov/Sandy/whereisthemoneygoing/maps/Pages /HudPmo.aspx

## REBUILDING STRATEGY GOAL: PROMOTING RESILIENT REBUILDING THROUGH INNOVATIVE IDEAS AND A THOROUGH UNDERSTANDING OF CURRENT AND FUTURE RISK[2]

It is increasingly important to take advantage of the latest data and technology to measure and manage risk. Flood risk maps need to incorporate what scientists know about the pace and impact of climate change on sea level and other environmental factors. At the same time, the demographics of at-risk communities—which change quickly and dramatically due to rapid urbanization and shifting work patterns—must be understood. In the Sandy region, and across the country, communities once thought to be safe from risk are now beginning to recognize they face greater vulnerability to extreme weather and other natural disasters than previously imagined.

A robust recovery must use good data and science to inform decision making. Evidence-based information, risk-based analysis, and robust cost-benefit analyses could help governments, businesses, and homeowners better invest in measures that increase resilience on the national, regional, and local levels. The National Climate Assessment represents the most recent science on climate-related impacts that highlight knowledge for improved policy decisions.

> **Lead Agencies**
>
> Department of Housing and Urban Development (HUD)
> National Oceanic and Atmospheric Administration (NOAA)
> Federal Emergency Management Agency (FEMA)
> United States Army Corps of Engineers (USACE)
> White House Council on Environmental Quality (CEQ)
> U.S. Global Change Research Program (USGCRP)

## Progress Update

The Task Force announced the implementation of its first recommendation – that all Sandy-related rebuilding projects funded by the Sandy Supplemental must meet a single uniform flood risk reduction standard – even before the release of the Rebuilding Strategy. The standard takes into account the increased risk the region is facing from extreme weather events, sea level rise and other impacts of climate change and applies to the rebuilding of structures that were substantially damaged and will be repaired or rebuilt with federal funding. In October 2013, NOAA and USACE in partnership with FEMA, CEQ, and USGCRP, completed a resiliency recommendation by releasing the sea-level rise viewer which offers access to data and information about the risks of sea level rise, storm surge, and flooding along the coastal United States. The web-based map has the potential to help business owners and community planners build, retrofit, or rebuild in a more resilient way.

The last recommendation in this area was to create a competition to inspire experts from around the world to develop innovative design solutions for the region. Launched in the summer of 2013 by HUD and the Task Force, the Rebuild by Design competition has produced regional, cross-disciplinary collaboration between state and local governments, international design teams, educational institutions, and the public.

After months of research and community engagement, ten Rebuild by Design teams unveiled their final proposals on April 3, 2014. The teams, along with hundreds of tri-state residents, local stakeholders, and government representatives, gathered to view the proposals. The resulting design innovations include growing breakwaters, the development of absorptive shorelines, off-shore islands, and regional tidal parks, and several proposals incorporate both ecological and financial resiliency. Winners have been selected and can be viewed at www.rebuildbydesign.org. Implementation of these winning projects will be undertaken by state and local stakeholders.

> **What this means for communities**
>
> Federal investments in resilience measures means that Sandy-affected communities will be **better protected against future storms and rising sea levels**. The region will soon benefit from the efforts of **world class design projects** developed specifically to address the needs and risks facing these communities, and community planners and businesses across the country now have **access to better** information about future risks to help them plan for a stronger, more resilient future.

## For More Information

- View NOAA's sea-level rise tool here: http://www.csc.noaa.gov/digitalcoast /tools/slrviewer
- Learn more about Rebuild by Design here: http://www.rebuildbydesign.org/
- Learn more about the National Climate Assessment here: http://www.globalchange. gov/what-we-do/assessment

# REBUILDING STRATEGY GOAL: ENSURING A REGIONALLY COORDINATED, RESILIENT APPROACH TO INFRASTRUCTURE INVESTMENT

The damage from Hurricane Sandy to infrastructure in the impacted region was unprecedented in scope and cost. The damage to a region from impacts to infrastructure is not only in the cost of repair and replacement, but in the severe and cascading impacts on assets and systems, and natural resources that form the framework of our communities. Impacts to infrastructure are especially hard on the most vulnerable in our communities as they have few options when needed services are not available. The goal of the Rebuilding Strategy is to ensure the rebuilding efforts are coordinated, timely, and effective and to encourage investment in systems, assets and nature-based protective features to help the region withstand and quickly recover from future disasters.

| **Lead Agencies** |
| --- |
| Department of Agriculture (USDA) |
| Department of Energy (DOE) |
| Department of Housing and Urban Development (HUD) |
| Department of Homeland Security (DHS) |
| Department of the Interior (DOI) |
| Department of Labor (DOL) |
| Department of Transportation (DOT) |
| Department of Health and Human Services (HHS) |
| Environmental Protection Agency (EPA) |
| Federal Emergency Management Agency (FEMA) |
| National Oceanic and Atmospheric Administration (NOAA) |
| National Telecommunications and Information Administration (NTIA) |
| US Army Corps of Engineers (USACE) |
| White House National Security Staff (NSS) |
| White House Council on Environmental Quality (CEQ) |
| Office of Management and Budget (OMB) |
| White House Office of Science and Technology (OSTP) |

## Progress Update

This section of the Rebuilding Strategy contains recommendations with the goal of ensuring a regionally coordinated, resilient approach to infrastructure investment. The first of these recommendations set forth a set of seven Resilience Guidelines for infrastructure projects. The seven Guidelines promote these concepts:

- Forward-looking, science-based comprehensive risk analysis
- Transparent and inclusive decision processes
- Regional coordination of resilience efforts
- Assurance of long-term efficacy and fiscal sustainability
- Environmentally sustainable and innovative solutions
- Use of targeted financial incentives
- Adherence to resilience performance standards

To date, key funding agencies, EPA, DOI, DOT/Federal Transit Administration (FTA), HUD, and USACE, have incorporated the Resilience Guidelines into their funding requirements to ensure grantees build back more resiliently and are measuring the effectiveness and impact of the Guidelines for Sandy recovery. In addition, an interagency policy team is currently looking at whether the Guidelines should be applied beyond the Sandy recovery efforts. Regional coordination, an integral part of the Guidelines, is underway at the Sandy Recovery Office through the Sandy Regional Infrastructure Resilience Coordination initiative, where a regional coordination effort that has brought Federal, state and local agencies together to discuss planned projects, shared funding opportunities, the required Federal review and permitting processes, and cascading benefits and impacts in the recovery process. The development of a Hurricane Sandy best practices template will help inform future federal recovery coordination.

Other efforts are underway to encourage the use of resilient energy strategies for key assets and systems, address the nexus between power and communications, power and public transportation, and between availability of funding and needed investment in infrastructure.[3] Each of these teams is identifying near term and longer term actions to address these issues.

In December of 2013, FTA released a Notice of Funding Availability allocating $3 billion in competitive grants for resiliency projects in the Sandy affected regions. The resiliency funds will be distributed to projects that reinforce the critical infrastructure necessary to support public transportation systems damaged by Hurricane Sandy. FTA's goal is to advance the best regionally coordinated projects, so taxpayers won't have to pay to restore the same transit services a second or third time.

DOT had also taken proactive steps to assist communities in preparing for, identifying infrastructure with the highest risk from, and strengthening resilience toward climate change and the potential for extreme weather events. In 2010-2011, the Federal Highway Administration (FHWA) funded 5 cities for a pilot program that conducted vulnerability and risk assessments of infrastructure to the projected impacts of global climate change. The purpose of the pilots was twofold; 1) to assist State DOTs and Metropolitan Planning Organizations (MPOs) more quickly advance existing adaptation assessment activities and 2) to assist FHWA in "test-driving" the model.

Based on the feedback and lessons learned through the pilots, FHWA revised the model into the Climate Change & Extreme Weather Vulnerability Assessment Framework. One such pilot program was awarded for New Jersey DOT/North Jersey Transportation Planning Authority that studied areas in Coastal and Central New Jersey.

To provide a base of scientific evidence for health officials, community members and leaders as they make decisions about health and social services, HHS awarded dozens of grants to conduct research in impacted communities on the health system's response, health care access, mental health, the health impacts of evacuation and other health resilience issues. Findings of these studies will be shared with the communities. A team of scientists, engineers, and policy analysts are also looking at how to better utilize nature-based (green) infrastructure alternatives (such as wetlands and open space) in projects.[4] The team is also looking at storm surge protection and how to share the data from these efforts in order to know what works best in different situations, as well as show how to best pursue a mixed approach – green and gray[5] infrastructure elements – to achieve the best results. To achieve this, the team is working to develop a better understanding of how to value green infrastructure to account for the extra benefits it may bring in the form of cleaner air, water, habitat for commercial species or recreational opportunities.

Finally, an interagency team lead by FEMA is working with stakeholders from across government and industry to promote better and stronger building codes so that all communities can benefit from a more resilient and safe approach to development.

---

**What this means for communities**

Federal infrastructure investments across the Sandy-affected region and nationwide will be **better coordinated** across federal agencies and **aligned with state and local stakeholders**, meaning that projects can be **delivered more efficiently** and with **more resilient outcomes for communities**.

---

## For More Information

- Learn more about FHWA's Climate Change Resilience Pilots here: https://www.fhwa.dot.gov/environmentclimate_change/adaptation/ongoing_and_current_research/vulnerability_assessment_pilots/
- Read the 2011 FHWA Coastal and Central New Jersey Pilot Study Report here: http://www.njtpa.org/Planning/Regional-Studies/Recently-Completed-Studies/Vulnerability-and-Risk-Assessment-of-NJTransporta/FHWAConceptualModel/CCVR_REPORT_FINAL_4_2_12_ENTIRE.aspx
- Read FTA's 2011 Flooded Bus Barns and Buckled Rails Report here: http://www.fta.dot.gov/documents/FTA_0001_-_Flooded_Bus_Barns_and_Buckled_Rails.pdf

## REBUILDING STRATEGY GOAL: RESTORING AND STRENGTHENING HOMES AND PROVIDING FAMILIES WITH SAFE, AFFORDABLE HOUSING OPTIONS

From the public housing projects in Queens and Brooklyn that remained without light and heat for days, to the beach front towns along the Jersey shore where surging tides plowed houses from their foundations and left them buried in sand, the storm upended tens of thousands of lives across the New York and New Jersey region. Sandy rendered individual homes and entire neighborhoods uninhabitable and, in some cases, unrecognizable.

Because the region has a high population density, a relatively expensive housing market, and low housing inventory, responding to the housing needs of affected residents raised challenges different from those faced in disasters such as Hurricanes Katrina, Ike, and Rita. Affordable, temporary housing units in close proximity to storm-affected neighborhoods were in short supply, which forced federal, state and local authorities to employ an array of policy tools to provide displaced individuals with a place to stay. Some of these tools had been used in past disasters, but many were significantly adapted or developed in real time to respond to Sandy.

---

**Lead Agencies**

Department of Housing and Urban Development (HUD)
Department of Treasury (Treasury)
Department of Health and Human Services (HHS)
Department of Homeland Security (DHS)
Environmental Protection Agency (EPA)
Federal Emergency Management Agency (FEMA)

---

## Progress Update

Lead agencies continue to make progress on completing the various housing recommendations, which range from speeding assistance to housing programs in the affected states and communities, to developing model affordable housing programs and interagency guidance on health related housing issues.

HUD allocated the first round of Community Development Block Grant - Disaster Recovery funding in just 8 days – faster than ever before. In total, HUD has now allocated $13 billion to the region to date.

A policy tool used to respond to Hurricane Sandy was HUD's Disaster Housing Assistance Program (DHAP), which provided temporary rental payments directly to landlords to help families displaced by the storm. Also, the IRS temporarily suspended tenant income limitations and non-transiency rules of the Low Income Housing Tax Credit to allow project owners to rent their vacant units to individuals and families who lost their homes due to Hurricane Sandy even if those individuals do not qualify as low-income persons.

FEMA's Sheltering and Temporary Essential Power (STEP) Pilot Program is a new policy tool that enabled States to work with residents to return to or remain in their homes by providing homeowners with funds for permanent repairs. This reduced the number of individuals in congregate shelters or in the FEMA Transitional Shelter Assistance (TSA) Program. Currently FEMA is in the middle of evaluating the effectiveness of STEP and has to date completed its customer surveys and is evaluating this feedback.

A model affordable housing program was created working with the Federal Housing Administration (FHA) and a New Jersey-based community development financial institution to purchase FHA single-family distressed loans in the most impacted counties, and to allow homeowners to make repairs while they remained in their homes. More than 125 homeowners (25% of the total portfolio of loans) already have loan modifications in progress and will be able to repair and retain their homes.

HUD and Treasury in partnership with New York City's Housing Development Corporation, continue to make progress in developing a multifamily risk-sharing model to finance affordable housing projects in New York City.

Finally, together FEMA, EPA, HHS and HUD are currently on target to issue consolidated guidance on the mediation of indoor air pollutants (e.g. mold, lead, and radon) with an anticipated publication date of late summer 2014.

---

**What this means for communities**

Agencies have worked to get money for housing to communities **faster than ever before,** are exploring new ways **to protect homeowners in disaster affected areas who are in danger of losing their homes to foreclosure,** and are working to ensure that homes impacted by disasters are rebuilt **healthy and safe.**

---

## For More Information

- Learn more about HUD's Community Development Block Grant – Disaster Recovery here: http://portal.hud. gov/hudportal/HUD?src=/program_offices/comm_ planning/communitydevelopment/programs/drsi
- For more background on FEMA's Sheltering and Temporary Essential Power (STEP) Pilot Program: http://www.fema.gov/media-library/assets/documents /29829?id=6709

## REBUILDING STRATEGY GOAL: SUPPORTING SMALL BUSINESSES AND REVITALIZING LOCAL ECONOMIES

Small businesses are particularly vulnerable to disasters because they often have small profit margins and cannot sustain extended business interruption. They also typically lack adaptive business management models, tend to be underinsured, and often depend on generating revenues from customers and clients who have also been impacted by the disaster. Disasters amplify existing economic issues for small businesses and entrepreneurs.

The Task Force recognized the role small businesses play in recovery and rebuilding after a disaster. Small businesses, such as grocery stores, pharmacies, and gasoline stations, provide services in their communities. Furthermore, small business contractors may contribute to economic recovery by taking on government contracts for rebuilding and long-term resilience and hiring a local workforce to do the work.

| **Lead Agencies** |
| --- |
| Department of Housing and Urban Development (HUD)<br>Department of Labor (DOL)<br>Department of the Treasury (Treasury)<br>Federal Emergency Management Agency (FEMA)<br>Small Business Administration (SBA) |

## Progress Update

The Rebuilding Strategy recommendations in this area are being implemented by SBA, HUD, Treasury, Labor, and the FEMA-led Recovery Support Function Leadership Group (RSFLG). Actions for all recommendations are in various stages of development.

SBA has completed several innovative improvements to its Disaster Loan Program, and published an interim final rule on April 25, 2014 that implements changes to expedite processing of applications from disaster victims with strong credit and to increase the amount of disaster assistance funds that can be disbursed to borrowers immediately following loan closings.

Further, SBA is developing legislative proposals to remove statutory barriers for some of its programs, to provide additional technical assistance to small businesses before and after disasters, and to better use business accelerators to promote recovery and growth following disasters. SBA also completed actions to improve small business contracting opportunities in Sandy rebuilding and has drafted language for statutory changes to the HUBZone program for disaster affected areas.

Treasury and HUD have continued to raise awareness of the use of Community Development Financial Institutions (CDFIs) for disaster recovery. HUD has encouraged Community Development Block Grant - Disaster Recovery (CDBG-DR) grantees to consider the provision of grant funds to a broad range of community organizations, including CDFIs, to help grantees address unmet needs through grantee training conferences, publication in the November 18, 2014 Federal Register Notice regarding CDBG-DR allocations, and in ongoing technical assistance with grantees.

Section 3 of the Housing and Urban Development Act of 1968 requires that certain HUD-assisted projects provide opportunities for training and employing low-income persons. The HUD Office of Fair Housing & Equal Opportunity, in coordination with the HUD Office of Community Planning and Development delivered Section 3 training to all three grantees (New York, New Jersey, and New York City). An ongoing process has been established to deliver additional training as necessary and in response to future monitoring.

DOL's Employment & Training Administration has provided more than $70 million in National Emergency Grants to affected states. Additionally DOL has assisted State Departments of Labor in sharing best practices. DOL representatives from the Occupational Safety & Health Administration, the Wage Hour Division, the Office of Federal Contract Compliance Programs & the Office of Congressional and Intergovernmental Affairs continue to work with the Regional Infrastructure Working Group to coordinate with every Federal and State agency that is financing recovery and resilience projects.

---

**What this means for communities**

Agencies are working to **speed funding to small businesses** after disasters, to expand the role of **community-based financial institutions** after disasters, to compile and align information about **federal resources available to small businesses** in the wake of a disaster, and to ensure that the Federal investments after a disaster **provide economic opportunities to those who need them most.**

---

## For More Information

- SBA Website with small business assistance information: www.sba.gov/sandy
- SBA Government Contracting Information: www.sba.gov/gcclassroom
- Federal Register Notice: www.gpo.gov/fdsys/pkg/FR-2013-11-18/pdf/2013-27506.pdf
- CDFI Research Information: http://cdfifund.gov/impact_we_make/research/CDFI_Response_to_Superstorm_Sandy_Impact_Assessment.pdf
- HUD Small Business Grant and Loan Program Toolkit: https://www.onecpd.info/cdbg-dr/toolkits/smallbusiness-loan-and-grant/
- HUD Section 3 Resources: http://portal.hud.gov/hudportal/HUD?src=/program_offices/fair_housing_ equal_opp/section3/section3

## REBUILDING STRATEGY GOAL: ADDRESSING INSURANCE CHALLENGES, UNDERSTANDING, AND AFFORDABILITY

When risks are known and disasters are imminent, individuals can take immediate precautions, such as boarding up windows when the forecast predicts high winds, seeking shelter during tornadoes, and clearing basements of valuables in the face of floods. Businesses can likewise prepare for disruption and, in some cases, plan to operate remotely. For risks less imminent and/or more difficult to predict, insurance can be an important line of defense against economic loss. In the absence of insurance, the cost of repairing damaged property is usually borne by the property/business owner or through Federal assistance and often has negative social consequences—disrupting lives and livelihoods.

There are two approaches to reducing the cost of recovery from future disasters. The first is to mitigate and reduce risk by moving out of harm's way or hardening properties to better withstand floods or other hazards. The second is to insure property and spread the risk. The

Task Force is proposing initiatives to encourage investment in both hazard mitigation and insurance. For these approaches to be effective, individuals need to understand their risks, take steps to reduce risk, and invest in applicable insurance products that will adequately transfer their risk in the case of a disaster.

| Lead Agencies |
| --- |
| Department of Housing and Urban Development (HUD)<br>Department of Treasury (Treasury)<br>Federal Emergency Management Agency (FEMA) |

## Progress Update

With the recent passage of the Homeowner Flood Insurance Affordability Act of 2014, there are legislative requirements that now further support and provide guidance to assist in implementing and completing the insurance recommendations in the Rebuilding Strategy.

For example, the legislation calls for the standing up of a Technical Mapping Advisory Council (TMAC) to provide guidance on various aspects of improving mapping, including incorporation of the best available climate science to assess flood risks and use of the best methodology for impact of sea level rise. The recommendation to improve the National Flood Insurance Program (NFIP) policyholder awareness of factors that affect flood risk and insurance rating decisions is supported by the Act which requires a Flood Insurance Advocate. In part, the Advocate will be responsible for educating policy holders about their individual flood risks, their options in choosing a policy and assisting property owners through the map appeal process. The TMAC will better equip FEMA to make accurate long-term rating decisions and is critical to the effectiveness of the Flood Insurance Advocate.

Another recommendation that will be implemented through the Homeowner Flood Insurance Affordability Act of 2014 is the analysis of the affordability of flood insurance and the impact of increased premiums on economically distressed households. The Act retains the provision from the Biggert-Waters Flood Insurance Reform Act of 2012 that requires FEMA to conduct an affordability study, but adds additional criteria to be included in the study, and also requires FEMA to draft an affordability framework to address the issues of affordability of flood insurance sold under NFIP.

A final example is the recommendation to encourage increased hazard mitigation activities, including elevation, in order to protect property against future losses. This recommendation will be met through the Act's requirement that FEMA establish guidelines for property owners that provide other alternative methods of mitigation, other than building elevation to reduce flood risk to residential buildings that cannot be elevated due to their structural characteristics. FEMA must also inform property owners about how the implementation of mitigation methods may affect their risk premium rates for flood insurance coverage under the NFIP. Upon implementation of these legislative requirements, the recommendations will be completed or revised accordingly.

> **What this means for communities**
>
> The new legislation will ensure that key components of the Task Force recommendations will be implemented and even expanded upon – resulting in **homeowners having more information** and a **new affordability framework** for the NFIP.

## For More Information

- For NFIP reform and updates: http://www.fema.gov/flood-insurance-reform

# REBUILDING STRATEGY GOAL: BUILDING STATE AND LOCAL CAPACITY TO PLAN FOR AND IMPLEMENT LONG-TERM RECOVERY AND REBUILDING

The scope and scale of Hurricane Sandy challenged the uneven capacities of state and local governments, which also faced differences in needs and readiness for disaster recovery. Many of the municipalities that experienced severe river flooding and the coastal towns along the New Jersey Shore and on Long Island are without full time planners, city managers, grants managers, engineers, and architects, and do not have the in-house capabilities to lead comprehensive, long-term recovery planning efforts on their own.

Planning for recovery from a catastrophic event like Sandy is a massive challenge for even the best prepared communities and it should not be postponed until the immediate response is complete. Recovery planning and decision-making take place under severe time constraints and deal with the rebuilding of multiple systems simultaneously. This effort involves stakeholders who have been traumatized and triggers funding sources not normally available. Successful recovery under such difficult circumstances depends on two critical factors: planning and capacity building.

> **Lead Agencies**
>
> Department of Housing and Urban Development (HUD)
> Federal Emergency Management Agency (FEMA)

## Progress Update

The FEMA-led Community Planning and Capacity Building Recovery Support Function (CPCB RSF) supported both New York and New Jersey in coordinating assistance from over 15 federal agencies to assist states and communities in organizing, planning and building recovery management capability across the affected area. FEMA and the CPCB RSF also drew on the support of a wide range of professional and community-based organizations (CBOs) and non-profits including: the American Planning Association in New York and New

Jersey, Sustainable Long Island, the Environmental Protection Agency's (EPA) Office of Research and Development and Office of Sustainable Communities, the National Renewable Laboratory, the New Jersey League of Municipalities, Sustainable Jersey, and New Jersey Future, among a host of organizations, to offer recovery planning training, consultation, and other forms of technical assistance to local community leaders across the declared counties.

Further, federal agencies have partnered with other state agencies as well as, CBOs and educational institutions to convene symposiums, forums, and roundtable discussions to better inform local communities and the general public on disaster preparedness and long-term community disaster recovery. One example of a best practice partnership between local government and an academic institution is the HHS-funded Extramural Hurricane Sandy Recovery Research program. Principal investigators from Columbia University and NYC Department of Health and Mental Hygiene collaborated to leverage existing guidelines and research on vulnerable populations affected by Hurricane Sandy in order to further augment the department's health  guidelines to address catastrophic flooding. CPCB RSF and its partners in New Jersey also worked with academic institutions to match academic programs with community needs. Participating institutions, such as Stockton, New Jersey Institute of Technology, Rowan and Rutgers Universities have worked together to provide qualified students for a variety of recovery activities such as "Alternative Spring Break" community recovery support, developing marketing and tourism plans, and grant writing assistance.

In New York, the CPCB RSF and its partners assisted the State in launching the New York Rising Community  Reconstruction Program by developing 11 guidance and recovery planning related documents and providing 104 "fact packs" containing Geographic Information System data and community conditions information for communities affected by Hurricanes Sandy, Irene and Tropical Storm Lee. The partnership between CPCB RSF, the Housing Recovery Support Function, and numerous non-governmental organizations created an interactive Resource Mapping Tool that links damaged New York communities to available information resources. State and local entities are already utilizing this decision-making tool to identify resource gaps. More than 150 Federal, State and county level recovery practitioners participated in community planning and capacity building training events organized through the Smart Growth Initiative (a working group comprised of representatives from EPA, FEMA, Metropolitan Transportation Authority – New York (MTA), and Nassau and Suffolk County) to build capacity for engaging community stakeholders in recovery planning. In New Jersey, CPCB RSF and partners held a Recovery Resource Summit where more than 100 representatives from federal, state, local, NGO, and philanthropic organizations had an opportunity to network with partners and identify potential resources. Also in New Jersey, CPCB RSF and its partners assisted Cumberland County to develop and implement a recovery planning process that resulted not only in a recovery strategy but additionally created a Local Resilience Partnership, as adjacent communities came together to build a more resilient future.

Early conversations between CPCB RSF and the philanthropic community resulted in the placement of recovery managers supporting six communities. Local disaster recovery management capacity has been increased throughout the affected area by providing training and funding for Local Disaster Recovery Managers (LDRMs). HUD encouraged the use of Community Development Block Grant - Disaster Recovery (CDBG-DR) grants to support the establishment of LDRMs in their Notice of Funding Availability in the Federal Register. LDRM job descriptions and information have been made available to local communities through interagency, state and non-profit partners. As a result, local disaster recovery staff have already been placed to support several New Jersey communities.

---

**What this means for communities**

Local leaders are getting **more information, training,** and **new resources** to help them **plan for and manage disaster recovery in their communities.**

---

## For More Information

- New York State Rising Program: http://stormrecovery.ny.gov/community
- Wall Street Journal article on FEMA symposia with Education and other institutions to improve resilience and local partnerships: http://online.wsj.com/news/articles /SB10001424052702304886904579475371378 044120
- CDBG-DR Second Allocation Federal Register Notice provides eligibility for funding Local Disaster Recovery Managers on page 69110 http://www.gpo.gov /fdsys/pkg/FR-2013-11-18/pdf/2013-27506.pdf
- Resource Mapping Tool: http://fema.maps.arcgis.com/home/webmap/viewer. html?webmap=c8e880eb4e7f4996ac26947884205da0
- New York City Department of Health and Mental Hygiene: http://www.nyc.gov/html /doh/html/ environmental/moldrpt1.shtml

## REBUILDING STRATEGY GOAL: IMPROVING DATA SHARING BETWEEN FEDERAL, STATE, AND LOCAL OFFICIALS

The use of data facilitates decision-making that is well-informed and leads to goals that are both clearly defined and realistically achievable. In post-disaster situations, data collection and application are especially important for on-the-ground recovery efforts, as well as for long-term policy formulation and program management. Data and information are extremely valuable to Federal, Tribal, State, and local governments, as well as to private citizens, businesses, non-profits, and other community groups.

---

**Lead Agencies**

Department of Housing and Urban Development (HUD)
Federal Emergency Management Agency (FEMA)
Small Business Administration (SBA)

---

## Progress Update

The Task Force report recommends improving data sharing between and among federal agencies and between and among federal, state, and local agencies. The agencies leading these efforts have made progress on many of these recommendations, and are working closely to implement longer-term goals.

Key accomplishments to date include increased flexibility for FEMA to share valuable recovery data with other federal agencies by renewing its Disaster Recovery Assistance Files System of Records Notice (SORN) and by publishing its Hazard Mitigation, Disaster Public Assistance (PA), and Disaster Loan Programs SORN. FEMA also issued a Policy for its Recovery data aimed at sharing data expediently and securely. FEMA launched a website explaining its information sharing processes and instructions to its key stakeholders (federal, state, local, tribal and certain established voluntary organizations). FEMA will soon place a data element glossary and sample report on the site. FEMA plans to create a similar, public-facing website. Further, HUD, SBA, and FEMA are working together to define disaster relevant data sets that will be published to the Administration's data.gov website.

Finally, FEMA and HUD are establishing an interagency data exchange that would allow both agencies to share and access critical information in real (or expedient) time, improving operations and program delivery at both agencies. The Disaster Assistance Improvement Program has finalized system requirements and design for an automated data exchange between FEMA and HUD that will allow the agencies to share relevant disaster data necessary to make eligibility determinations and reduce duplicative payments for housing assistance following a disaster. Though the initial focus is on HUD and FEMA, once built, this system could in the future be expanded to include data from other agencies as well.

---

**What this means for communities**

State and local partners will be able to **access and understand valuable federal agency disaster data.** Federal agencies will be able to expediently and securely **share information** among one another and other stakeholders, thus accelerating **disaster relief efforts and assistance.**

---

## For More Information

- FEMA's Hazard Mitigation, Disaster Public Assistance (PA), and Disaster Loan Programs SORN: http://www. gpo.gov/fdsys/pkg/FR-2014-03-24/pdf/2014-06361.pdf

# DATA SHARING AND ACCOUNTABILITY THROUGH THE PROGRAM MANAGEMENT OFFICE (PMO)

The Program Management Office (PMO) provides a concrete example of the ways in which open and transparent data sharing practices between agencies can encourage smarter and more effective decision making in recovery and rebuilding efforts. The size, complexity, and urgency of the funding for Hurricane Sandy recovery made it clear -- even before the Sandy Supplemental was enacted -- that the Task Force needed a central coordinating office that would work closely with agencies, OMB, and the oversight community, such as the agency Inspectors General and the Recovery Accountability and Transparency Board (RATB). PMO was also established to leverage lessons learned from Hurricane Katrina, as well as best practices from the American Recovery and Reinvestment Act of 2009 (ARRA).

| Lead Agencies |
| --- |
| Department of Housing and Urban Development (HUD)<br>Federal Emergency Management Agency (FEMA) |

## Progress Update

Since the Hurricane Sandy Rebuilding Task Force and its Program Management Office (PMO) disbanded on time and under budget on September 30, 2013, the PMO function has successfully continued through the Sandy PMO within HUD. In partnership with FEMA, the Sandy PMO has completed its two recommendations.

The Sandy PMO continued and expanded upon the role of the Task Force PMO, by growing its monitoring system beyond the supplemental funding and performance data to include implementation tracking for the 69 recommendations of the Rebuilding Strategy. The Sandy PMO has also organized and provided data for three Sandy Principals' meetings, co-chaired by the Secretary of HUD and the FEMA Administrator, ensuring continued cabinet-level engagement in this important work, even after the sunset of the Task Force.

The PMO has partnered with the RATB to improve transparency of the supplemental funding by providing regular data to the public in the form of maps and downloadable files. Finally, the PMO created a new resource for federal agencies - a PMO Toolkit - which documents and compiles key lessons, tools, and tips for the development of a PMO so that they may be replicated in the event of a future disaster, or in response to other large, cross-agency Supplemental appropriations.

The PMO has ensured that longer-term recovery continues by monitoring implementation of the Sandy recommendations and the Sandy Supplemental funding progress by supporting cabinet-level engagement through quarterly Principals meetings.

| What this means for communities |
| --- |
| The PMO provides **transparency for the public on the progress of recovery**, and **accountability for Federal agency partners**, by providing detailed information on the progress of the Supplemental funding, and periodic reports on the implementation of the Rebuilding Strategy recommendations. |

## For More Information

- State level Sandy Supplemental Financial Data: http://www.recovery.gov/Sandy/whereisthemoneygoing/maps/Pages/HudPmo.aspx

## APPENDIX: RECOMMENDATIONS FROM THE HURRICANE SANDY REBUILDING STRATEGY

### Resilience: Promoting Resilient Rebuilding through Innovative Ideas and a thorough Understanding of Current and Future Risk

1) Facilitate the incorporation of future risk assessment, such as sea level rise, into rebuilding efforts with the development of a sea-level rise tool.
2) Develop a minimum flood risk reduction standard for major Federal investment that takes into account data on current and future flood risk.
3) Create a design competition to develop innovative resilient design solutions that address the Sandy-affected region's most pressing vulnerabilities.

### Infrastructure: Ensuring a Regionally Coordinated, Resilient Approach to Infrastructure Investment

4) Apply Infrastructure Resilience Guidelines to all Federal infrastructure investments and projects for Sandy recovery.
5) Consider applying the Infrastructure Resilience Guidelines nationally.
6) Federal, State, and local agencies should continue to coordinate Sandy recovery infrastructure resilience projects.
7) Institutionalize regional approaches to resilience planning in the NDRF and the National Mitigation Framework.
8) Establish a Sandy Regional Infrastructure Permitting and Review Team that leverages the Executive Order 13604 framework for Sandy projects.
9) Leverage the Executive Order 13604 framework to identify opportunities to expedite and improve other types of review processes through programmatic agreement or consultation where appropriate.
10) Disaster recovery efforts should account for the temporary staffing needs of Federal agencies and State and local governments who conduct reviews and permitting of Federal disaster recovery projects.
11) Provide technical assistance to States and localities to help optimize Sandy recovery infrastructure funding, share best practices, leverage resources, advance sustainability, and meet the needs of vulnerable communities.
12) Ensure that Sandy recovery energy investments are resilient.
13) Mitigate future impacts to the liquid fuels supply chain like those experienced during the Sandy recovery.
14) Encourage Federal and State cooperation to improve electric grid policies and standards.
15) Mobilize the private sector and non-profit community to develop innovative solutions that support and integrate whole community efforts for disaster relief.
16) Develop a resilient power strategy for wireless and data communications infrastructure and consumer equipment.
17) Expedite flow of Sandy transportation funding to needed repairs.

18) Align Sandy transportation funding expenditures with national policy goals.

19) Consider green infrastructure options in all Sandy infrastructure investments.

20) Improve the understanding and decision-making tools for green infrastructure through projects funded by the Sandy Supplemental.

21) Create opportunities for innovations in green infrastructure technology and design using Sandy funding, particularly in vulnerable communities.

22) Develop a consistent approach to valuing the benefits of green approaches to infrastructure development and develop tools, data, and best practices to advance the broad integration of green infrastructure.

23) Ensure Sandy recovery water infrastructure investments are timely, resilient, sustainable, and effective.

24) Ensure Sandy recovery water infrastructure projects are coordinated with other infrastructure investments.

25) States and localities should adopt and enforce the most current version of the IBC and the IRC. *(IBC: International Building Code; IRC: International Residential Code)*


## Housing: Restoring and Strengthening Homes and Providing Families with Safe, Affordable Housing Options

26) For future disasters that affect high-density and high cost areas, shelter-in-place programs like New York City's Rapid Repair and FEMA's Sheltering and Temporary Essential Power (STEP) programs should be implemented to reduce the number of people displaced from their homes who would otherwise require short term housing. Evaluate the effectiveness of STEP and compare outcomes to other forms of temporary emergency sheltering implemented in response to Sandy. In addition, evaluate the New York, New Jersey, and New York City implementation of sheltering in place programs.

27) HUD should expedite future allocations from the remaining CDBG-DR funds for Sandy recovery and other eligible disasters, as well as other allocations (if appropriated) for future disasters. HUD should continue to provide consistent and appropriate standards for the use of CDBG-DR funding. In addition, HUD should encourage grantees to use toolkits and other existing resources to expedite program implementation.

28) Require grantees to use CDBG-DR funding to support public and HUD-assisted multi-family housing as well as subsidized and tax credit-assisted affordable housing with recovery and risk mitigation efforts.

29) Align the foreclosure prevention policies of the FHA and the FHFA – including policies on moratoria, forbearance, and refinancing.

30) HUD should explore ways to assist State and local governments to develop model affordable housing programs that leverage funding from the public, private, and philanthropic sectors for affordable housing development and preservation in Sandy-affected areas, as well as in other regions that could potentially be affected by future disasters.

31) Encourage and promote the Insurance Institute for Business and Home Safety (IBHS) FORTIFIED home programs/ Resilience STAR development standards.

32) Help identify opportunities for state and local housing programs to leverage funds and create public-private partnerships.

33) FEMA, EPA, HUD, and HHS should issue consolidated guidance on remediation of indoor air pollutants (e.g. mold, lead, radon, and asbestos) that can pose health hazards for workers and residents in the Sandy-affected region. In addition, these agencies should recommend or establish region and housing stock specific toolkits related to indoor air pollutants for States and localities responding to disasters. Tribal, State, and local governments should include the remediation of these indoor environmental pollutants in their rebuilding construction/rehabilitation programs.

34) Bring together the Housing RSF and Emergency Support Function six partner agencies to review and integrate existing housing plans, as well as existing statutes, regulations, and policies for potential changes (statutory, regulatory or policy) to improve the delivery of housing solutions for future disasters.

## Small Business: Supporting Small Businesses and Revitalizing Local Economies

35) Build a Disaster Preparedness and Operations Team (DPOT) focused on planning to help SBA district offices, including those in the Hurricane Sandy region, ensure clear and consistent guidance on how to access both local and Federal aid following a disaster.

36) Institute a "No Wrong Door" approach to federal information sharing after disasters by building on existing information platforms and cross-referencing Hurricane Sandy disaster recovery resources. Furthermore, measures should be taken to ensure that information about economic recovery from Hurricane Sandy is accessible to vulnerable populations.

37) Encourage HUD CDBG-DR grantees to address the needs of a broad range of affected small businesses, including through the provision of grant funds to community organizations that work closely with businesses whose needs might otherwise be unmet.

38) Remove statutory barriers for SBA programs that provide additional technical assistance to small businesses before, during, and after a disaster.

39) Provide SBA statutory authority to fund incubators and accelerators.

40) Institute new and innovative process improvements to SBA's Disaster Loan program.

41) Modify regulations to adopt and "alternative size standard" for small businesses for SBA's Economic Injury Disaster Loans similar to the standard for SBA business loan programs, to enable more businesses to qualify for loans.

42) Increase SBA's unsecured disaster loan limits and expedite the disbursement of small dollar loans.

43) Defer loan payments due to SBA from Microloan Intermediaries, when appropriate as determined by SBA Administrator, if a certain percent of the Intermediary's portfolio is made up of loans to micro-borrowers in major disaster areas, including the Hurricane Sandy region.

44) Encourage HUD CDBG-DR grantees and private sources to fund additional CDFI outreach and support to small businesses in vulnerable communities.

45) Raise awareness that Treasury's SSBCI Program can be used for disaster recovery, including Hurricane Sandy recovery.

46) Create opportunities and tools to increase access for small businesses to rebuild their businesses and participate in Hurricane Sandy rebuilding.

47) Make statutory changes to existing SBA initiatives to make it easier for small and local businesses to access Federal contracts for Hurricane Sandy rebuilding.

48) Promote best practices of local workforce agencies that are integrating disaster recovery and long-term Hurricane Sandy rebuilding into their ongoing efforts.

49) Encourage HUD CDBG-DR grantees, in complying with Section 3 regulations, to maximize efforts to create specialized skills training programs in the areas needed most for Sandy rebuilding, ranging from mold remediation and construction to ecosystem and habitat restoration, green infrastructure, and coastal engineering. Furthermore, the Task Force recommends that these training programs include low-income individuals and other vulnerable populations and create local Hurricane Sandy recovery jobs that pay wages and benefits at industry standards.

50) Pursuant to Executive Order 13502, executive agencies should be encouraged to consider consideration of Project Labor Agreements (PLAs) on large-scale construction projects in the Hurricane Sandy region in order to promote economy and efficiency in federal procurement.

## Insurance: Addressing Insurance Challenges, Understanding, and Affordability

51) Establish Unified Insurance Disbursement Process.

52) Support efforts to reduce consumer confusion regarding risk and insurance coverage while working to increase hazard preparedness.

53) Improve National Flood Insurance Program (NFIP) policyholder awareness of factors that affect flood risk and insurance rating decisions.

54) Encourage increased hazard mitigation activities including elevation in order to protect property against future losses.

55) Continue to assess actuarial soundness of decreasing premiums based on mitigation activities other than elevation.

56) Analyze affordability challenges of flood insurance and the impact on economically distressed households facing premium increases.

## Community Planning and Capacity Building: Building State and Local Capacity to Plan for and Implement Long-Term Recovery and Rebuilding

57) Work with States and local jurisdictions to consider funding strategies and raise awareness about the need to fill LDRM positions. *(LDRM: Local Disaster Recovery Manager)*.

58) Support the New York Rising Community Reconstruction Program.

59) Support New Jersey planning efforts, including pilots for New Jersey Local Resilience Partnerships, and encourage Federal agencies, the State of New Jersey, non-profits, and philanthropic organizations to provide both financial and technical support for the formation and operation of the Local Resilience Partnerships.

60) Package the variety of existing Federal resources and tools related to disaster recovery and create new ones specific to community planning and capacity building in order to establish a coordinated suite of assistance that enhances and streamlines access to the recovery expertise needed by impacted communities.

61) Facilitate and expand opportunities for philanthropic and non-profit engagement in recovery, including opportunities for organizations that work with vulnerable populations. The CPCB RSFs in New York and New Jersey should actively support funder collaboratives that provide grants to nonprofits working in coordination with government. This should include encouragement of sub-grants to NGOs that would assist in accomplishing the Federal outreach requirements, including those specific to vulnerable populations to ensure they are included in the recovery planning process.

## Data: Improving Data Sharing Between Federal, State and Local Officials

62) Agencies should make aggregated, PII-scrubbed data about disaster-affected populations available to the public using a central website similar to http://www.data.gov. Specifically, FEMA, HUD, and SBA should coordinate to create a new website or adapt an existing one (such as FEMA's openFEMA site) for data posting during disasters. In addition, FEMA, HUD, and SBA should create a process for digesting raw data into an aggregated form that the public can view.

63) Each agency and each State should identify a "data steward" who serves as a point of contact for data requests. This contact should not only be available after disasters, but also serve as an informational resource in advance of disasters. FEMA, HUD, and SBA should each designate an individual within their agencies that is permanently available to receive data sharing requests and related questions from States, local governments, and non-governmental entities. Each agency should then distribute the name and contact information of that individual to all 50 States. In the event of a disaster, agencies should send affected States a reminder that the data steward is available to assist them and that each State is responsible for identifying a central point of contact within the governor's office or within the primary disaster response agency to coordinate requests with Federal agencies.

64) Each agency should catalogue its disaster data in a "menu" that describes the data that it may share with States and local governments. Specifically, each agency's data steward (see recommendation 63) should create a document containing a list of all data sets that are typically requested during a disaster. Each data item description should include the fields in the data set and the units of measurement, as well as a brief description of how the data can be used by States responding to a disaster and describe the limitations of the data (privacy requirements, aggregation, data latency, etc.). This document should be distributed to disaster agencies in each State.

65) FEMA, HUD, and SBA should adopt a common data sharing agreement template so that data requestors do not have to familiarize themselves with three separate forms. Attorneys and privacy officials from these agencies should meet to compare their current data sharing agreement formats and identify common boilerplate language that can serve as the basis for an interagency template. Once drafted, this template should then be distributed by each agency's data sharing steward to the States.

66) Work towards a multi-agency integrated data repository, or "data hub," shared and operated by FEMA and HUD, that, to the extent permitted by law and Federal policy, allows those agencies to access and store one another's data and to pass these data along to States in the event of a Federally declared disaster. FEMA and HUD should provide technical support and personnel resources to further this tool's development in preparation for the next disaster. In addition, agency attorneys and privacy officials should discuss what steps will be necessary to begin preparing the legal framework for a multi-agency data portal.

67) To help make Federal data available to States, agencies should review "routine use" language in relevant SORNs to determine whether any changes are warranted that could provide greater flexibility to share information for planning purposes, to share information across State agencies and with local governments and to broaden categories of records to cover data from other sources. Attorneys in FEMA's Office of Chief Counsel who have considered this issue have offered to make themselves available to provide guidance.

## Program Management Office (PMO): Data Sharing and Accountability

68) Continue functions of PMO to track the progress of the Sandy supplemental funding and performance.

69) Document the functions and processes used by the Task Force recovery in a "PMO toolkit" which could be quickly deployed in the event of future supplemental funding.

## End Notes

[1] While the Rebuilding Strategy identified specific agencies (such as the Department of Housing and Urban Development) to lead implementation, in some cases these leads have changed, or more specific subcomponents of or offices within an agency (such as the Office of Community Planning and Development) have been identified. Further, for some recommendations, the Rebuilding Strategy also identified contributing or supporting agencies. This progress report reflects the latest lead agencies only, and does not include contributing agencies, which in some cases have played a significant role to support implementation.

[2] Resilience is the ability to anticipate, prepare for, and adapt to changing conditions and withstand, respond to, and recover rapidly from disruptions. Disruptions can include deliberate attacks, accidents, potential threats, and naturally occurring incidents.

[3] Energy investment refers to assets, rather than investment in the grid, and their resilient power systems, which includes combined heat and power systems (CHP), microgrids, renewable energy sources, and backup generation.

[4] Storm surge associated with Hurricane Sandy caused dune and beach erosion, island breaching, and transport and deposition of sediment inland (i.e., overwash) in coastal communities from New England to Florida. Coastal

flooding also caused significant erosion to existing natural infrastructure, inundation of wetland habitats, removal of or erosion to coastal dunes, destruction of coastal lakes, and new inlet creation.

[5] Green and Gray Infrastructure are terms used to differentiate between the integration of natural systems and processes (such as wetlands) or engineered systems that mimic natural systems (such as artificial reefs) which are known as "green infrastructure" and more traditional built systems (such as concrete culverts and flood walls) which are known as "gray infrastructure."

# INDEX

## C

## F

## N

## O

## P

## Q

## R